Producing Pleasure in the Contemporary Uni

Bold Visions in Educational Research
Volume 59

Series Editors:

Kenneth Tobin, *The Graduate Center, City University of New York, USA*
Carolyne Ali-Khan, *College of Education & Human Services, University of North Florida, USA*

Co-founding Editor:

Joe Kincheloe (with Kenneth Tobin)

Editorial Board:

Barry Down, *School of Education, Murdoch University, Australia*
Daniel L. Dinsmore, *University of North Florida, USA*
Gene Fellner, *College of Staten Island, City University of New York, USA*
L. Earle Reybold, *College of Education and Human Development,*
   George Mason University, USA
Stephen Ritchie, *School of Education, Murdoch University, Australia*

Scope:
Bold Visions in Educational Research is international in scope and includes books from two areas: *teaching and learning to teach* and *research methods in education*. Each area contains multi-authored handbooks of approximately 200,000 words and monographs (authored and edited collections) of approximately 130,000 words. All books are scholarly, written to engage specified readers and catalyze changes in policies and practices. Defining characteristics of books in the series are their explicit uses of theory and associated methodologies to address important problems. We invite books from across a theoretical and methodological spectrum from scholars employing quantitative, statistical, experimental, ethnographic, semiotic, hermeneutic, historical, ethnomethodological, phenomenological, case studies, action, cultural studies, content analysis, rhetorical, deconstructive, critical, literary, aesthetic and other research methods.

Books on *teaching and learning to teach* focus on any of the curriculum areas (e.g., literacy, science, mathematics, social science), in and out of school settings, and points along the age continuum (pre K to adult). The purpose of books on *research methods in education* is **not** to present generalized and abstract procedures but to show how research is undertaken, highlighting the particulars that pertain to a study. Each book brings to the foreground those details that must be considered at every step on the way to doing a good study. The goal is **not** to show how generalizable methods are but to present rich descriptions to show how research is enacted. The books focus on methodology, within a context of substantive results so that methods, theory, and the processes leading to empirical analyses and outcomes are juxtaposed. In this way method is not reified, but is explored within well-described contexts and the emergent research outcomes. Three illustrative examples of books are those that allow proponents of particular perspectives to interact and debate, comprehensive handbooks where leading scholars explore particular genres of inquiry in detail, and introductory texts to particular educational research methods/issues of interest to novice researchers.

Producing Pleasure in the Contemporary University

Edited by

Stewart Riddle
University of Southern Queensland, Australia

Marcus K. Harmes
University of Southern Queensland, Australia

Patrick Alan Danaher
University of Southern Queensland, Australia
Central Queensland University, Australia

SENSE PUBLISHERS
ROTTERDAM / BOSTON / TAIPEI

A C.I.P. record for this book is available from the Library of Congress.

ISBN 978-94-6351-177-3 (paperback)
ISBN 978-94-6351-178-0 (hardback)
ISBN 978-94-6351-179-7 (e-book)

Published by: Sense Publishers,
P.O. Box 21858,
3001 AW Rotterdam,
The Netherlands
https://www.sensepublishers.com/

All chapters in this book have undergone peer review.

Printed on acid-free paper

All rights reserved © 2017 Sense Publishers

No part of this work may be reproduced, stored in a retrieval system, or transmitted in any form or by any means, electronic, mechanical, photocopying, microfilming, recording or otherwise, without written permission from the Publisher, with the exception of any material supplied specifically for the purpose of being entered and executed on a computer system, for exclusive use by the purchaser of the work.

TABLE OF CONTENTS

Acknowledgements		vii
1.	Partaking of Pleasure: Regenerating the Working Lives of University Academics *Marcus K. Harmes, Patrick Alan Danaher, and Stewart Riddle*	1
2.	Producing Moments of Pleasure within the Confines of the Neoliberal University *Eileen Honan*	13
3.	'Do What Sustains You': Desire and the Enterprise University *Stewart Riddle*	25
4.	The Pleasure of Writing: Escape from the Dominant System *David Bright*	37
5.	Wild Choreography of Affect and Ecstasy: Contentious Pleasure (*Joussiance*) in the Academy *Jennifer Charteris, Adele Nye, and Marguerite Jones*	49
6.	The Joy in *Writingassemblage* *Sarah Loch, Linda Henderson, and Eileen Honan*	65
7.	Female Pleasure in the Academy through Erotic Power *Cecily Jensen-Clayton and Rena MacLeod*	81
8.	The Intrinsic Pleasure of Being Present with/in Humanistic Research *Gail Crimmins*	95
9.	For Hermann: How Do I Love Thee? Let Me Count the Ways. Or, What My Dog Has Taught Me about a Post-personal Academic Life *Carol A. Taylor*	107
10.	Where Have All the Flowers Gone? The Future for Academics *Pauline Collins*	121
11.	Reducing the Drag: Creating V Formations through Slow Scholarship and Story *Alison L. Black, Gail Crimmins, and Janice K. Jones*	137

TABLE OF CONTENTS

12. Testimonio and the *Idios Kosmos* of the Contemporary Academic: Charting the Possibilities for Pleasure in Personal Accounts from Inside the Academy   157
    Andrew Hickey and Robyn Henderson

13. Self-Determination Theory and Academic Life: Strategies for Reclaiming Pleasure and Professionalism Distilled from Universities in Australia and Europe   171
    Erich C. Fein, Rahul Ganguly, Thomas Banhazi, and Patrick Alan Danaher

14. The Pleasure and Pain of Aboriginal Being in the University   185
    Kathryn Gilbey and Tracey Bunda

15. Academic Writing, Creative Pleasure and the Salvaging of Joy   201
    Susanne Gannon and Jo Lampert

16. From Frustration to Flow: Finding Joy through Co-teaching   213
    Judith Gouwens and Kenneth P. King

17. Pleasure, Pain and the Possibilities of Being and Becoming: Robustly Hopeful Reflections by an Australian Personal Fitness Trainer and His University Academic Client   229
    Samuel Davies and Patrick Alan Danaher

18. "Don't Cry – Do Research!" The Promise of Happiness for an Academic Killjoy   243
    Fred Dervin

List of Contributors   255

ACKNOWLEDGEMENTS

We wish to thank Meredith Harmes, the project officer for this book, for her many and inestimable contributions to making this book a reality. We also thank Michel Lokhorst and Jolanda Karada from Sense for their ongoing support.

MARCUS K. HARMES, PATRICK ALAN DANAHER, AND
STEWART RIDDLE

1. PARTAKING OF PLEASURE

Regenerating the Working Lives of University Academics

INTRODUCTION

Universities are fascinating places to work. A "provocative social cocktail" (Symes, 2004, p. 395) is one particularly apt description, although for some, the fascination could be ironically expressed as a reaction to the giddying changes and restructures and revisionings that define the contemporary university. As a result, academics with a taste for history may feel some empathy for the legendary Vicar of Bray, a clergyman who kept his job and his head during the tumults of English religious history by abiding strictly to this principle:

> And this is law, I will maintain unto my Dying Day, Sir. That whatsoever King may reign, I will be the Vicar of Bray, Sir!

The sentiment is self-serving, true, in that higher authority may change but should be at worst followed and at best ignored, but any academic who has experienced yet another programme being restructured or a department re-organized, or encountered yet another institutional vision statement, should feel kinship with someone determined to keep going no matter how often or how drastically things change.

The institutional, policy and employment changes against and about which the contributors to this collection are writing are well known. Academia finds itself, however reluctantly, in a neoliberal world. The *enterprise university*, as recognized and elaborated by Marginson and Considine (2000), is an approach to a corporatized and de-regulated vision of higher education that governments around the world have found irresistible.

Many universities maintain traditions such as a motto in Latin, but the old classical adage, *Atque inter silvas academi quaerere verum*, or "Seek for truth in the groves of academe", conjures up the ghosts of a genteel world that is perhaps now lost for ever. In the age of the enterprise university, it sometimes seems that the groves of academe have been cut down and salt sown where once they grew. As such, the affordances and aspirations framing academics' work differ markedly from those of previous generations. These circumstances place unprecedented pressures on academics to enact their roles in new ways, yet what this collection of chapters demonstrates is that these same circumstances also create space for alternative approaches to reimagining who and what academics are and the character and purposes of academic enterprise.

Each contribution to this volume upholds the proposition that universities and the academic enterprise that they promote matter more than ever. It is certainly possible to put a money value on their importance. Universities are a major source of revenue and in many countries they rank highly as an export industry because of international students. The teaching, the research and the scholarship continue to matter to those responsible for these activities. Given how heavily universities weigh in with regard to cultural and economic capital, the fact that this volume also suggests that the ways that this teaching, research and scholarship can be carried out should matter as well.

That is not to suggest that the volume is Pollyanna-ish. Certainly there are references to dogs, cats, cross-stitching, writing fiction, and other realms of activity that may not come immediately to mind when thinking of academic activity. But these are starting points. Nor are the contributions introspections. Instead the issues that they raise – of finding meaning in work, of taking pride in that work, of the place of first nations peoples in the knowledge systems of the colonizers, of withstanding bullies, working with professional courtesy, amongst others – surely matter regardless of the workplace or the type of work.

Admittedly, some of the context is specific and the pressures discussed are distinctive to the contemporary university. What then is this academia and who are the academics populating it? Shifts in identity, in purpose, in governance and in other realms of existence have led to there being many possible answers to these crucial questions. Perhaps at one-time academia may have been a self-governing community of scholars, although such apparently benign ideals are long past. Nonetheless, academics retain significant amounts of power. They also maintain high levels of professional autonomy, but what is the price of this autonomy?

IN THE GROVES OF ACADEME?

Attention has been given to the growing pressure on academics working in contemporary university systems across the globe to produce research outputs at increasing speeds and intensities. From this perspective, the academic institution produces multiple tensions and moments of crises, where it seems that there is limited space left for the intrinsic enjoyment arising from scholarly practices. The civilized sense of academic activity taking place "in the groves of academe" is far removed from the realities of contemporary pressures.

Few would doubt the transformation of universities. The factors and causes of change vary in tone and emphasis from country to country, but the outcomes have remarkable levels of similarity in terms of implications and outcomes. In Australia, the Dawkins Review (1987) was one iteration of the changes to universities, but the United States of America (USA), the United Kingdom (UK), Europe and elsewhere all have similar tales of economic stresses and identity crises (Kwiek, 2005). What have been the results? Are the people who inhabit universities now different? Are the incentives and disincentives now different, especially for research? Does public scholarship for the public good become more akin to working for private enterprise?

These are not very positive questions on the whole. By contrast, in this book, we examine on a global level how pleasure is both possible in and central to the endeavours of academics working in universities. Here pleasure is defined and experienced variously as: affirmation, affordance, flow, focus, fulfilment, happiness, heightened consciousness, immersion, joy, motivation, and self-actualization in various academic environments. The contributions to this volume address in their different ways the issues of work intensification in the university, seeking the spaces and opportunities for pleasure. To be clear, pleasure means the affective engagement with work that feels meaningful. What is affective for one may not be a pleasure for others.

The importance of what follows lies in the ways that the contributors engage with this issue in personal, academic and sometimes political ways. In doing so, they pursue some of the ingenious and often subversive opportunities that academics have pursued to craft meaning, create pleasure, or let off steam. Some of the contributors to this collection have discussed the pleasure in writing, not necessarily about their field of research. In doing so, they follow a long and intriguing tradition. Possibly one of the naughtiest ways that academics have created pleasure is through their writing. Some like the academic detective novelists Michael Innes, Dorothy L. Sayers and Robert Barnard took gleeful pleasure in setting their murder mysteries in universities and colleges and bumping off in print and with great relish fictional analogues of their colleagues.

At the same time, not all pleasure is so murderous. More recently, Jorge Cham's beloved *Piled Higher and Deeper* (www.phdcomics.com), has given relief and release to countless beginning academics. Academics being what they are, many also take to blogs and other sharing sites such as the *Thesis Whisperer* (www.thesiswhisperer.com) to discuss stressors, debate strategies and generally share experiences in a spirit of solidarity. Social media also share pleasurable and humorous accounts of academic life, such as the popular *Shit Academics Say* (@AcademicsSay) Twitter account.

Inevitably, such dialogue can seem inward and precious; after all, any job has its stresses, and one contributor to the blog, *Why do academics work so much?* (Thesis Whisperer, 2013), provided the healthily corrective point of view: "For most academics it's not a life-and-death situation – if a paper isn't published the sky will not fall". That is very true, but other comments stressed other distinctive challenges: "There is NO SUCH THING AS TIME OFF IN ACADEMIA. You cannot escape your own brain, your own thoughts, or the notion that you have to plan ahead …. [T]he only way to take time off is to leave the profession and do something else". Or, on the experience of doing a PhD, "It is something that MUST be suffered through!" These attitudes are actually quite alarming and perhaps academics are too hard on themselves. A recent opinion piece (Watson & Battle, 2016) published in the online research-news site, *The Conversation*, urged academics to lighten up, and even to experiment with comedy as a means of communicating findings:

> To be a humorous academic appears to be an unacceptable oxymoron and those who use humour in their work run the risk of being seen as non-serious, and therefore trivial. Even Erving Goffman, one of the greatest social scientists of the 20th century, is regarded in some quarters with suspicion for his 'sparkling' humorous prose. (n.p.)

These points contribute to thinking about why this book, and why this book now? Already it seems that there might have been too much written about the problems with universities. The educational historian Hannah Forsyth (2014) attempted to call time on what she dubs the "jeremiad genre of university literature across the world". She continues: "It has got to the point where I have come to admire such authors' inventiveness in finding new phrases for 'academics complain about'". Mind you, Forsyth's book, a history of Australian universities, itself finds plenty to complain about, including gender and pay imbalances, the corporatisation of universities, the overpaid executive tiers and the small 'scraps' over which disenfranchised academics fight.

Nor is it automatic that all change is bad. Universities in the past were on the whole elitist and places for the highly-privileged. They were far from inclusive (Symes, 2004), and their staff members were often unregulated rather than recognizably professional. There is a younger generation of academics who have no particular reason to look back with nostalgia at earlier notions of an academic *Golden Age* (Archer, 2008; Bryson, 2004). There is also the possibility that even a painful experience can bring pleasure. At one level why should there even be an assumption of pleasure? Presumably academics are there to work, and pleasure is not required in a workplace.

Many of the chapters that follow grapple with these binaries, including pleasure and pain, private and public, and personal and institutional (see also: Macfarlane, 2015). But there may be a desire to experience pleasure partly in order to do more and better work. In many ways this book is disruptive – disruptive of notions of untrammelled professionalism, of the unfettered right to say what one likes as a public intellectual, yet also of the contrary and counter-intuitive assumption that academics (like all workers and producers) are unthinking ciphers who contribute nothing from their own identities to their work.

PARTAKING OF PLEASURE

It is vital at this juncture to emphasise that we see the "partaking of pleasure" taken from the title of this chapter as mobilizing multiple meanings and as evoking varied values, thereby resisting a homogenising and potentially reductionist understanding. Consequently readers are likely to respond to the subsequent accounts in this book in equally diverse ways. Some or perhaps all of these renditions of academic pleasure might be seen as being solipsistic and self-indulgent. By contrast (or perhaps in addition), these studies might be regarded as demonstrating the agential, deliberative and resilient character of contemporary academics whose efforts to partake of various forms of pleasure constitute important strategies to enhance their own wellbeing and in the process to maximise their prospects of serving their respective communities and constituencies.

As we foreshadowed in the previous section of this chapter, there are several possible approaches to conceptualizing academics' work and their associated identities and subjectivities. Here we elaborate on three such approaches – the philosophical, political and practical parameters of the partaking of pleasure – that provide a structure for the book.

At the deepest and the broadest levels, the philosophical parameter of the partaking of pleasure accentuates the ontological, epistemological and axiological dimensions of past, present and potential future existences. These dimensions in turn highlight the significance of multiple influences on how individual academics live their lives, the affordances of and constraints on their lives and how they live them, how they conceptualize pleasure and its possible place in their work, and the meanings that they ascribe to that work. These dimensions also help to frame how academics approach the three generally recognised aspects of their work: teaching, research and service or engagement. For instance, individual academics' respective epistemological understandings of what knowledge/knowledges is/are, how it/they is/are created and circulated, and the appropriate values attending its/their reception and influence are likely to flow through into their specific approaches to planning and enacting their teaching programs, their supervision of higher degrees by research students and their research trajectories.

From this perspective, some of the ideas about academic pleasure introduced in the previous section of this chapter can be placed in the wider perspective of being situated against the backdrop (and on occasion of working against the grain) of the sometimes intrinsic and invisible but no less influential outworkings of deeper philosophical ideas.

For instance, a distinctive leitmotif in several of the subsequent chapters is the (usually deleterious) impact of an absence of productive, uninterrupted time on academics' work. This leitmotif was summarized neatly in a study of the careers of academic managers in universities in the UK: "New managerialism ... may place different emphasis on time usage and be more concerned to regulate and account for its use by professionals previously allowed considerable autonomy" (Deem & Hillyard, 2002, p. 127).

From a philosophical perspective, time has been theorized in diverse ways, including the conceptualization of temporality in the context of neoliberalism (Herzfeld, 2009), which is another recurring theme in many of the following chapters. In this way, time and its absence or its short supply function simultaneously as an empirical encapsulation of the concerns of many contemporary academics and researchers and as a metaphor for broader affordances and challenges characterising their work. Similarly, a study of UK academics' work concluded that:

> ... [the] additive effects of job demands and control on psychological well-being and of job demands and support on both burnout and job satisfaction were shown, corroborating research showing that high job strain is linked to

ill health and job dissatisfaction in this homogeneous occupational sample. (McClenahan, Giles, & Mallett, 2007, p. 85)

A more explicitly philosophical interpretation of the same phenomenon of academics' work stress and burnout (which again resonates with some of the subsequent chapters) is likely to be alert to greater diversities of experience and nuances of meaning-making that in turn are liable to generate a wider range of understandings of this phenomenon. This is not to deny the authenticity and urgency of emotions (whether positive or negative) experienced by individual academics, but it is to assert that pursuing the philosophical parameter of the partaking of pleasure is likely to place those emotions against the backdrop of other considerations that function both to affirm and to enrich personal perspectives. This is less a plea for some kind of inappropriate generalisability than it is a call for conversation and dialogue among and across academics and researchers whose experiences are diverse yet whose potential interest in and take-up of pleasure are in our view worth cultivating.

This call for conversation and dialogue in turn accentuates the political parameter of the partaking of pleasure that is also explored in diverse ways and to considerable effect in the following chapters. We see this political parameter as recognizing the exercise of multiple forms of power. In some respects this power is centred on the seemingly totalizing capacity of the contemporary state (Finnemore & Goldstein, 2013; Hirst, 2001), and/or of the global forces of late capitalism (Büscher & Igoe, 2013; Crary, 2013) and neoliberalism (Bates, 2014; Newman, 2013), to frame and constrain what academics and researchers can and cannot do. For instance, distilling a growing body of scholarship about this theme, Slaughter (2014) contended "…how marketization has become deeply imbricated in so many aspects of the academy" (p. ix), and she also recorded with words that resonate pointedly and powerfully with many of the subsequent chapters:

> We understood the academic swivel toward the market as being framed by opportunities created by the rise of the neoliberal state, the knowledge economy, globalization, and the growth of transnational capitalism. We tried to work out mechanisms that connected academics to the market possibilities opening up and focused on organizational processes – new circuits of knowledge, interstitial organizational emergence, intermediating organizations, expanded managerial capacity – and also narratives, discourses, social technologies, resources, rewards, and incentives that moved actors within the university from the public good knowledge/learning regime to the academic capitalist knowledge/learning regime. (p. vii)

Relatedly, although from a different perspective, Tuck (2016) identified a parallel among 14 university teachers in the UK between positioning the teaching of academic writing as 'skills' rather than as 'learners' (p. 1612) on the one hand and devaluing the work of the teachers of that academic writing.

At the same time, the political parameter draws attention to the capacity to resist and subvert these exercises of power over academics and researchers. We have noted above this contestatory capability of pleasure against the increasingly politicized backdrop of the conditions in which academics and researchers work. Several scholars have analysed the potential to undermine the supposedly invincible onrush of the forces of the contemporary world. For example, O'Brien (2017) insisted on both the need and the feasibility to resist 'neoliberal education'. Intriguingly, one demonstration of this resistance could be seen in Al Lily's (2016) initiative of "crowd-authoring" (p. 1053), whereby "…101 scholars of education and technology spread across the globe collaborated in three rounds via email to write a 9000-word manuscript" (p. 1053). Moreover, Al Lily used the evident success of this initiative to call for "… an intercontinental group of academics to form an 'assembly of authoring'" (p. 1053). Additionally, he advocated "Such an assembly of authoring … [developing] into an 'assembly of *action*', with its members explicitly seeking to bring about changes and social interventions" (p. 1053; emphasis in original).

Furthermore, semi-structured interviews with 20 researchers at one Canadian university yielded that "Participants demonstrated agency on behalf of themselves and their institution by engaging in practices they thought would provide space for research that 'really mattered'" (Martimianakis & Muzzin, 2015, p. 1454). The authors proposed something of a generational dimension of this agency: "Younger participants were more likely to resist being 'disciplined'; they identified strongly with conceptual forms of interdisciplinarity and derived both satisfaction and creativity from working in the margins of knowledge spaces" (p. 1454).

Likewise, Collyer (2015) used her qualitative study in four Australian universities to analyse the universities "as sites of contestation between the new professional managers and the established academic profession over the control of the conditions of work, the production of expert knowledge and the worksite itself" (p. 315). She observed, among other findings, that there was "… a dynamic process in which academics innovatively respond to threats to reduce their autonomy, to increased levels of surveillance and other constraints on practice" (p. 315).

This reference to practice evokes the practical parameter of the partaking of pleasure by and for academics and researchers in contemporary universities that is also pursued by a number of the following chapters. From this perspective, practice is neither mundane nor pedestrian, but instead it frames and describes what academics and researchers do, and also why, how, with whom and with which effects they do it. Accordingly, practice generates a prism that enables otherwise implicit and invisible actions by academics and researchers to be analysed and understood.

As the next section of this chapter explains, the subsequent chapters take up the notion of practice in relation to the partaking of pleasure in contemporary universities in diverse ways. More broadly, we see this form of practice as a kind of constrained and contained agency, with individual authors – or pairs or groups of authors – striving for opportunities and outlets for their creativity, intelligence and sense of responsibility, however that sense was manifested. In this regard, the practice parameter both resonates with and builds on the philosophical and the political parameters articulated earlier in this section.

Similarly, considerable scholarly literature attests both to the importance of the practice parameter and to the complexities of enacting that practice within the material contexts of current university life. For instance, a study of "… a practice of division of labour between teaching-oriented and research-oriented staff" (Geschwind & Broström, 2015, p. 60) members in three Swedish universities found that academic managers' strategies for rewarding research agendas "… seem to reinforce existing patterns of division of labour among academic staff" (p. 60) by assigning teaching responsibilities "… to less research-active staff" (p. 60). While the respective researchers and teachers involved in these practices might well take pleasure from them, from another perspective one individual's pleasure is sometimes at the cost of a colleague's less pleasurable experience of the same situation.

This crucial point about differential experiences of situations and about the relativities of participating of pleasure in practice emphasises the material conditions that frame and constrain such relativities in academics' and researchers' work:

> Material resources are an important prerequisite for any research [and university teaching], whether in the form of well-equipped laboratories, up-to-date libraries or fast internet connections, and these in turn provide access to the all-important disciplinary networks that set the ground rules for community membership …. Similarly, it is a country's economic situation that largely determines its level of social development, and ultimately, its academic culture. (Bennett, 2014, p. 2)

These material relativities – which are actually deeply embedded structural inequalities – are manifested in multiple enactments of practice, such as the challenges and opportunities attending early career academics in African universities developing the distinctive knowledge and skills required for effective university teaching (Teferra, 2016), and the equivalent challenges and opportunities characterizing academics' access to and use of electronic journals for scholarly communication at the University of the Punjab (Arshad & Ameen, 2017).

Furthermore, McKenzie (2017) identified another form of structural inequality in relation to practice with regard to what she termed "a precarious passion" (p. 31) prompted by the difficulty of many Australian academics securing full-time, continuing employment in universities today. As McKenzie noted, "These casual employees are disproportionately female …" (p. 31), and they are also younger academics and researchers.

RECLAIMING PLEASURE IN THE CONTEMPORARY UNIVERSITY

It is necessary to situate individual researchers' partaking of pleasure in the context of broader institutional and trans/national flows of power and politics. There are important questions to be asked about the kinds of scholarship that are made possible within the contemporary university. The philosophical, political, and practice parameters of academic work need to be better understood, so that we might find more meaningful ways of producing scholarly work that is deeply connected to academics' lives. At the same time, we need to be mindful that what constitutes pleasure for one person or group of people might not be feasible or relevant for others, owing partly to differences in personalities and preferences, and partly to the highly varied material conditions and empirical contexts framing the work of academics and researchers in universities today.

The following chapters deploy a range of strategic conceptual and methodological tools in order to provide various accounts of producing pleasure within the contemporary university. While the book is not intended to be read in a set order, chapters have been grouped into broad themes so that common themes and narrative threads might emerge and entwine each other. The mixture of scholarly voices and experiences from around the world, from different disciplinary fields and different levels of rank, also serves to highlight our point that there is no one measure of pleasure, nor of what constitutes the production of pleasurable academic subjectivities. Indeed, we see these chapters as a vibrant collection of different academic lives being performed through the sharing of scholarly writing, whether the writing is conceptual, empirical, creative, fictional, and so on.

Several chapters take their theoretical and conceptual cues from the work of French philosopher, Gilles Deleuze, employing notions of desire and assemblage through writing encounters and experiments. Others have a distinctly feminist ethics, drawing on a range of devices to trouble the taken-for-grantedness of the neoliberal and enterprise regimes of the contemporary university. Some chapters provide reflective accounts of researchers' experiences in teaching, research and scholarly activity, while others develop themes of dis/connection, subjective agency and collective activism within the academy.

We believe that each contribution provides a unique take on the notion of how pleasure can be produced within the confines of universities, while also acknowledging the problematic tension of wanting to produce meaningful scholarly work while also being recognised as a scholar within the particular confines of research metrics, productivity measurements and research quality assessments. The irony is not lost on us, that while edited books and book chapters count for very little in the knowledge production game of the university system, the opportunity to produce a book that is interested in the production of pleasure, is in itself a pleasurable act.

Through the contributions in this book, we seek to create opportunities for the strategic refusal of the quantifying, stultifying and stupefying delimiters of what is possible for academic production, and instead to open up spaces for conversation, reflection and thought, in order to think, to be and to do differently – pleasurably. In pursuing this goal, we posit that, far from being reprehensible or self-indulgent, the partaking of pleasure is actually crucial to regenerating the working lives of university academics around the world.

In some ways this book may be therapeutic or recuperative, and it is certainly a counter narrative to the onrush of the enterprise university and the devaluing of its students and academics. Yet ironically the book also counts towards the knowledge production of academics' profiles and outputs measures. This doubling up of potential outcomes of this volume encapsulates the complexities attending contemporary academic work and the multiplicities of meanings and value(s) ascribed to that work by diverse stakeholders with equally diverse interests. From this perspective, the partaking of pleasure "in the groves of academe" in order to regenerate the working lives of university academics is as controversial as it is crucial.

In particular, this volume shows how researchers are able to rupture the bounds of what is permissible and possible within their daily lives, habits and practices. As such, we pose and address several increasingly significant questions. What are some of the multiple and different ways that we can reclaim pleasure and enhance the durations and intensities of our passions, desires and becomings within the contemporary university? How might these aspirations be realised? What are the spaces for the pleasurable production of research that might be opened up? How could we reconfigure the neoliberal university to be a place of more affect, where desire, laughter and joy join with the work that we seek to undertake and the communities whom we serve? And perhaps, most of all, how might we reclaim pleasure in the contemporary university?

REFERENCES

Al Lily, A. E. A. (2016, December). Crowd-authoring: The art and politics of engaging 101 authors of educational technology. *International Journal of Information Management, 36*(6), 1053–1061. doi: 10.1016/j.ijinfomgt.2016.07.004

Archer, L. (2008). The new neoliberal subjects? Young/er academics' constructions of professional identity. *Journal of Educational Policy, 23*(3), 265–285.

Arshad, A., & Ameen, K. (2017). Scholarly communication in the age of Google: Exploring academics' use patterns of e-journals at the University of the Punjab. *The Electronic Library, 35*(1), 167–184. doi: 10.1108/EL-09-2015-0171

Bates, J. (2014, July). The strategic importance of information policy for the contemporary neoliberal state: The case of Open Government Data in the United Kingdom. *Government Information Quarterly, 31*(3), 388–395. doi: 10.1016/j.giq.2014.02.009

Bennett, K. (2014). Introduction: The political and economic infrastructure of academic practice: The 'semiperiphery' as a category for social and linguistic analysis. In K. Bennett (Ed.), *The semiperiphery of academic writing: Discourses, communities and practices* (pp. 1–9). Basingstoke, UK: Palgrave Macmillan.

Bryson, C. (2004). What about the workers? The expansion of higher education and the transformation of academic work. *Industrial Relations Journal, 35*(1), 38–57.

Büscher, B., & Igoe, J. (2013). 'Prosuming' conservation? Web 2.0, nature and the intensification of value-producing labour in late capitalism. *Journal of Consumer Culture, 13*(3), 283–305.

Collyer, F. M. (2015). Practices of conformity and resistance in the marketization of the academy: Bourdieu, professionalism and academic capitalism. *Critical Studies in Education, 56*(3), 315–331. doi: 10.1080/17508487.2014.985690

Crary, J. (2013). *24/7: Late capitalism and the ends of sleep*. London, UK: Verso.

Dawkins, J. S. (1987). *Higher education: A policy discussion paper*. Canberra: Australian Government Publishing Service.

Deem, R., & Hillyard, S. (2002). Making time for management: The careers and lives of manager-academics in UK universities. In G. Crow & S. Heath (Eds.), *Social conceptions of time: Structure and process in work and everyday life (Explorations in sociology)* (pp. 126–143).

Finnemore, M., & Goldstein, J. (Eds.). (2013). *Back to basics: State power in a contemporary world.* Oxford, UK: Oxford University Press.

Forsyth, H. (2014). *A history of the modern Australian university.* Sydney, NSW, Australia: NewSouth Books.

Geschwind, L., & Broström, A. (2015). Managing the teaching–research nexus: Ideals and practice in research-oriented universities. *Higher Education Research & Development, 34*(1), 60–73. doi: 10.1080/07294360.2014.934332

Herzfeld, M. (2009). Rhythm, tempo, and historical time: Experiencing temporality in the neoliberal age. *Public Archaeology: Archaeological Ethnographies, 8*(2-3), 108–123. doi: 10.1179/175355309X457178

Hirst, P. (2001). *War and power in the 21st century: The state, military conflict and the international system.* Cambridge, UK: Polity Press.

Kwiek, M. (2005). The university and the state in a global age: Renegotiating the traditional social contract. *European Educational Research Journal, 4*(4), 324–341.

Marginson, S., & Considine, M. (2000). *The enterprise university: Power, governance and reinvention in Australia.* Oxford, UK: Oxford University Press.

Martimianakis, M. A., & Muzzin, L. (2015). Discourses of interdisciplinarity and the shifting topography of academic work: Generational perspectives on facilitating and resisting neoliberalism. *Studies in Higher Education, 40*, 1454-1470. doi: http://dx.doi.org/10.1080/03075079.2015.1060708

McClenahan, C. A., Giles, M. L., & Mallett, J. (2007). The importance of context specificity in work stress research: A test of the Demand–Control–Support model in academics. *Work & Stress: An International Journal of Work, Health & Organisations, 21*(1), 85–95. doi: 10.1080/02678370701264552

McKenzie, L. (2017). A precarious passion: Gendered and age-based insecurity among aspiring academics in Australia. In R. Thwaites & A. Pressland (Eds.), *Being an early career academic feminist academic: Global perspectives, experiences and challenges* (pp. 31–49). Basingstoke, UK: Palgrave Macmillan.

Macfarlane, B. (2015, January). Dualisms in higher education: A critique of their influence and effect. *Higher Education Quarterly, 69*(1), 101–118. doi: 10.1111/hequ.12046

Newman, J. (2013). Spaces of power: Feminism, neoliberalism and gendered labor. *Social Politics, 20*(2), 200–221. doi: https://doi.org/10.1093/sp/jxt008

O'Brien, S. (2017). Resisting neoliberal education: For freedom's sake. In T. Rudd & I. F. Goodson (Eds.), *Negotiating neoliberalism: Developing alternative educational visions* (Studies in professional life and work, Vol. 3) (pp. 149–166). Rotterdam, The Netherlands: Sense Publishers.

Slaughter, S. (2014). Foreword. In B. Cantwell & I. Kauppinen (Eds.), *Academic capitalism in the age of globalization* (pp. vii–x). Baltimore, MD: John Hopkins University Press.

Symes, C. (2004). Revolting campuses: Novel impressions of Australian higher education. *Teaching in Higher Education, 9*(4), 395–406.

Teferra, D. (2016). Early career academics in Africa – induction into the teaching praxis. *Studies in Higher Education, 41*(10), 1735–1740. doi: 10.1080/03075079.2016.1221651

Thesis Whisperer. (2013). *Why do academics work so much?* Retrieved from https://thesiswhisperer.com/2013/01/15/why-do-academics-work-so-much-2/

Tuck, J. (2016). 'That ain't going to get you a professorship': Discourses of writing and the positioning of academics' work with student writers in UK higher education. *Studies in Higher Education, 41*(9), 1612–1626. doi: http://dx.doi.org/10.1080/03075079.2014.999320

Watson, K., & Battle, I. C. (2016, April 4). *An education in irony: Why academics need to be funny.* Retrieved from https://theconversation.com/an-education-in-irony-why-academics-need-to-be-funny-55261

Marcus K. Harmes
University of Southern Queensland, Australia

Patrick Alan Danaher
University of Southern Queensland, Australia
and
Central Queensland University, Australia

Stewart Riddle
University of Southern Queensland, Australia

EILEEN HONAN

2. PRODUCING MOMENTS OF PLEASURE WITHIN THE CONFINES OF THE NEOLIBERAL UNIVERSITY

THERE'S A FINE LINE BETWEEN PLEASURE AND PAIN

Pleasure is in no way something that can be attained only by a detour through suffering; it is something that must be delayed as long as possible because it interrupts the continuous process of positive desire. There is, in fact, a joy that is immanent to desire as though desire were filled by itself and its contemplations, a joy that implies no lack or impossibility and is not measured by pleasure since it is what distributes intensities of pleasure and prevents them from being suffused by anxiety, shame, and guilt. (Deleuze & Guattari, 1987, p. 155)

In this chapter, I explore the productive possibilities of becomingacademic through the "continuous process of positive desire" that Deleuze and Guattari describe in the above quote. The neoliberal apparatus of the university constructs us as a subject "suffused by anxiety, shame and guilt", as lacking the scores or wins or publications or prizes or grants that will create a successful academic. Yet there is a 'fine line between pleasure and pain'[1] as we all yearn to become success; we appear to relish in the anxiety and overwork; we engage with the inherent contradictions in the technologies of performance and agency (Davies & Petersen, 2005). This is what the performative regime of the neoliberal university does – works within us not on us (Ball, 2012). We relish in the praise and reward system, we panic in the failed state of non-funded grants, we envy those successful, and we delight in the inner glow shining from the google citations on our screens. We are drawn to the clickbait of messages, 'someone just searched for you on google', we boast on Facebook and Twitter of our 'h-indexes' and latest publications, we moan about long hours, time away from families, piles of marking.

How is it then that we can create a space to find joy in our academic careers that is not based on the incessant search to fill the gaps, to plug up the holes? Is it possible to be satisfied, sufficient, satiated, to experience joy "that implies no lack or impossibility"? If, as Deleuze suggests, control operates through "continual monitoring", the challenge is "to create vacuoles of non-communication, circuit breakers so that we can elude control" (Deleuze, 1995, p. 175). To create vacuoles (or little storage bubbles of non-communication), moments when we take up the position of Bartleby – the man who simply says 'I prefer not to' (Savat & Thompson, 2015, p. 280; Tamboukou, 2012, p. 860). In Deleuzeguattarian terms, this is not just a matter of 'deterritorialisation' or a deconstruction of the systems and machines that hold the neoliberal university together. There is a politics involved as Wallin (2012) and Savat and Thompson (2015) remind us, in taking up modes of thought from Deleuze and Guattari to re-think the relations between institutions and subjects, between the social and the individual, between us and the forms of disciplinary power that are enacted within these contemporary societies of control (Deleuze, 1992). With Buchanan (2000, p. 8), I am interested in understanding how Deleuze and Guattari contribute to an "apparatus of social critique".

Bronwyn Davies has been undertaking such a critique of neo-liberal constructions of academic life and the rise of new managerialism techniques of control in universities for some years (see Davies, 2005; Davies & Bansel, 2010; Davies & Petersen, 2005). Over ten years ago, she challenged us to rethink how we constitute ourselves and others within the confines of the neo-liberal university, using a series of questions, unanswerable questions, those that have puzzled her and others as we grapple with the complex ambivalence of becoming academic.

> How might we catch ourselves mouthing the comfortable cliches and platitudes that together we use to shape that same world that we shake our heads at with sorrow and resignation – or that we secretly in our darkest hearts applaud? How might we put to one side our own safety and comfortable certainties and ask the impossible questions that exist outside of the already known, the already asked, the comfortably conservative discursive universe that shores up our certainties and keeps the world a safe place – for us? How are we to resist engaging in the neoliberally induced surveillance of ourselves and each other, surveillance that limits, that holds us neatly packaged within economic and utilitarian discourses? How can we dare to ask, in the face of that discourse and its constraints, the questions that unsettle, the questions that disrupt the certainties and securities, the questions that honour a passionate ideal of the academy where intellectual work is without fear, where it does not know, necessarily, where its questions might lead – passionate work that recognizes no boundaries that might prevent its development and where it also cares passionately about its effects? (Davies, 2005, p. 7)

Hold these questions in your hearts and minds while you read this chapter, think about how you can engage with these ideas, those of collaboration, collegiality, and communication, to produce joy, to engage in a critical political project that creates a space for doing the 'passionate work' that ignites and drives us in our academic lives.

MAPPING THE TERRITORY

Maria Tamboukou (2012) says these are 'dark times' for academics, but the darkness is not only created through the overshadowing of our lives by the audit culture and the performativity regimes created through the practices of the neoliberal managers who control our work. It is also a darkness that we seek out, she argues, as we hide in caves and withdraw "from public academic spaces" (p. 860).

It is cold outside. A biting westerly wind blows through the suburbs, clouds build and sun bursts through. It is quiet, I can hear a truck two streets away, the cockatoos have stopped their raucous cries for today, I can see the wind in the trees but not hear it.

I am comfortable, warm.

The ping of incoming mail is intermittent, there are no urgent tasks, I have the day to write, to create, to express my thoughts, ideas and opinions.

This is a privileged life.

Understanding and deconstructing the "matrices of complex practices, values and discourses" (Tamboukou, 2012, p. 860) that form the "Auditland" territory (Murphie, 2014) requires not only recognizing the ambivalent positions of both oppression and compliance, of pleasure and pain, but also the privilege of these positions, especially for those of us in continuing tenured appointments. There is privilege and pleasure in "choosing to work when and where" (Gornall & Salisbury, 2012, p. 143). Indeed, Gornall and Salisbury argue that the "very intense, intensive, and in some ways, extensive kinds of working" (p. 146) are not only pleasurable but also provide "motivation, curiosity and engagement" (p. 145).

Yet acknowledgement of our positions of comfort should not, must not, "forestall resistance" (Davies & Petersen, 2005, p. 93).

> We therefore need urgently to think about how some of the pleasures of academic work (or at least a deep love for the 'myth' of what we thought being an intellectual would be like, but often seems at far remove from it) bind us more tightly into a neoliberal regime with ever-growing costs, not least to ourselves (Gill, 2009, p. 241)

We must come out of our solitary confinement in the dark caves of "academic escapism" (Tamboukou, 2012, p, 861), move away from "reflecting upon, analysing and writing about academic performativity, audit cultures and the panopicisation of the academy" (p. 86), and take some action, even if that action is just channeling Bartleby.

These actions, of activism, of resistance, of seeking out a form of activity that cannot be counted or audited (Murphie, 2012, p. 37), will necessarily take place within and across the territory that has been colonized by the audit society, yet at the same time will require a rethinking of the edges of those territories, moving into the borderlands:

> The map is open and connectable in all of its dimensions; it is detachable, reversible, susceptible to constant modification. It can be torn, reversed, adapted to any kind of mounting, reworked by an individual, group, or social

formation. It can be drawn on a wall, conceived of as a work of art, constructed as a political action or as a meditation. (Deleuze & Guattari, 1987, p. 2)

If the Auditland creates an "existential territory of crisis, competition and digitized data" (Savat & Thompson, 2015, p 293), then our brave new land must create collegiality and slow scholarship (Mountz et al, 2015). If the control society brings with it "the language of efficiency, effectiveness, impact and lifelong learning", then we must use a language of failure (Halberstam, 2011; O'Gorman & Werry, 2012), a language that doesn't count. We must refuse to engage in the creation of the climate of crisis - so for example when the new year begins each and every year with a warning about an operational budget crisis that requires us all to tighten our belts, reduce sessional staff hours, increase class sizes – can we take up the challenge not to engage?

The society of control, the auditland territory, produces us as "compliant workers, depoliticized consumers, and passive citizens" (Giroux, 2003, p. 181). Can we instead think about subversion and challenging what is taken for granted as acceptable? Can we be failures, fools and ironists (McWilliam, 2000), can we celebrate "joy as a force, an excess of the type that does not solely originate in the body nor is solely an effect of the body, but both"? (Kern et al., 2014, p. 847)

FOOLISH FAILURES

To celebrate this kind of joy, to experience pleasure that does not interrupt the active processing of desire, to delight in subversion and critique may mean taking up positions that are unknown to us as academics. An exploration of what it might mean to become a 'foolish failure' draws also on the possibilities of laughter and irony, and of engaging in these acts with others, in a sense of collegiality, community, and collaboration that moves beyond that encouraged by neoliberal market forces that insist that collaboration must have outputs, that collegiality can be measured by the number of professors on grant applications, that the organizational shell of a 'school' or 'faculty' can replace a community of scholars.

Celebrating failure is an act of activism, a way to succeed in resisting the "measure and mantra of the corporatizing university" (O'Gorman & Werry, 2012, p. 3).

> Failure's promise lies in its capacity to unravel the certainties of knowledge, competence, representation, normativity and authority. Failure ... is the inevitable and critical counterpoint to modernity's empty promises (O'Gorman & Werry, 2012, p. 1).

As well as celebrating failure, and engaging with pleasure and joy, delighting in subversion and critique may also allow us to enact the position of the Fool.

> We recommend the cultivation of foolishness, especially when it is dangerous, as one kind of antidote to the unassailability that neo-liberalism achieves for itself. (Davies & Petersen, 2005, p. 94)

After all, it appears that there has been a long and complicated history between knowledge, the academy and the Fool. As Foucault (1988, p. 25) reminds us, "Erasmus, in his dance of fools, reserves a large place for scholars", and in the original 'ship of fools':

> The first canto of Brant's poem is devoted to books and scholars; and in the engraving which illustrates this passage in the Latin edition of 1497, we see enthroned upon his bristling cathedra of books the Magister who wears behind his doctoral cap a fool's cap sewn with bells. (1988, p. 25)

The trope of the 'wise fool' echoes throughout literary criticism, especially in relation to Shakespeare. The Fool in *King Lear*, but elsewhere as well, is articulate and clever. Like academics, the Fool needs an "acute sense of the semantics and rhetoric of language" (Mullini, 1985, p. 102). Like the Fool, academics can use language that is "rhetorically rich, semantically ambiguous, ontologically disruptive of the order of the fictional world" (Mullini, 1985, p. 104).

Taking up this position then, of the foolish failure, requires an active disruption, an open and public dismantling of the "masters house" (Lorde, 1984), which in itself can be dangerous, dangerous for those engaged in the demolition, but also dangerous for those looking on, the passers-by who may be trapped by the falling timbers.

The foolish failure rejects the position offered within the neoliberal academy of "the individual as a career-seeking entrepreneur" (Cannizzo, 2016, p. 8). After all, it is this discourse that "devours us like a flesh-eating bacterium, producing its own toxic waste – shame: I'm a fraud, I'm useless, I'm nothing. It is (of course) deeply gendered, racialised and classed, connected to biographies that produce very different degrees of 'entitlement' (or not)" (Gill, 2009, p. 240). The successful academic hides failure, is ashamed, is constituted as lacking the right numbers, citations, grants, teaching scores. The foolishfailure in contrast, actively searches for other ways of beingacademic, looks out for "subjugated knowledges", engages in "a refusal of mastery, a critique of the intuitive connections within capitalism between success and profit, and … a counterhegemonic discourse of losing" (Halberstam, 2011, pp. 11–12).

The foolish failure focusses (if paying attention for more than 5 minutes is possible) on subjugated knowledges that Foucault describes as "nonconceptual knowledges, as insufficiently elaborated knowledges: naive knowledges, hierarchically inferior knowledges, knowledges that are below the required level of erudition or scientificity" (2003, p. 7). These are the small, local, "regional or differential, incapable of unanimity and which derives its power solely from the fact that it is different from all the knowledges that surround it" (2003, p. 8). The language is a 'minor language', "less a product than a process of becoming minor, through which language is deterritorialized immediately social and political issues are engaged, and a collective assemblage of enunciation makes possible the invention of a people to come" (Bogue, 2010, p. 171). A minor literature is political, asubjective, collective, and revolutionary, existing "only in relation to a major language and [as] investments of that language for the purpose of making it minor" (Deleuze & Guattari, 1987, p. 105).

MEDIATING EXPERIMENTATION

So then, "how does it work"? (Deleuze, 1995). In the remainder of this chapter I offer ideas about how this position of foolish failure can open up specific possibilities for engaging with/in pleasurable academic work. The foolish failure is a mediator, underlining the "affective and relational nature of thought where potentially 'joyful' affects are Spinozan (Deleuze, 1988, p. 50, p. 124) in that they enhance the power to act" (Done et al., 2014, p. 269). The mediator is much more interested in collaboration and collective modes of inquiry than in individual success and grandstanding. The mediator offers advice that she never takes herself, she teaches others about the strategies and tactics required to survive the neoliberal jungle, while at the same time wallowing in the mud at the bottom of the pile. She refuses to eat her young (Zipin & Nuttall, 2016), instead leading them by the hand to greener pastures, helping and guiding them "to pursue theoretical interests and experiment with less positivist modes of inquiry" (Done et al., 2014, p. 278).

But this is not a rulebook, or a self-help survival guide for the early career academic. There are no paths to follow, no steps hollowed out of the sand or mud for others to use:

> What distinguishes the map from the tracing is that it is entirely oriented toward an experimentation in contact with the real. The map does not reproduce an unconscious closed in upon itself; it constructs the unconscious. (Deleuze & Guattari, 1987, p. 2)

It is an experimentation.

Mediators "facilitate the production of alternative truths" (Done et al, 2014, p. 269). For me this facilitation has three parts to it: deconstruction of the language that creates and orders our systems of order; creation of writing that is vitalist and heterogeneous; and a collective collaboration that forms a writingacademicassemblage (see Loch et al. in this book).

Deconstruct Language

Institutional education is stratified through a double pincer movement, an "unstable equilibrium" such that there are always "two distinct formalizations in reciprocal presupposition and constituting a double-pincer ... We are never signifier or signified. We are stratified" (Deleuze & Guattari, 1987, p. 67). Partly this stratification proceeds through language, through those order-words that "order always and already concerns prior orders" (Savat & Thompson, 2015, p. 278). For me the creation of circuit breakers and vacuoles are aided at least partly by a critical examination of language, how language helps to create this unstable equilibrium, how language contains always and already the ordering and orders of our systems of control.

So foolish failing academics examine the language that contains and controls us, questions and critiques and even laughs at its use. Here's an example of this language:

Build Process Improvement Capability

At the heart of service delivery lies the processes through which customer needs are identified and services delivered. A robustly designed process is critical to delivering the desired quality of service consistently and efficiently. Creating standard and streamlined processes for common activities can deliver benefits through reducing variability and enabling sharing of best practice. Variability at the local level (which do not add value to customers) is an impediment to a consistent service and customer experience and a barrier to the successful implementation of enterprise-wide systems.[2]

First look at the title: four words randomly assigned a syntactic place. Are they verbs? adjectives? adverbs? nouns? If we moved them around would that make any difference? Process Capability Build Improvement? Does that carry any more or less meaning?

These are the weasel words so loathed by Don Watson (2004). Whenever I read this type of management speak I am reminded of these lines from *Macbeth*:

it is a tale
Told by an idiot, full of sound and fury,
Signifying nothing.

And I think that this helps us understand what Deleuze was writing about when he tried to pull us away from the eternal signifier – from the fixation of ascribing a meaning to a word or series of words – because these words mean nothing, they are empty, hollow, or as Toni Morrison says:

It is the language that drinks blood, laps vulnerabilities, tucks its fascist boots under crinolines of respectability and patriotism as it moves relentlessly toward the bottom line and the bottomed out mind. (Morrison, 1993)

Yet while hollow, Helene Cixous reminds us that this language is also not idle, but actually works to crush us, to castrate or decapitate.

And I think we're completely crushed, especially in places like universities, by the highly repressive operations of metalanguage, the operations, that is, of the commentary on the commentary, the code, the operation that sees to it that the moment women open their mouths-women more often than men-they are immediately asked in whose name and from what theoretical standpoint they are speaking, who is their master and where are they coming from: they have, in short, to salute ... and show their identity papers. (Cixous & Kuhn, 1981, p. 51)

The foolish failing academic works continually against this language, against the movements to block us into a system that not only creates such vacuous language but urges us to use it. "We catch ourselves mouthing the comfortable cliches and platitudes" (Davies, 2005, p. 7). We engage in "that form of play called irony" (McWilliam, 2000, p. 174)

> Where sarcasm is ruled out of proper language deployment in education on the grounds of its intention to wound, where cold humor may be cold comfort, and where overt opposition is anticipated as the first step to unemployment, irony is a bright and shiny bauble among modernity's store of tarnished playthings. (McWilliam, 2000, p. 174)

This playful irony may appear through comments on social network pages, through 'following' and 'sharing' the humour and satire produced by others and each other (http://chronicle.com/article/AcademicsSay-The-Story/231195). It may even be found in academic manuscripts (Honan et al 2015), maybe even in chapters in this book.

Vitalist Writing

It is not enough though to play with deconstruction, to ironically point out platitudes and weasel words. Foolish failures also engage with subversion through making use of subjugated knowledge and minor literature to "de-form" academic writing (Kraemer, 1991, p. 58). Most of my current work is with PhD students and early career researchers who are subverting 'pre-existing' structures and thinking differently about research writing (see for example, Honan & Bright 2016; Honan et al., 2015). We write about how to think about doing a thesis differently, how to avoid the dangers of a structure that is repeated to the point of orthodoxy. We write about publishing in journals that 'don't count', we stretch the boundaries of the academic genres (Somerville, 2012) to include poetry, and images, lyrics, and screengrabs. We try to find words to use to replace the tired and trite, to rethink the language we use to write about method (Honan, 2014).

This requires a rethinking of academic writing, not as an act of applying the pre-existing, to create a style that is against style and structure. Writing that is vitalist,

> something unstable, always heterogeneous, in which style carves differences of potential between which things can pass, come to pass, a spark can flash and break out of language itself, to make us see and think what was lying in the shadow around the words, things we were hardly aware existed. (Deleuze, 1995, p. 141)

The sparks of this style of writing are produced through an irreverent "straining toward something that isn't syntactic nor even linguistic (something outside language)" (Deleuze, 1995, p. 164). This would be a writing that produces a language that is not "arid" but that can "vibrate with a new intensity" (Deleuze & Guattari, 1986, p. 19). Not writing according to what is expected, but writing to create – to bring something to life. This kind of writing is hard, and fascinating, and joyous, and difficult, and, and and ….

For Deleuze, writing is and was experimentation,

> Writing is a question of becoming, always incomplete, always in the midst of being formed, and goes beyond the matter of any liveable or lived experience. It is a process, that is, a passage of life that traverses both the liveable and the lived. (Gao, 2013, p. 414)

Writingassemblage

So how do we do it? How does it work? Well one way is to rethink the individual and once again this is a subversive act, possibly because as Deleuze and Guattari remind us, we are always being moved, pushed towards an ideal noble individual. How might we begin to actualize less individualistic academic subjectivities? Can we subvert traditional expectations of academic merit that requires a competitive, combative individual?

> The various forms of education or "normalization" imposed upon an individual consist in making him or her change points of subjectification, always moving toward a higher, nobler one in closer conformity with the supposed ideal. (Deleuze and Guattari, 1987, p. 129)

We need to remind ourselves of the joy of community, of collaboration, not collaboration because we have to do it, or it's strategic, or important for our careers, but seeking out those with collective interests, sustaining collegiality, and most importantly developing what Hil calls a counternarrative "that speaks of cooperation, collegiality, communality, civic engagement, citizenship rather than simply acquiescing to the competitive ethos of the market" (Hil, 2014, p. 65).

And finding the spaces to do this is quite hard; not even a physical space, but a gap, a vacuole, in our thinking about what it means even to do collective work. Is it possible to think of collaboration without assuming that "there are separate writers who exist in advance of writing who can come together to collaborate, to write a text together. I wonder whether one can think collaboration without the humanist subject" (Wyatt et al., 2014, p. 414). In another chapter in this book, three of us attempt to demonstrate this "writing as an assemblage– not the sum of separately existing identities" (Wyatt et al., 2014, p. 407). It is a joyous writing, a writing without responsibility, without our faces turned outwards to citation counts and journal rankings, but turned within to each other, we write to and through each other. One mentions a walk on the beach with a dog, and the other writes this image into their work, one uses the word 'crochety' to describe her feelings and they all take this up to write about crocheting together a piece of writing. We do not own words or pieces, we don't track changes or compare versions, we write.

–*Write messily*
–*Write assemblages*
–*Write pleasurably, monstrously, vitally*

–Spit it out, pour the words onto the page, ignore structures, recipes, top ten tips

AND SO

How can we dare to ask the questions that honour a passionate ideal of the academy where intellectual work is without fear, where it does not know, necessarily, where its questions might lead - passionate work that recognizes no boundaries that might prevent its development and where it also cares passionately about its effects. (Davies, 2005, p. 7)

Join with me in this pleasurable work, engage passionately in ideas and ideals, find a joy that is productive. Relish the opportunity to demonstrate your foolish failures, revel in ironic deconstructions of the linguistic binds that tie us into the positions of compliance. Find the moments of pleasure within these confined spaces.

In the other chapters in this book you will find opportunities to engage in this passionate work. The writers here use many different methods, write from many different theoretical perspectives, and produce many different meanings of the words, *pleasure* and *joy*. But, as the wordcloud image below reflects, the connections are closer than the disconnections, the questions asked are those that Bronwyn Davies urges upon us, questions that know no boundaries or answers, but help us engage with the political project of reclaiming the academic space as one with integrity, with passion, with creativity and pleasure.

NOTES

1. https://en.wikipedia.org/wiki/Divinyls
2. https://www.uq.edu.au/ess/process-architecture. I am not singling out this particular university, could have chosen any example randomly from any university's webpages.

REFERENCES

Ball, S. J. (2012). Performativity, commodification and commitment: An I-Spy guide to the neoliberal university, *British Journal of Educational Studies*, *60*(1), 17–28. doi: 10.1080/00071005.2011.650940

Bogue, R. (2010). Minoritarian+literature. In A. Parr (Ed.), *The Deleuze dictionary* (Revised ed., pp. 170–171). Edinburgh: Edinburgh University Press.

Buchanan, I. (2000). *Deleuzism: A metacommentary*. Edinburgh: Edinburgh University Press.

Cannizzo, F. (2016). The transformation of academic ideals: An Australian analysis. *Higher Education Research & Development*. doi: 10.1080/07294360.2016.1138454

Cixous, H., & Kuhn, A. (1981). Castration or decapitation? *Signs*, *7*(1), 41–55.

Davies, B. (2005). The (im)possibility of intellectual work in neoliberal regimes. *Discourse: Studies in the Cultural Politics of Education*, *26*(1), 1–14. doi: 10.1080/01596300500039310

Davies, B., & Bansel, P. (2010). Governmentality and academic work: Shaping the hearts and minds of academic workers. *JCT (Online)*, *26*(3), 5.

Davies, B., & Petersen, E. B. (2005). Neo-liberal discourse in the Academy: The forestalling of (collective) resistance. *Learning & Teaching in the Social Sciences*, *2*(2), 77–97.

Deleuze, G. (1992). Postscript on the Societies of Control. *October*, *59*, 3–7.

Deleuze, G. (1995). *Negotiations, 1972–1990*. Columbia University Press.

Deleuze, G., & Guattari, F. (1986). *Kafka: Toward a minor literature* (D. Polan, Trans.). Minneapolis: University of Minnesota Press.

Deleuze, G., & Guattari, F. (1987). *A thousand plateaus. Capitalism and schizophrenia*. London: The Athlone Press.

Done, E. J., Murphy, M., & Knowler, H. (2014). Post-identitarian postgraduate pedagogy: Deleuzian mediation and resistance to 'measuring up'. *Power and Education*, *6*(3), 268–282.

Foucault, M. (1988). *Madness and civilization: A history of insanity in the age of reason* (R. Howard, Trans.). New York: Vintage.

Foucault, M. (2003). *Society must be defended: Lectures at the College De France, 1975–1976* (D. Macey, Trans.). New York: Picador.

Gao, J. (2013). Deleuze's conception of Desire. *Deleuze Studies*, *7*(3), 406–420.

Gill, R. (2009). Breaking the silence: The hidden injuries of neo-liberal academia. In R. Flood & R. Gill (Eds.), *Secrecy and silence in the research process: Feminist reflections* (pp. 228–244). London: Routledge.

Giroux, H. A. (2003). Selling out higher education. *Policy Futures in Education*, *1*(1), 179–200.

Halberstam, J. (2011). *The queer art of failure*. Durhan & London: Duke University Press.

Hil, R. (2014). Post Whackademia? Putting the brakes on the neoliberal university juggernaut. *Social Alternatives*, *33*(2), 64–67.

Honan, E. (2014). Disrupting the habit of interviewing. *Reconceptualizing Educational Research Methodology*, *5*(1), 1–17.

Honan, E., & Bright, D. (2016). Writing a thesis differently. *International Journal of Qualitative Studies in Education*, *29*(5), 731–743.

Honan, E., Henderson, L., & Loch, S. (2015). Producing moments of pleasure within the confines of an academic quantified self. *Creative Approaches to Research*, *8(*3), 44–62.

Kern, L., Hawkins, R., Falconer Al-Hindi, K., & Moss, P. (2014). A collective biography of joy in academic practice. *Social & Cultural Geography*, *15*(7), 834–851. doi: 10.1080/14649365.2014.929729

Kraemer, D. (1991). Abstracting the bodies of/in academic discourse. *Rhetoric Review*, *10*(1), 52–69.

Lorde, A. (1984). The master's tools will not dismantle the master's house. *Sister outsider: Essays and speeches by Audre Lorde* (pp. 110–113). Trumansburg, NJ: Crossing Press.

McWilliam, E. (2000). Laughing within reason: On pleasure, women, and academic performance. In E. A. St. Pierre & W. S Pillow (Eds.), *Working the ruins: Feminist poststructural theory and methods in education* (pp. 164–178). New York: Routledge.

Mountz, A., Bonds, A., Mansfield, B., Loyd, J., Hyndman, J., Walton-Roberts, M., Basu, R., Whitson, R., Hawkins, R., Hamilton, T., & Curran, W. (2015). For slow scholarship: A feminist politics of resistance through collective action in the neoliberal university. *ACME: An International E-Journal for Critical Geographies, 14*(4), 1235–1259.

Mullini, R. (1985). Playing the fool: The pragmatic status of Shakespeare's clowns. *New Theatre Quarterly, 1*, 98–104. doi:10.1017/S0266464X00001457

Murphie, A. (2014) 'Auditland'. *PORTAL Journal of Multidisciplinary International Studies, 11*(2), 1–41.

O'Gorman, R., & Werry, M. (2012). On failure (on pedagogy): Editorial introduction. *Performance Research: A Journal of the Performing Arts, 17*(1), 1–8. doi: 10.1080/13528165.2012.651857

Savat, D., & Thompson, G. (2015). Education and the relation to the outside: A little real reality. *Deleuze Studies, 9*(3), 273–300.

Somerville, M. J. (2012). Textual genres and the question of representation. In S. Delamont & A. Jones (Eds.), *Handbook of qualitative research in education* (pp. 533–541). Cheltenham: Edward Elgar.

Tamboukou, T. (2012). Truth telling in Foucault and Arendt: Parrhesia, the pariah and academics in dark times, *Journal of Education Policy, 27*(6), 849–865. doi: 10.1080/02680939.2012.694482

Wallin, J. (2012) 'Bon Mots for Bad Thoughts'. *Discourse: Studies in the Cultural Politics of Education, 33*(1), 147–162.

Watson, D. (2004). *Death sentence: The decay of public language*. North Sydney, NSW: Vintage.

Wyatt, J., Gale, K., Gannon, S., Davies, B., Denzin, N. K., & St. Pierre, E. A. (2014). Deleuze and collaborative writing: Responding to/with "JKSB". *Cultural Studies ↔ Critical Methodologies, 14*(4), 407–416.

Zipin, L., & Nuttall, J. (2016). Embodying pre-tense conditions for research among teacher educators in the Australian university sector: A Bourdieusian analysis of ethico-emotive suffering. *Asia-Pacific Journal of Teacher Education, 44*(4), 348–363. doi: 10.1080/1359866X.2016.1177164

Eileen Honan
School of Education
The University of Queensland, Australia

STEWART RIDDLE

3. 'DO WHAT SUSTAINS YOU'

Desire and the Enterprise University

DO WHAT SUSTAINS YOU PART I

early career researcher workshop
Strategic Capacity Building for Academic Career Development
eager for answers – the plan – the road map
here comes the advice …
lean in and listen closely

"Do what sustains you"

sustains me? Dear Google, what is?
sustain – 1. to strengthen or support, physically or mentally
2. to undergo or to suffer something unpleasant, especially an injury
I'll take the first option, thanks

late capitalism, neoliberalism, humanism, modernity
we have made quite a mess of things
but surely someone will clean it up
if not us, then who?
if we can't sustain our world
how can we hope to sustain ourselves?
Eomer warns: look to your friends
but do not look to hope, for it has forsaken these lands

what is this thing, the enterprise university?
who called it into being?
what does it produce?
how does it produce us, its subjects?
we are coded and striated
ranked and labelled and sorted
unrecognizable to ourselves
knowable as academics
produce more, produce faster, produce better
Quartile 1, Category 1

Rank File Sort Coded 1
1, 1, 1, 1 ...

desire, desiringmachines, desiring production
do we really desire our own oppression?
fascism as a war machine
mobilising the desire for self-destruction

I lack a sense of certainty, a clarity, a finality
I fear the one who has the answer
to the thing
I'm not sure I even know what the thing is
where are the gaps
the breaks in the assemblage
the places for rupture and interruption?

LIVING THE ENTERPRISE UNIVERSITY

Peer-reviewer's comments on a paper:

It started off well, but it's like the author gave up halfway through

Academics live in strange times. Everywhere we are coded and constructed within the machine of the enterprise university to faithfully produce high quality research outputs and secure competitive external research funding grants. We are counted and graded, chopped up and classified, found to be acceptable (or otherwise) within the logical bounds of a system that rewards entrepreneurial and innovative research that secures large grants and is published in high-ranked research journals.

We are the new hyper-performers, outdoing ourselves and each other on each metric devised and implemented in local institutions and across nations. There are very real effects on the physical and mental health of academics who are unable or unwilling to reject the self-defeating logic of a system that appears determined to eat its young in a race to produce outputs in ever increasing speeds and intensities. It is little wonder that such an alarming situation has resulted in a widespread malaise of disaffection, anxiety and stress among academics (Petersen, 2011).

Researchers are formed as knowable subjects through the machine of the enterprise university. Individuals plug in and produce outputs in the service of the larger machines of institutional academia, connecting and disconnecting at various places and times, depending on the functions being fulfilled and the various flows of desire. Yet, we know that this is not necessarily how it *should* be just because it *is* this way. The contemporary university might seem like no accident, yet it is a contingent effect of particular political, social and economic circumstances that might well be otherwise, should we desire it to be so. Along with Cupples and Pawson (2012), I desire "moments and spaces of tactical re-appropriation, in which it might be possible to imagine and construct alternative narratives" (p. 15) for our academic labours.

In this chapter I seek to engage with some advice that was given at an early career research workshop, where the presenter proposed a simple formula: *Do what sustains you*. Working with Deleuze and Guattari's (1983, 1987) notion of desire, I am interested in experimenting and playing within a space of strategic refusal, creative and affirming, in order to find a way that both works within and against the grain of the enterprise university. By tapping into the immanent forces and flows of an academic vitality, I suggest that we might meaningfully and collectively sustain ourselves through a slower, more care-full, creative and collaborative scholarship. At the same time, I am mindful of the dangers of desire, where we might find ourselves desiring our own oppression (Deleuze & Guattari, 1983) and behaving in ways that run counter to our ethical principles through a desire to be known as successful academic subjects (Petersen, 2009). As an early career researcher, I desire longevity as an academic and also to do work that is meaningful (not that I am sure I know what the measure of this might be), and to do work that sustains me. This is a challenge in the contemporary enterprise university.

Marginson and Considine (2000) describe the *enterprise university* as being characterised by a range of strategies designed to enhance institutional prestige and income, including: corporatized executive control and governance, enterprise culture and focus on entrepreneurship and the creation of pseudo-markets. A powerful effect of the enterprise mission is on academic subjectivities, which are "subordinated to the mission, marketing and strategic development of the institution and its leaders" (Marginson & Considine, 2000, p. 5). The past couple of decades have seen an intensification and acceleration of the enterprise university, evident in the manta of *constant change* and corporate-driven restructures across many universities in places such as Australia and the United Kingdom.

Additionally, individual academics themselves have become sites for acceleration in the enterprise university, both in therapeutic and entrepreneurial terms. At the same time, the structural relations of people, institutions and nature are often deliberately ignored. For example, in one day from my university, I took great satisfaction in deleting three official university emails that explained that the university was 1) forming a digital hub that would focus on innovation, entrepreneurship and digital lives; 2) exterminating native bees on the university campus, and 3) offering mindfulness workshops to help increase employee self-awareness and satisfaction. I cannot shake the feeling that the mindfulness workshops are a manoeuvre to ensure that *well-being* is maintained for a productive set of knowledge workers in the enterprise university. It makes good economic sense to have a happy, productive workforce if you want to maximize your outputs.

Kelly (2015) writes of a day in the life and death of the enterprise university, of fissures and slippages between dominant and subversive discourses. Perhaps in my deleting of the three emails I was being subversive, but perhaps their messaging had already filtered into my academic subjectivity, a small but significant part of the ongoing creeping permeation of the performativity of the enterprise university ... until one day I wake up and find that I myself have become the monster I most fear.

A long-time friend and musician (not an academic) recently suggested to me that the pinnacle of academic success would be having my portrait hung in a university boardroom. I laughed and said that if that ever happened to me, I would have gone horribly wrong somewhere along the way. But it does speak to my whispering uncertainty that while I think I might be doing scholarly work that goes against the grain of the enterprise university, such as this chapter, all the while I am drawn in deeper.

The enterprise university is an effect of a wider socio-political system of neoliberalism, which can be understood as a series of governmental techniques with particular social, economic and political formations. Ball (2012) describes how neoliberalism "gets into our minds and our souls, into the ways in which we think about what we do, and into our social relations with others" (p. 18). These relations themselves become a factor in the knowledge production of universities, where innovation and agility become much more than glib words spoken by politicians. Lynch (2015) argues that there is a danger in the transactional and product-led set of relations, where "constant appraisal leads to the internalization of an actuarial and calculative mind set both at the individual and collective levels" (p. 199). It seeps not only into the behaviours of academics, but into their very being: an ontological becoming of the academic-entrepreneur.

Perhaps most concerning is that there appears to be an unquestioning acceptance of continuous appraisal and audit at the heart of the enterprise university. From annual performance reviews to promotion and tenure applications, competitive grant rounds, and the valorization of impact metrics such as citation counts, H-indices, publication quartiles and journal rankings, the work and worth of academics is reduced to what is knowable through such apparatuses. Davies and Bansel (2010) argue that these technologies of audit and appraisal work to "standardise and regularise expert knowledges so that they can be used to classify and diagnose populations of workers and the potential risks in managing them" (p. 7). If knowledge is the new capital, then knowledge workers are the new proletariat, a necessary source of labour for the knowledge-capital machine, but certainly not to be trusted. Shore (2008) argues that the disciplinary technologies of audit are not simply thrust upon academics, but that academics themselves are complicit in its shaping of academic subjects. A colleague from another university once showed me a shiny new *continuous improvement matrix* that they had designed for their university department. I could barely contain my horror.

The performative culture of the enterprise university that demands hyper-accountability from academics calls forth new skills of "presentation and of inflation, making the most of ourselves, making a spectacle of ourselves. As a consequence, we become transparent but empty, unrecognisable to ourselves" (Ball, 2012, p. 19). However, this is no matter, so long as there are growing research outputs matching an increasingly strict set of 'quality' requirements. I find the idea of becoming unrecognizable of particular interest, given the emphasis that

Deleuze and Guattari (1987) give to the process of *becoming*, where the myriad constant formation of new multiplicities replaces the humanist ideal of the stable, rational subject. Why should it not be so with the academic subject, who is in a state of constant flux and always becoming-academic? I wonder then, what a circuit-breaker to the enterprise university might produce, or what might happen if academics everywhere were to take up Bartleby's formula and say, "I prefer not to". I am not convinced that this is something that will happen any time soon. In the meantime, I will try to stick with the formula of doing work that sustains me.

Part of the normalizing effect of the enterprise university comes from its *responsibilization* of academic citizens (Ferguson, 2009), who are treated like miniature firms within a broader competitive network, incentivized to perform in ways that adhere to the university mission and research plan. It is worth noting that perhaps what is being produced through these efforts is "endless activity and innovation that may add up in accord with the university's metrics, but from a transformational perspective rarely adds to" (Meyerhoff, Johnson. & Braun, 2011, p. 489). This begs the question; why do we do these activities?

Davies and Petersen (2005) ask us to consider how it has become normalized and viable for academics to "control, regulate and report on their own work and on the work of others" (p. 34) through the technologies of audit and appraisal that are so widespread in the enterprise university. It seems to be an important question, one that goes to the heart of this chapter's concern with the role of desire and the academic as a desiring-machine. Indeed, "we collaborate, we conspire, we accede, we encourage each other to produce ourselves as quantified" (Honan, Henderson, & Loch, 2015, p. 47). Along with Petersen (2009), I wonder whether we are able to "not-further, to not-sanction, in word and action, the construction of the university and of academic life rolled into many of the rationalities, apparatuses and practices at work in the enterprise university" (p. 410). How might we do this? Is it even a desirable thing?

ACADEMICS AS DESIRINGMACHINES

A conversation with a colleague:

I would like to be a professor at some point in the next ten years or so

Why?

To prove that I can do it, I guess

Okay, but are going to need many more high-profile publications

I know

For Deleuze and Guattari (1983), the notion of desire is straightforward: "desire is a machine, a synthesis of machines, a machinic arrangement—desiringmachines" (p. 296). Buchanan (2008) argues that Deleuze and Guattari's view of desire is an "affirmative notion of production, setting aside the standard negative notion of desire as lack or need" and that "desire does not need to be stimulated by an exogenous force such as need or want, it is a stimulus in its own right" (p. 47). Deleuze and Guattari (1983) say:

> To a certain degree, the traditional logic of desire is all wrong from the very outset: from the very first step that the Platonic logic of desire forces us to take, making us choose between *production* and *acquisition*. From the moment that we place desire on the side of acquisition, we make desire an idealistic (dialectical, nihilistic) conception, which causes us to look upon it as primarily a lack: a lack of an object, a lack of the real object. (p. 25)

Desire flows and produces modes of intensities (Deleuze & Guattari, 1983), a migratory and nomadic traversing of vibrations and flows. Perhaps Deleuze and Guattari's (1987) notion of the *body without organs* comes closest to how I think a move towards knowing the academic as a desiringmachine. They say that the body without organs involves the "connection of desires, conjunction of flows, continuum of intensities. You have constructed your own little machine, ready when needed to be plugged into other collective machines" (Deleuze & Guattari, 1987, p. 161). Indeed, the body without organs is desire itself: blocs of becoming, intensities, particles and fluxes (Deleuze & Parnet, 2002). It is not what desire means but what desire does that is important (Deleuze & Guattari, 1983). How does the academic as desiringmachine work? What does is produce? What effect might the desiringmachine have on the enterprise university?

Colebrook (2014) describes how the micro-perceptions of sympathies, affects and desires work to produce us as social and political beings. She says that, "it is true that for the most part our desires follow the paths of least resistance, perhaps accepting what has always been deemed to be acceptable" (pp. 119-120). This might, in some way, explain how it is that academics might work in ways that run counter to their own sense of justice and purpose, in order to gain recognition, acceptance and reward within the enterprise university. It is hard to argue with an annual performance review proforma or promotion application after all.

Of course, we understand that "desire can be made to desire its own repression (Deleuze & Guattari, 1983, p. 105). The very desire for success as an academic (whatever criteria might be employed to determine this) call forth a particular submission to the machinery of performativity and accountability that come with working in the enterprise university. But does that mean that we should simply accede to our desire for being seen as successful? I don't think so. Deleuze and Guattari (1987) provide a further warning about desire:

> Desire is never separable from complex assemblages that necessarily tie into molecular levels, from microformations already shaping postures, attitudes, perceptions, expectations, semiotic systems, etc. Desire is never an

undifferentiated instinctual energy, but itself results from a highly developed, engineered setup rich in interactions: a whole supple segmentarity that processes molecular energies and potentially gives desire a fascist determination. Leftist organizations will not be the last to secrete microfascisms. It's too easy to be antifascist on the molar level, and not even see the fascist inside you, the fascist you yourself sustain and nourish and cherish with molecules both personal and collective. (p. 215)

The turning of desire against itself in order to desire one's own subjugation to the microfascisms of the enterprise university is a clear outcome of the academic as desiringmachine. For Deleuze and Guattari (1987), much attention is given to molar fascism, while the real danger perhaps comes from the microfascism of individuals themselves. In the enterprise university, molar fascisms might include the institutional policies and procedures of particular universities' research strategies or national research measurements such as the Research Excellence Framework in the United Kingdom and the Excellence in Research for Australia. While our attention might be focussed on the effects of these large exercises on academics' lives, less is given to the microfascist acts that come from self-interest and survival within the academy. As Petersen (2009) points out, the ultimate tyranny in the enterprise university is that "it is nice people who enforce monstrous policies" (p. 419).

There is a significant tension between practices of self-interest and survival, with the dual "discourses of individualisation and autonomy and de-individualisation and regularisation" (Davies & Bansel, 2010, p. 9) constantly at work on academic subjectivities. Bansel et al. (2008) remind us that academics engage in contradictory survival tactics of compliance and subversion in the enterprise university. It is a dangerous tightrope to walk, yet one that sits at the centre of the academic experience. What is it that we desire when we do so? Petersen (2009) asks how we become "complicit in upholding practices and desires that we also and otherwise reject. What does desire for promotion, for instance, make us vulnerable to? How are such desires produced and upheld, and how are they constituted as legitimate?" (p. 419).

Perhaps there is some hope in the notion that "desire is revolutionary because it always wants more connections and assemblages" (Deleuze & Parnet, 2002, p. 79). If we are always seeking to make a bigger impact with research (however that might be measured in this particular research audit or that one), then perhaps that might open up productive circuits for research-creation that were not otherwise possible. At the same time, in the desire to become "calculable rather than memorable" (Ball, 2012, p. 17) through metrics and other performative devices, there is a decreasing number of acceptable forms of creative activities available to academics (Meyerhoff, Johnson, & Braun, 2011). When the only thing that counts is that which is countable, other possible ways of acting on the world are foreclosed. This is a serious concern, given that there is a real pressure from appraisal and audit technologies in the university.

For example, Honan, Henderson and Loch (2015) argue that our institutional selves are constructed as lacking and our desire is mobilised to 'fill' that lack. They say, "We spend our days and nights, hours and hours, trying to plug up the holes, trying to stuff them with the cotton wool stuffing of appeasement, of reassurance, endlessly completing futile and empty tasks, searching for that moment of completeness, of success" (p. 47). It seems that the enterprise university relies on a Freudian-Lacanian desire of lack, where academics are required to perform ever-more contradictory and self-defeating microfascist acts of preservation in order to compete within the system and thus become complete.

While Deleuze and Guattari do not necessarily provide a 'way out' of the machine in which we find ourselves, their productive desire does allow for a more molecular understanding of the academic as a desiringmachine. By seeing the fascist within, perhaps we are then able to better negotiate the complex and contradictory sets of political, social and economic relations that form the assemblage of the enterprise university. Or maybe not. At the very least, we might seek for a more permissive and pleasurable approach to the performativities of producing ourselves as academics.

TOWARDS A SLOWER, MORE CARE-FULL ACADEMIC DESIRINGMACHINE

An annual performance review:

Do you want to be promoted to the next level?

Yes

You need a six-figure external research grant; otherwise, don't even bother

The pressure to be known as a productive academic is present across all aspects of the academic machine, but is especially pronounced in our desire for writing outputs. Things such as impact factors and H-indexes exist because we desire that we be "constituted and regulated through technologies of audit and writing" (Bansel et al., 2008, p. 673). There is a certain sense of achievement and comfort provided from the quantified, ranked and sorted indices of audit technologies, which can be seductive to the unwary researcher. At the same time, there is promise in writing which breaks free, as Deleuze and Guattari (1986) argue, "writing has a double function: to translate everything into assemblages and to dismantle the assemblages. The two are the same thing" (p. 47). Much like desire, this double function often sees academic *freedom* both found and lost, through the act of writing. Of course, all of this is unimportant. The only thing of interest for the enterprise university is that the writing *counts*.

Yet the focus on outputs and metrics as the measure of academic worth has an effect of configuring relationships in the enterprise university as a means to a particular end (Lynch, 2015), "the end being high performance and productivity that can be coded and marketed. This reduces first order social and moral values to second-order principles; trust, integrity, care and solidarity are subordinated to regulation, control and competition" (p. 195).

I wonder what a refusal of audit and accountability structures might produce. What would be the consequence of changing from a focus of accountability to responsibility (Cupples & Pawson, 2012), which involves a significant tactical shift of academic subjectivities? What might result from reversing the focus on regulation, control and competition back to trust, integrity, care and solidarity as first-order principles? As Ball (2012) argues, in the enterprise university the re-orientation of scholarly activities towards measurable performance outcomes is a first-order effect of performativity, and these deflect "attention away from aspects of social, emotional or moral development that have no immediate measurable performative value" (p. 20). What would happen if we were able to focus instead on the social and emotional aspects of academic labour?

There is a double-edge to the affective dimensions of the academic desiringmachine. For example, "one of the predominant emotions of the neo-liberal university is resentment rather than pleasure" (Meyerhoff, Johnson, & Braun, 2011, p. 493). I would add envy and pride to this mix, which are powerful motivating agents in the individualized and competitive environment of the contemporary university. It is very nearly a Hobbesian state of affairs, where individual academics compete against others for tenure, promotion, grants, incentives and other accolades, while being produced as effective and efficient knowledge workers who are innovative and entrepreneurial. Petersen (2009) describes the delicate balance of resistance and enrolment in the enterprise university. She says:

> resistance to neoliberal rationalities and practices must consist of deliberate promotion and nurturing of counter-neoliberal rationalities and practices, in order to prevent neoliberal discourses from coagulating and becoming hegemonic. The deliberate promotion and nurturing must happen at both the collective and individual level; collective and persistent critique of the naturalisation of monstrous practices and desires will make individual courage increasingly possible and likely, but individual responsibility for upholding counter-neoliberal discourse should not be stalled in the meantime. (p. 420)

Mountz and colleagues (2015) remind us that there is a "need amid the chaos to slow – things – down" (p. 1238). In the contemporary enterprise university, how might it be possible to decelerate … to just slow down? The call for a slower, collective and care-full scholarship seems particularly important, given the troubling effects of acceleration and compression of time-space of the enterprise university on academic lives (Davies & Bansel, 2005).

Ulmer (2016) calls for a slow ontology, which brings forth "modes of writing scholarly research that are not unproductive, but are differently productive" (p. 1) in the desire for more pleasurable forms of scholarly activity. Alongside a slower scholarship that provides for pleasurable academic work, I would place a more *care-full* scholarship (Mountz et al., 2015). Lynch (2015) argues that care is "not open to measurement in terms of quality, substance and form within a metric measurement system" (p. 201), with measurement, surveillance, control and regulation being at odds with the need for care. Working from an ethic of care requires a slower temporality, one that resists the auditability of the measured and instead gives rise to multiple academic and non-academic outcomes (Evans, 2016).

At the same time, slow and care-full scholarship is not just about individual academics finding the cracks and spaces from which to create pleasure, but should form a bigger picture of remaking the university through "cultivating caring academic cultures and processes" (Mountz et al., 2015, p. 1238). I wonder, what does a more caring university look like? Can it still be an enterprise university if we all resisted enrolment in its work intensification and instead practised care-full and slow scholarship that connected deeply to the rich veins of our individual and collective knowledges?

Refusal is also at the heart of a slower, care-full scholarship. Meyerhoff, Johnson and Braun (2011) consider the potential of events of individual and collective disruption and refusal, where the possibility of new subjectivities and temporalities arise. At the same time, I am cautious about simply replacing *ninja-like productivity* with an overly-simplified or regressive ethic of slowness (Vostal, 2014) as I am not sure what a more radical slowness might mean. It seems to me that there is promise in creating different refusal spaces where we might speak, think, write, create and play in different ways (Lather & St. Pierre, 2013) that perhaps more expressively tap into our academic desiringmachines.

I fear the potential damage of a learned docility that results from constant appraisal and audit, the *being seen to be seen* of accountability and performativity regimes of the enterprise university. How is it possible to be radical, to be slow, to reconfigure the academic desiringmachine in a less fascist way? I am not sure that simply slowing down will be enough. No doubt a certain strategy and tendency to the tactical is necessary. I am reminded of the advice to do work that sustains me and wonder whether it might be the way out of the bind of performativity in which the enterprise university places us.

Cupples and Pawson (2012) envisage an enterprise university that is inhabited by tactical AND responsible academics engaging in more critical and democratic citizenship. I am not entirely sure how to reconcile the notion of tactical playing-the-game alongside a care-full and caring scholarship, but it is intriguing nonetheless. Perhaps a commitment to resistance within a framework of general compliance is the only way to *survive* as an academic. Perhaps not. Along with Honan, Henderson and Loch (2015), I am seeking the moments "when desire is released from the restricted codes of the academy, when the transformative production of desire moves us beyond and away" (p. 52). What does it move us toward? I am not sure. That is why it is so exciting and terrifying.

DO WHAT SUSTAINS YOU PART II

music
coffee, whiskey, laughter

words sinuously stretching
time compresses a little and then wanders on ...
– email – DING!
um, no thanks
alright, but then I will keep writing
what happened to the day?

words and then more words
choose them carefully, creatively, concisely
be quotable but not too much
seeking flow, cohesion, clarity, focus

I remember some advice = do what sustains me
... this sustains me ... this does
not the crazy stuff that litters my working hours
all the thousand tiny things
instead, the pleasures of a writing project
or a cabal of renegade academics
who refuse to be simply coded and counted
as nothing more than the sum of their outputs

academic desiringmachines
desiring something other than what we've been told we must
doing something because it feels good
to work together
sharing a collective desire for wisdom
a slow, care-full refusal

This is what sustains me

REFERENCES

Ball, S. (2012). Performativity, commodification and commitment: an I-spy guide to the neoliberal university. *British Journal of Educational Studies*, *60*(1), 17–28. doi: 10.1080/00071005.2011.650940

Bansel, P., Davies, B., Gannon, S., & Linnell, S. (2008). Technologies of audit at work on the writing subject: a discursive analysis. *Studies in Higher Education*, *33*(6), 673–683. doi: 10.1080/03075070802457017

Buchanan, I. (2008). *Deleuze and Guattari's Anti-Oedipus: A reader's guide*. London: Continuum.

Colebrook, C. (2014). *Sex after life: Essays on extinction, Vol 2*. Ann Arbor, MI: Open Humanities Press.

Cupples, J., & Pawson, E. (2012). Giving an account of oneself: The PBRF and the neoliberal university. *New Zealand Geographer*, *68*, 14–23. doi: 10.1111/j.1745-7939.2012.01217.x

Davies, B., & Bansel, P. (2005). The time of their lives? Academic workers in neoliberal time(s). *Health Sociology Review*, *14*(1), 47–58. doi:10.5172/hesr.14.1.47

Davies, B., & Bansel, P. (2010). Governmentality and academic work: shaping the hearts and minds of academic workers. *Journal of Curriculum Theorizing*, *26*(3), 5–20.

Davies, B., & Petersen, E. B. (2005). Intellectual workers (un)doing neoliberal discourse. *International Journal of Critical Psychology, 13*, 32–54.

Deleuze, G. (1997). *Essays critical and clinical* (D. Smith & M. A. Greco, Trans.). Minneapolis, MN: University of Minnesota Press.

Deleuze, G., & Guattari, F. (1983). *Anti-Oedipus: Capitalism and schizophrenia* (R. Hurley, M. Seem, & H. R. Lane, Trans.). Minneapolis, MN: University of Minnesota Press.

Deleuze, G., & Guattari, F. (1986). *Kafka: toward a minor literature* (D. Polan, Trans.). Minneapolis, MN: University of Minnesota Press

Deleuze, G., & Guattari, F. (1987). *A thousand plateaus: Capitalism and schizophrenia* (B. Massumi, Trans.). Minneapolis: University of Minnesota Press.

Deleuze, G., & Parnet, C. (2002). *Dialogues II* (H. Tomlinson & B. Habberjam, Trans.). London: Continuum.

Evans, R. (2016). Achieving and evidencing research 'impact'? Tensions and dilemmas from an ethic of care perspective. *Area, 48*(2), 213–221. doi:10.1111/area.12256

Ferguson, J. (2009). The uses of neoliberalism. *Antipode, 41*(1), 166–184. doi:10.1111/j.1467-8330.2009.00721.x

Honan, E., Henderson, L., & Loch, S. (2015). Producing moments of pleasure within the confines of an academic quantified self. *Creative Approaches to Research, 8*(3), 44–62.

Kelly, F. (2015). A day in the life (and death) of a public university. *Higher Education Research & Development, 34*(6), 1153–1163. doi:10.1080/07294360.2015.1024628

Lather, P., & St. Pierre, E. A. (2013). Post-qualtitative research. *International Journal of Qualitative Studies in Education, 26*(6), 629–633. doi: 10.1080/09518398.2013.7887520

Lynch, K. (2015). Control by numbers: new managerialism and ranking in higher education. *Critical Studies in Education, 56*(2), 190–207. doi:10.1080/17508487.2014.949811

Marginson, S., & Considine, M. (2000). *The enterprise university: Power, governance and reinvention in Australia*. Cambridge University Press.

Meyerhoff, E., Johnson, E., & Braun, B. (2011). Time and the university. *ACME: An International E-Journal for Critical Geographies, 10*(3), 483-507.

Mountz, A., Bonds, A., Mansfield, B., Loyd, J., Hyndman, J., Walton-Roberts, M., ... Curran, W. (2015). For slow scholarship: a feminist politics of resistance through collective action in the neoliberal university. *ACME: An International E-Journal for Critical Geographies, 14*(4), 1235–1259.

Petersen, E. B. (2009). Resistance and enrolment in the enterprise university: an ethnodrama in three acts, with appended reading. *Journal of Education Policy, 24*(4), 409–422. doi:10.1080/02680930802669953

Petersen, E. B. (2011). Staying or going? Australian early career researchers' narratives of academic work, exit options and coping strategies. *Australian Universities' Review, 53*(2), 34–42.

Shore, C. (2008). Audit culture and Illiberal governance Universities and the politics of accountability. *Anthropological Theory, 8*(3), 278–298. doi: 10.1177/1463499608093815

Ulmer, J. B. (2016). Writing slow ontology. *Qualitative Inquiry*. doi:10.1177/1077800416643994

Vostal, F. (2015). Academic life in the fast lane: The experience of time and speed in British academia. *Time and Society, 24*(1), 71–95. doi: 10.1177/0961463X13517537

Stewart Riddle
School of Teacher Education and Early Childhood
University of Southern Queensland, Australia

DAVID BRIGHT

4. THE PLEASURE OF WRITING

Escape from the Dominant System

God doesn't want me to be a writer. But I have no choice.
(Kafka)

INTRODUCTION

It may be – I'm not really sure yet – that I am committing a certain kind of error in employing Deleuze to write about the pleasure of writing, given that Deleuze, in his own words, could "hardly bear the word 'pleasure'" (Deleuze, 1997, p. 189). Whether this is the case remains to be seen, but for now, at least, it is the elaboration of the possibility of this mistake that forms of the basis of this chapter: in other words, writing about (the possibility of the mistake of writing about) the pleasure of writing with Deleuze. Here is my declaration of intent[1]: it is my argument that the pleasure (though, as we shall see, pleasure may be the wrong idea here) of writing can be read *inter alia* as the creative and productive aspects of desire as the production of new forms of subjectivity through the process of writing itself. And that this production may, at least, be found in the processes of what Deleuze and Guattari (1986) term a 'minor literature' and Ronald Bogue (1997, p. 111) describes as 'minor writing': writing that produces escape from dominant modes of being. As such, this chapter is written around the problem of reading writing as the work of how writing writes the self – synthesising a self – rather than a self producing writing. I use the work of Deleuze and Guattari here to suggest that a minor literature might offer possibilities for desiring-production in academic writing. This is writing that, in the words of Deleuze and Guattari, that "is affected with a high coefficient of deterritorialization" (1986, p. 16), that is, writing that produces movement and change, forming new connections and producing new and innovative forms of subjectivity that diverge from the dominant (major) modes of being writerly.

~~THE~~ MY (DIS-)PLEASURE ~~OF~~ ⁁WITH THE ⁁ACADEMIC TEXT

In *The Pleasure of the Text*, Roland Barthes proposes two kinds of texts: those of pleasure (*plaisir*), and those of *jouissance*.[2] The text of pleasure, Barthes writes, is "the text that contents, fills, grants euphoria; the text that comes from culture and does not break with it, is linked to a comfortable practice of reading" (1975, p. 14). This is a text that does what it is supposed to do, that conforms to expectations and is, thus, recognisable as such – satisfying, as Miklitsch (1983, p. 103) writes, the "convention-derived expectations of the kind of text it is ... (so much so that, while or after reading it, he feels: This is what a text should be)".

Not exactly opposed to the text of pleasure, yet different, for Barthes, is the text of *jouissance*. Unlike the text of pleasure, the text of *jouissance* is unsettling, subversive, unconventional, a text that produces a moment opposed to convention, expectation, and recognition:

> the text that imposes a state of loss, the text that discomforts (perhaps to the point of a certain boredom), unsettles the reader's historical, cultural, psychological assumptions, the consistency of his tastes, values, memories, brings to a crisis his relation with language. (Barthes, 1975, p. 14)

Texts of pleasure; texts of bliss. So far, so neat and tidy. But as Miklitsch (1983, p. 105) notes, "a particular text is neither wholly a "text of pleasure" nor a "text of bliss": it is always already both". For Barthes, neither the conformist, conventional text of pleasure nor the unsettling, disruptive text of *jouissance* is to be privileged; he remains opposed to instituting and institutionalizing a hierarchy of the pleasure of the text, where pleasure is inferior to *jouissance* (Miklitsch, 1983). Pleasure and *jouissance* are, though different, not opposed in kind. As Duncan and Duncan (1992, p. 26) write,[3] "*plaisir* is the more comforting form of pleasure and *jouissance* the more demanding and tension-producing" Miklitsch, meanwhile, notes that there is also the problem of there being no clear point of distinction where one becomes the other:

> Part of the problem of describing the difference between 'pleasure' (*plaisir*) and 'bliss' (*jouissance*) or, in English, 'forepleasure' and 'orgasm', is that there is no absolute difference between them, no 'point' (the Aristotelian *stigme*) at which it is possible to say that one ends and the other begins: When does pleasure end and orgasm begin? (1983, pp. 109–110)

In his later work, *S/Z*, Barthes (1974) proposes another two kinds of text: the *readerly*, "what can be read, but not written", and the *writerly,* the goal of which "is to make the reader no longer a consumer, but a producer of the text" (p. 4). This distinction seems in some ways analogous with the earlier distinction between the readable and recognizable texts of pleasure and the difficult and provocative texts of *jouissance*, however, here the privileging of the *writerly* is explicit:

> Our literature is characterized by the pitiless divorce which the literary institution maintains between the producer of the text and its user, between its owner and its customer, between its author and its reader. This reader is thereby plunged into a kind of idleness – he is intransitive; he is, in short, *serious*: instead of functioning himself, instead of gaining access to the magic of the signifier, to the pleasure of writing, he is left with no more than the poor freedom either to accept or reject the text: reading is nothing more than a *referendum*. (Barthes, 1974, p. 4)

It seems not very difficult to read much of academic writing (and here I refer, in the main, to what St. Pierre (2011, 2016) has described as "conventional humanist qualitative" inquiry) as *referenda*: an academic literary institution in which serious academic texts are submitted to serious academic publishers and journals to be accepted or rejected by serious academic readers according to the serious conventions and expectations of the various and serious epistemological and methodological disciplines from which they emerge – texts that come from culture and do not break with it in order to be recognisable and acceptable as such.[4] Laurel Richardson (1994) has described this model of social-scientific academic writing as static and mechanistic, "scientific" in its belief in objectivity, precision, unambiguity, truth and reality. St. Pierre (in Richardson & St. Pierre, 2005, p. 967) describes being *trained* to think of writing in this way: 'as a tracing of thought already thought, as a transparent reflection of the known and the real – writing as representation, as repetition'. This is the type of writing that constitutes what Deleuze and Guattari call the "root-book", that which:

> imitates the world, as art imitates nature: by procedures specific to it that accomplish what nature cannot or can no longer do. The law of the book is the law of reflection, the One that becomes two. ... what we have before us is the most classical and well reflected, oldest, and weariest kind of thought. (Deleuze & Guattari, 1987, p. 5)

This is comforting, readerly, scientific, academic writing that intends and claims to signify in a neatly binary fashion. Beginning with what "really happened", writing forms a copy, standing in for "the real", tracing the already thought, the already occurred, imitating the world, the One. Such writing brooks no crises in language; it can only be read and judged on its communicative intent and achievements – Does it do what it is supposed to do? Does it conform to the expectations of the discipline? Is it recognisable as conventional humanist qualitative inquiry?

But, to read and write language in this way ignores, as Richardson (1994, p. 346) explains, "the role of writing as a dynamic, creative process". Deleuze and Guattari's concepts of language and writing have little to representing the world and communicating the word. In the introduction to *A Thousand Plateaus: Capitalism and Schizophrenia*, they write:

> We will never ask what a book means, as signified or signifier; we will not look for anything to understand in it. We will ask what it functions with, in connection with what other things it does or does not transmit intensities, in which other multiplicities its own are inserted and metamorphosed, and with what bodies without organs it makes its own converge. (1987, p. 4)

Here, language and writing and reading have "nothing to do with signifying" (Deleuze & Guattari, 1987, pp. 4–5). Language is no mere mechanism for objectivity, precision, and unambiguity, but rather, as Bogue (2005, p. 111) describes it, language is "a mode of action, a way of doing things with words", the primary function of which is "not to communicate neutral information but to enforce a social order by categorizing, organizing, structuring and coding the world". Writing *functions*, inscribing and producing a social order as opposed to reflecting and representing what really happens/happened.[5] All kinds of texts *function*, both the comforting and the discomforting, the pleasurable and the orgasmic, the readerly and the writerly. What, then, of writing that claims simply to signify and communicate? 'What a vapid idea,' write Deleuze and Guattari (1987, p. 6), "the book as the image of the world".

DESIRE
OR,
THE COMPLETE ROTTENNESS OF ˅ᵀᴴᴱ PLEASURE ˅ᴼᶠ ᵀᴴᴱ ᵀᴱˣᵀ

For Deleuze both pleasure and *jouissance* are inadequate concepts inasmuch as they function as maledictions of *desire*, reducing (cursing) desire as an assuageable lack to be momentarily satisfied, trapped in a "pious circle" of desire-lack/desire-pleasure/desire-*jouissance*: 'The idea of pleasure,' he writes, "is a completely rotten (*pourrie*) idea" (2001, p. 96). Barthes, Deleuze (2001) thinks, would lead us astray with his focus on texts of pleasure and *jouissance*, liquidating desire within this pious circle:

> Broadly speaking, desire is lived as such a disagreeable tension that—a horrible, hideous word is required here, that's how bad this thing is—a discharge is necessary. And this discharge, this is what pleasure is! People will have peace, and then, alas! desire is reborn, a new discharge will be necessary. (Deleuze, 2001, p. 96)

As Buchanan (2008, p. 47) notes, for Deleuze (and Guattari), "desire does not need to be stimulated by an exogenous force such as need or want, it is a stimulus in its own right'", This is a radical reformulation of the concept, at odds with common sense notions of subjects who desire objects they both lack and want and who experience pleasure in their attainment. As Deleuze explains:

> For me, desire implies no lack; neither is it a natural given. It is an *agencement* of heterogenous elements that function; it is process as opposed to structure or genesis; it is affect as opposed to sentiment; it is "*haec*-eity" (the individuality of a day, a season, a life) as opposed to subjectivity; it is an event as opposed to a thing or person. (1997, p. 189)

Desire is neither desire for an object, nor a drive, nor a structure (Massumi, 1992). Rather, and here it becomes clear why the malediction of desire is so disagreeable for Deleuze, 'desire produces reality, or stated another way, desiring-production is one and the same thing as social production' (Deleuze & Guattari, 1983, p. 30). Buchanan (2000, p. 15) argues that this correlation of desire with production "is without doubt the most important postulation in the whole of *Anti-Oedipus*".[6] Desiring-production is pre-personal: a synthetic, machinic process that functions to-machine (Bogue, 2003), forming syntheses and producing flows and intensities:

> If desire produces, its product is real. If desire is productive, it can be productive only in the real world and can produce only reality. Desire is the

set of *passive syntheses* that engineer partial objects, flows, and bodies, and that function as units of production. The real is the end product, the result of the passive syntheses of desire as autoproduction of the unconscious. Desire does not lack anything; it does not lack its object. It is, rather, the *subject* that is missing in desire, or desire that lacks a fixed subject. (Deleuze & Guattari, 1983, p. 26)

For Deleuze and Guattari, then, it is not subjects that desire, but desire that subjects; desiring-production is a process that autoproduces the unconscious, creating bodies and intensities and flows. As Patton (2000, pp. 70–71) puts it, "desire produces intensities and the consumption of intensities, wherever and in whatever form these may be found. Subjectivity is an effect of this process rather than its origin". Desire is not derived from need, but rather 'needs are derived from desire: they are counterproducts within the real that desire produces' (Deleuze & Guattari, 1983, p. 27). Turning to desire, then, means abandoning lack, need, pleasure, *jouissance,* and the like as rotten ideas, ideas that only obscure the nature and function of desire as production, such that 'desire simultaneously loses any link with lack, with pleasure or orgasm, or with *jouissance'* (Deleuze, 2001, p. 98).

DESIRING-WRITING/BECOMING-WRITING

Perhaps, then, it is neither pleasure nor *jouissance* that we should look to find in writing, but desire, conceiving of writing as investments of desiring-production rather than thinking the pleasure or *jouissance* that results from writing as the irruption of desire-lack/desire-pleasure/desire-*jouissance*. Conceiving of writing in this way, desiring-writing, would be to focus on the productive flows, intensities, and connections of writing, not asking what writing says or means, not reading as *referenda*, but reading the capacities of writing to produce things, bodies, intensities, and flows.

If desire is taken as a productive process that stimulates writing, then it is not the subjective desire of the author to ameliorate some disagreeable absence of writing, to produce some discharge of words, but the productive force of desire to produce someone who writes, something that is written, and someone who reads. Michel Foucault said of Roussel that:

> after his first book he expected that the next morning there would be rays of light streaming from his person and that everyone on the street would be able to see that he had written a book. That's the obscure desire of a person who writes. It is true that the first text one writes is neither written for others, nor for who one is: one writes to become someone other than who one is. Finally there is an attempt at modifying one's way of being through the act of writing. (1986, p. 184)

This obscure desire, writing to become someone other than who one is, is not typically taken to be the function of conventional humanistic qualitative writing within the academy; yet it is the case that the scholar's persona is constituted by the text, or, in other words, that the investment of desire in writing functions to constitute the writer, as Atkinson notes of ethnographic research:

> the monograph also constitutes the field and its author. ... Whyte is Street Corner Society (1981); Willmott and Young are Bethnall Green; Lacey is Hightown Grammar (1971). They have other personae too, but we know scholars and their fields through the work of the monograph. (1992, pp. 10–11)

Or as Foucault (1996, p. 405) puts it, 'The work is more than the work: the subject who is writing is part of the work', But if Foucault's focus is on becoming someone other than who one *is*, Deleuze's interest lies firmly in becoming-in-itself, which implies no state of *being* as such, neither that who one *is* nor that who one *will be*: 'becoming produces nothing other than itself ... What is real is the becoming itself, the block of becoming, not the supposedly fixed terms through which that which becomes passes' (Deleuze & Guattari, 1987, p. 238). Writing is always a matter of becoming, a matter of the becoming-subject who is becoming-writing, but who is always becoming rather than being:

> Writing is a question of becoming, always incomplete, always in the midst of being formed, and goes beyond the matter of any livable or lived experience. It is a process, that is, a passage of Life that traverses both the livable and the lived. Writing is inseparable from becoming: in writing, one becomes-woman, becomes-animal or -vegetable, becomes-molecule, to the point of becoming-imperceptible. (Deleuze, Smith, & Greco, 1997, p. 225)

Desiring-writing is becoming, the machining of a block of becoming through the functions of language and writing, producing languages, subjects, objects, predicates; bodies of writing: passages of Life. 'Tomorrow,' Kafka writes, 'I shall begin writing again, and I shall go at it full tilt: for I know that if I don't write I shall be thrust out from among the living without mercy' (Blunden, 1980, p. 18).

TOWARDS A MINOR ACADEMIC LITERATURE(S) OR, HOW TO GO AT IT FULL TILT

What academic writing can form investments of or in desiring-production? Becoming, as May notes, is always "minoritarian",

> a matter of becoming something other than what is offered by the dominant conceptual categories of a given society; it is a movement away from the given toward that which a society refuses or is as yet unable to recognize. (2001, p. para. 19)

The minoritarian is that which discomforts and unsettles, which exceeds or transgresses the dominant social and cultural conceptions of what is recognizable. Not determined numerically, minority exists rather in the 'political potential of its divergence from the norm [and] provides an element capable of deterretorializing the norm' (Patton, 2000, p. 7). Investments of desire in writing as minoritarian-becoming are 'a process of becoming minor, through which language is deterritorialized immediately social and political issues are engaged' (Bogue, 2010, p. 171). Deleuze and Guattari term this a minor literature, not the language of a minority, but rather a different use of the major language "which a minority constructs within a major language" (Deleuze & Guattari, 1986, p. 16) and existing 'only in relation to a major language and [as] investments of that language for the purpose of making it minor' (Deleuze & Guattari, 1987, p. 105).

Lecercle (2002, p. 195) writes that the aim of a minor literature "is not to foster or extract meaning, but to give rise to intense, and intensive, expression ... not to make recognisable sense, but to express intensities, to capture forces, to act". This is at odds with the major language of conventional qualitative inquiry: one of disinterested and objective Enlightenment humanism (St. Pierre, 2011) that presents texts as *referenda*, intended to foster and extract meaning, and to make recognisable, objective, unambiguous, transmittable sense, to be accepted or rejected as what texts ought to be. A minor utilisation of this major language in a way that opposes the 'oppressive quality' (Deleuze & Guattari, 1986, p. 27) of an "overdetermined qualitative inquiry" (St. Pierre, 2011, p. 611) might represent an investment of desiring-writing, re-introducing, into language, disruption, uncertainty, ambiguity, discomfort, unrecognizability and so on. Functioning rather than communicating. Acting rather than making sense. Expressing intensities rather than meaning. The *function* of this minor literature might be precisely to (re)introduce crises into the language itself, to make the language itself stutter, machining forces, intensities, and bodies that constitute becomings which are always minoritarian in quality, in their divergence from the dominant norms of culture. As writing, a minor literature:

> opens up a kind of foreign language within language, which is neither another language nor a rediscovered patois but a becoming-other of language, a "minorization" of this major language, a delirium that carries it off, a witch's line that escapes the dominant system. (Deleuze et al., 1997, p. 229)[7]

Perhaps the investment of desire in academic writing can be found in this work: machining becomings, minorizations, disruptions, experimentations: writing to become when becoming produces nothing other than becoming itself, writing to force rays of light to stream from one's person such that everyone on the street would recognize one as a writer, even as the writer is becoming-imperceptible. Writing as Beckett (1989, p. 101) wrote, "All of old. Nothing else ever. Ever tried. Ever failed. No matter. Try again. Fail again. Fail better". Deleuze (1998) writes that when authors proceed this way, they "express themselves entirely".

So how does one proceed to write in such a way: inventing, minorizing, becoming, expressing, going at it full tilt? There is little to be recommended in the way of method here, indeed to do so would do a violence to the idea of minorization:

> We learn nothing from those who say: "Do as I do". Our only teachers are those who tell us to "do with me", and are able to emit signs to be developed

in heterogeneity rather than propose gestures for us to reproduce. (Deleuze, 1994, p. 23)

Deleuze does, however, offer some hint of his approach in his final conversations with Claire Parnet, saying:

> One must settle in at the extreme point of one's knowledge or one's ignorance, which is the same thing, in order to have something to say. If I wait to know what I am going to write – literally, if I wait to know what I am talking about – then I would always have to wait and what I would say would have no interest. If I do not run a risk ... If I settle in also and speak with a scholarly air on something I don't know, then this is also without interest. But I am speaking about this very border between knowing and non-knowing: it's there that one must settle in to have something to say. (Boutang, Deleuze, & Parnet, 2012)

Here, then, finally, we return to what writing will do: not the transparent and neutral and unambiguous communication of objective and neutral information and truth, but the disruption of dominant social codes of academic thought and writing where 'writing *is* thinking, writing *is* analysis, writing *is* indeed a seductive and tangled *method* of discovery' (Richardson & St. Pierre, 2005, p. 967). This, say Deleuze and Guattari, 'is what style is':

> or rather the absence of style – asyntactic, agrammatical: the moment when language is no longer defined by what it says, even less by what makes it a signifying thing, but what it causes it to move, to flow, and to explode – desire. For literature is like schizophrenia: a process and not a goal, a production and not an expression. (Deleuze & Guattari, 1983, p. 133)

CONCLUSION

It seems, now, having settled in to have something to say, that the pleasure of writing (with Deleuze, at least) is not pleasure at all – a rotten idea – but desire, or more precisely the investment of desire in becoming, where becoming is always minoritarian and always diverges from dominant social and cultural codes. Uncoupled from the pious circuit of lack-pleasure-*jouissance*, no longer obsessed with the desire to discharge words and possess writing, desiring-writing is a productive and creative stimulus for Life, capturing flows, expressing intensities, effecting and affecting all kinds of bodies. The academic writing with which I am familiar, conventional humanist qualitative inquiry, seems overdetermined and oppressive, legislating fixed representations of writing as objective, recognisable, neutral communication which obscure the creative and dynamic aspects of writing as a process of thinking and becoming. A minor academic literature, one which re-introduces crises in language, may provide a means to express a self and style in writing, a process of writing that says something at the extreme point of ignorance or knowledge, where indeed there remains something interesting to be said.

And so I have written, once more. Writing about writing, where writing has more to do with function than form, more to do with ordering than communicating, more to do with thinking than knowing. Writing functioning to produce writers who have written rather than the other way around. Bodies of writing produced as an effect of writing, as the effect of investments of desire in writing. What kind of text has resulted? Was it pleasurable? Contenting? Discomforting? Or perhaps all of these? Or none? In any case, I have written. (Though you wouldn't know it if you saw me on the street.) I have placed myself at the frontier of my knowledge, at the border of knowledge and ignorance. I am becoming, still in the midst of being formed, still among the living, still alive.

NOTES

[1] 'The weaknesses of a book are often the counterparts of empty intentions that one did not know how to implement. In this sense, a declaration of intent is evidence of real modesty in relation to the ideal book' (Deleuze, 1994, p. xix).

[2] Buchanan (2010, p. 367) describes the translation of "*jouissance*" as "bliss" as unhappily blunting the significance of the distinction. Here I use the original *jouissance*, though as Barthes himself disclaims:

> (Pleasure/Bliss: terminologically, there is always a vacillation – I stumble, I err. In any case, there will always be a margin of indecision; the distinction will not be the source of absolute classifications, the paradigm will falter, the meaning will be precarious, revocable, reversible: the discourse incomplete.) (1975, p. 4)

[3] Perhaps tautologically?

[4] 'What now seems problematic,' Deleuze argues,

> is the situation in which young philosophers, but also all young writers who're involved in creating something, find themselves. They face the threat of being stifled from the outset. It's become very difficult to do any work, because a whole system of "acculturation" and anticreativity specific to the developed nations is taking shape. It's far worse than censorship. (1995, p. 27)

[5] 'Language,' Deleuze writes,

> is presented to us as basically informative, and information as basically an exchange. Once again, information is measured in abstract units. But it's doubtful whether the schoolmistress, explaining how something works or teaching spelling, is transmitting information. She's instructing, she's really delivering precepts. And children are supplied with syntax like workers being given tools, in order to produce utterances conforming to accepted meanings. We should take him quite literally when Godard says children are political prisoners. Language is a system of instructions rather than a means of conveying information. (1995, pp. 40–41)

[6] Indeed, Buchanan argues that understanding production is crucial to understanding Deleuze (and Guattari's) concept of desire, writing: 'It would not be wrong to say that desire and production are synonymous; in fact, one could say the basic hypothesis of Anti-Oedipus is that desire should be conceived as production (hence the concept of desiring-production)' (2011, p. 15).

[7] As St. Pierre observes, Deleuze and Guattari themselves provide a model for such work, creating a "foreign language within language":

> they introduce new concepts that replace earlier concepts; their concepts interact, overlap, and their meaning shifts; they create a minor language within the major language we're

comfortable with so we feel like foreigners in our own language. They make language stutter and stammer. They make thought stutter. We're not used to this kind of writing, this kind of thought, and their work often seems too hard to read. Who wants to work so hard? On the other hand, their concepts are immediately, almost dangerously useful. And they are often playful. (2016, p. 8)

REFERENCES

Atkinson, P. (1992). *Understanding ethnographic texts*. Thousand Oaks, CA: Sage.
Barthes, R. (1974). *S/Z* (R. Miller, Trans.). Malden, MA: Blackwell.
Barthes, R. (1975). *The pleasure of the text* (R. Miller, Trans.). New York, NY: Hill and Wang.
Beckett, S. (1989). *Nohow on*. London, England: John Calder.
Blunden, A. (1980). A chronology of Kafka's life. In J. P. Stern (Ed.), *The world of Franz Kafka*. London, England: Weidenfeld and Nicolson.
Bogue, R. (1997). Minor writing and minor literature. *symploke, 5*(1), 99–118. doi: http://dx.doi.org/10.1353/sym.2005.0051
Bogue, R. (2003). *Deleuze on literature*. New York, NY: Routledge.
Bogue, R. (2005). The minor. In C. J. Stivale (Ed.), *Gilles Deleuze: Key concepts* (pp. 110–120). Chesham, England: Acumen.
Bogue, R. (2010). Minoritarian+literature. In A. Parr (Ed.), *The Deleuze dictionary* (Revised ed., pp. 170–171). Edinburgh, Scotland: Edinburgh University Press.
Boutang, P. A., Deleuze, G., & Parnet, C. (2012). *Gilles Deleuze from A to Z* [DVD]. Los Angeles, CA: Semiotext(e).
Buchanan, I. (2000). *Deleuzism: A metacommentary*. Durham, NC: Duke University Press.
Buchanan, I. (2008). *Deleuze and Guattari's Anti-Oedipus: A reader's guide*. London, England: Continuum.
Buchanan, I. (2010). *A dictionary of critical theory*. Oxford, England: Oxford University Press.
Deleuze, G. (1994). *Difference and repetition* (P. Patton, Trans.). London, England: The Athlone Press.
Deleuze, G. (1995). *Negotiations: 1972–1990* (M. Joughin, Trans.). New York, NY: Columbia University Press.
Deleuze, G. (1997). Desire and pleasure (D. W. Smith, Trans.). In A. I. Davidson (Ed.), *Foucault and his interlocuters* (pp. 183–192). Chicago, IL: The University of Chicago Press.
Deleuze, G. (1998). *Essays critical and clinical* (D. W. Smith & M. A. Greco, Trans.). London, England: Verso.
Deleuze, G. (2001). Dualism, monism and multiplicities (Desire-Pleasure-Jouissance). *Contretemps: An Online Journal of Philosophy, 2*(May), 92–108.
Deleuze, G., & Guattari, F. (1983). *Anti-Oedipus: Capitalism and schizophrenia* (R. Hurley, M. Seem & H. R. Lane, Trans.). Minneapolis, MN: University of Minnesota Press.
Deleuze, G., & Guattari, F. (1986). *Kafka: Toward a minor literature* (D. Polan, Trans.). Minneapolis, MN: University of Minnesota Press.
Deleuze, G., & Guattari, F. (1987). *A thousand plateaus: Capitalism and schizophrenia* (B. Massumi, Trans.). Minneapolis, MN: University of Minnesota Press.
Deleuze, G., Smith, D. W., & Greco, M. A. (1997). Literature and life. *Critical Inquiry, 23*(2), 225–230.
Duncan, J. S., & Duncan, N. G. (1992). Ideology and bliss: Roland Barthes and the secret histories of landscape. In T. J. Barnes & J. S. Duncan (Eds.), *Writing worlds: Discourse, text and metaphor in the representation landscape* (pp. 18–37). London, England: Routledge.
Foucault, M. (1986). *Death and the labyrinth: The world of Raymond Roussel* (C. Raus, Trans.). London, England: Continuum.
Foucault, M. (1996). *Foucault live: Interviews, 1961–1984*. New York, NY: Semiotext(e).
Lecercle, J.-J. (2002). *Deleuze and language*. New York, NY: Palgrave.

Massumi, B. (1992). *A user's guide to capitalism and schizophrenia: Deviations from Deleuze and Guattari*. Cambridge, MA: MIT Press.
May, T. (2001). The ontology and politics of Gilles Deleuze. *Theory & Event, 5*(3). doi: 10.1353/tae.2001.0017
Miklitsch, R. (1983). Difference: Roland Barthes's Pleasure of the Text, Text of Pleasure. *boundary 2, 12*(1), 101–114. doi: 10.2307/302940
Patton, P. (2000). *Deleuze and the political*. London, UK: Routledge.
Richardson, L. (1994). Writing: A method of inquiry. In N. K. Denzin & Y. S. Lincoln (Eds.), *Handbook of qualitative research* (pp. 516–529). Thousand Oaks, CA: Sage Publications.
Richardson, L., & St. Pierre, E. A. (2005). Writing: A method of inquiry. In N. K. Denzin & Y. S.Lincoln (Eds.), *The Sage handbook of qualitative research* (3rd ed., pp. 959–978). Thousand Oaks, CA: SAGE Publications.
St. Pierre, E. A. (2011). Post qualitative research: The critique and the coming after. In N. K. Denzin & Y. S. Lincoln (Eds.), *The Sage handbook of qualitative research* (4th ed., pp. 611–625). Thousand Oaks, CA: SAGE Publications.
St. Pierre, E. A. (2016). Deleuze and Guattari's language for new empirical inquiry. *Educational Philosophy and Theory*, 1–10. doi: 10.1080/00131857.2016.1151761

David Bright
Monash University, Australia

JENNIFER CHARTERIS, ADELE NYE, AND
MARGUERITE JONES

5. WILD CHOREOGRAPHY OF AFFECT AND ECSTACY

Contentious Pleasure (Joussiance) in the Academy

And Joy, whose hand is ever at his lips
Bidding adieu; and aching Pleasure nigh,
Turning to poison while the bee-mouth sips:
Ay, in the very temple of Delight
Veil'd Melancholy has her sovran shrine,
Though seen of none save him whose strenuous tongue
Can burst Joy's grape against his palate fine;
His soul shalt taste the sadness of her might,
And be among her cloudy trophies hung.
(John Keats, 1819)

INTRODUCTION

Higher education institutions comprise entangled assemblages of bodies, material objects, discourses, spaces and diverse technologies. These entanglements are affective intensities that manifest embodied prepersonal relationality. As a prepersonal construct, affect is the social, physical and emotion change, or variation that is co-produced when assemblages of bodies and objects contact (see Coleman, 2005). The corpus of the academy is a constantly changing phenomenon "intermingling with other human and non-human entities and forces in dynamic collective assemblages" (Mayes, 2016, p. 106). Affective assemblages produce a kind of existential agitation (Massumi, 2015) that comprise sensations of time/motion, speed and heat (Ringrose, 2014). This existential agitation is captured in Keats' poem (above) where melancholy and joy ravel together. The poem highlights the embodiment of pleasure, leveraged from knowledge of melancholy and flows of affect.

In feminist scholarship, the Lacanian concept of jouissance has been appropriated to encapsulate affective flows felt in both body and mind (Khasnabish, 2006). We use the term jouissance to both recognize and mobilize the feeling of transition in bodily states (Sellar, 2014), in order to both consider and even reconfigure new perspectives for higher education politics. Our reading of jouissance suggests a recognition of affective intensities that exceed, accompany and continually modulate consciousness (Sellar, 2014). Feminist poststructural scholarship in affect and jouissance (Ahmed, 2010a; Berlant, 2011; Irigaray, 1985) enable us to consider how happiness is a narrowly prescribed aspect of biopower (Rabinow & Rose, 2006) in the academy. Rejecting forms of happiness that align with the biopower of neoliberal capitalist discourse, we consider the affective intensities of jouissance as a contentious ecstasy of escape and deterritorialization. Feminist onto-epistemology is premised on an understanding of the dynamics of knowledge and politics. Hemmings (2012) points out that feminism both challenges objectivity, through prioritizing embodiment and location, and also through a focus on "knowing differently, as well as knowing different things or knowing difference" (p. 151).

In our work as three teacher education scholars in a regional university, we relish tensions, refutations and moments of crises that arise when normalized, hegemonic scholarly practices are placed under scrutiny. This scrutiny threatens the promise of the sublime happiness that is associated with success in the academy – in particular when that success links with an unquestioned alignment of academic practice and the politics of "academic capitalism" (Slaughter & Leslie, 2001, p. 154). We adopt a stance of "joyful and generous disobedience" (Braidotti, 2002, p. 110) in our conception of jouissance. However, when embedded in the politics of affect, as a contentious ecstasy, joy can be "disruptive" and even "painful" (Massumi, 2015, p. 44). It is a moment where bodily becoming can be overwhelming. In considering artistic practice, Massumi (2015) writes:

> [It] is all about intensifying bodily potential, trying to get outside or underneath the categories of language and affective containment by those categories, trying to pack vast potentials for movement and meaning in a single gesture, or in words that burst apart and lose their conventional meaning, becoming like a scream of possibility, a babble of becoming, the body bursting out through an opening in expression. (p. 45)

Through this work, a wild choreography of affect, we consider ecstatic moments in relation to the transgressive notion of the feminist killjoy. We illuminate the paradoxical tension of this "feminist killjoy" position (Ahmed, 2010b, 2014) as willful disobedience that challenges the happiness associated with going with the (prescribed) flows in the academy. This disobedience is a refusal and resistance to the opiate of acquiescence with academy biopolitics and in particular a rejection of complacent happiness in the status quo. The focus for our collective project is a consideration of the rupturous embodied moments of jouissance that are embedded in an academy that we conceptualise as a rhizomatic Body without Organs (BwO) (Deleuze & Guattari, 1987).

A BwO is an assemblage of flows that can plug into other assemblages and has no beginning, end or restriction (Ibrahim, 2015). The academic machine can be seen as relational power that functions through the liquid language of networks associated with academic capitalism (Kroker, 1992). In writing this chapter, we refuse the stealthy climb over the dead bodies to get to the top that mark the normalized, individualistic career trajectory in the academy. It is an academic climb that is fostered through competitive grants and the track record profile. We therefore take up the BwO concept in the context of this chapter to focus on functionality in the academy, rather than the (rather pointless) process of unraveling some contrived, attributed meaning or definition. Inspired by Deleuze and Guattari (1987), we are interested in how we can continually dismantle the organism of the academy to map affective assemblages, in particular to learn how "intensities [can] pass or circulate. The academy assemblage "has only itself, in connection with other assemblages and in relation to other bodies without organs" (p. 4). We use the concept, BwO, to ask about the functionality of the academy in relation to other organs – what are these connections? To what extent and in what ways are intensities transmitted? How are other multiplicities inserted and metamorphosed and what convergences are there with other bodies without organs?

We extend previous considerations of affective flows in the academy (Charteris et al., 2016) by "kicking a hole out of the old boundaries of the self" (Anzaldúa, 1987, p.71), and rupturing simplistic conceptions of happiness. Through collective biography (Davies & Gannon, 2006), we provide accounts of affective intensities as rupturous and embodied moments of jouissance. Although in Irigary's work 'jouissance' has connotations of sexuality, we use it for its embodiment of pleasure (Russell, 2009). Our collective biography is a choreography of jouissance, both in its embodied construction, and its presentation in this chapter. A feminist research methodology (Davies & Gannon, 2006), collective biography offers a process to deterritorialise biopower in the academy. It also offers a deterritorialization of itself as research that provokes "a shift beyond any remnant attachment to the speaking/writing subject towards her dispersal and displacement via textual interventions that stress multivocality" (Gannon, Walsh, Byers, & Rajiva, 2014, p. 181).

This chapter proceeds by providing an account of the jouissance of feminist killjoys and a critique of an emphasis on happiness in the Higher Education milieu. We go on to discuss the ecstasy of contentious pleasure through our collective biography choreography as embodied flows of BwO.

JOUISSANCE OF FEMINIST KILLJOYS

The notion of jouissance provides a 'new material' (Coole & Frost, 2010) reading of embodied affect. By evoking affect as a prepersonal intensity (Massumi, 1987) we circumvent the entrapment of binary conceptions that pit happiness against sadness or strife. Braidotti (2014) tells us that joy (what we see as jouissance) is not a psychological state. It is a mythical state that pertains to levels on ontological energy: of being able to confront "the ugliness, the perversity and the vulgarity of the times and still act and not be squashed by it". Moreover, we consider that to think politically and ethically one must transcend the easy capture of immediate sensory acquiescence to knowledge systems that reproduce social and cultural inequities. This acquiescence can be seen as a gendered response so as not to cause ripples or make waves. Ahmed (2010b) argues that there is agency in the feminist project of taking up a voice. She writes, "whilst hearing feminists as killjoys might be a form of dismissal, there is an agency that this dismissal rather ironically reveals" (p. 2). She also observes that happiness can be used "to justify social norms as social goods (a social good is what causes happiness, given happiness is understood as what is good)". The bestowal of happiness can be seen as an "incorporeal transformation" as a language that acts upon and informs relational activity (Deleuze & Guattari, 1987, p. 93). Ahmed (2010a) illustrates her point with an allusion to the feminist critique of the 'happy housewife' as a docile caricature of complementary patriarchal society. She notes that happiness follows a "relative proximity to a social ideal" (p. 53). The desire to be the 'good academic' subject (Petersen, 2007) is a case in point. To be happy in the academy requires being complicit in taking on the prescribed set of goals. Ahmed (2010a) points out, "imagination is what makes women look beyond the script of happiness to a different fate ... We might explore how imagination is what allows women to be liberated from happiness and the narrowness of its horizons" (p. 62).

Appealing to the imaginary, we envisage jouissance can provide "an 'outside' that exceeds biopolitical mechanisms" (Anderson, 2011, p. 30). Engagements with affect in the form of jouissance become "political counters" to "forms of biopower that work through processes of normalization" (Anderson, 2011, p. 28). Biopower are strategies for governing life that entail

> one or more truth discourses about the 'vital' character of living human beings; an array of authorities considered competent to speak that truth; strategies for intervention upon collective existence in the name of life and health; and modes of subjectification, in which individuals work on themselves in the name of individual or collective life or health .... (Rabinow & Rose, 2006, p. 195)

Deleuzoguattarian theory enables us to consider biopolitics. The notion of BwO provides a means to contend the regimentation of biopolitical power that produces us as academic subjects, in particular a sense of lack that is inherent in our desire for happiness and pleasure. (Examples of biopolitical mechanisms driven through lack, can include the acquisition of positive student evaluations of teaching, having articles accepted by scholarly journals, receiving awards for teaching, scholarship and service.) Deleuze and Guattari (1987) construe 'lack' as less a universal prerequisite for desire, than a social construction within a particular socio-historical milieu. McLaren (1995) describes the cultural configuration that produces desire. "Objects of desire are shaped not in a value-free laboratory or homogenizing sphere but by the often conflictual social and cultural forms in which desiring takes place" (p. 71). As the first systematic theorists of technological fascism (Kroker, 1992), Deleuze and Guattari (1987) appropriated the term "body without organs" (BwO) from dramatist Antonin Artaud's work. The BwO does not pertain to an absence of organs but rather is a rejection of "the organization of the organs insofar as it composes an organism" (Deleuze & Guattari, 1987, p. 30). With its emphasis on 'becoming', we use the BwO to pertain to affective flows in academy assemblages that exceed the achievement of specific goals. The BwO are not "a notion or a concept but a practice, or a set of practices. You never reach the Body without Organs, you can't reach it, you are forever attaining it, it is a limit"

(Deleuze & Guattari, 1987, p. 166). BwO practices are rhizomatic, in that they deterritorialize striated organizing machines and offer scope for freedom. Deleuze & Guattari, (1987) describe how BwO can manifest.

> Lodge yourself on a stratum, experiment with the opportunities it offers, find an advantageous place on it, find potential movements of deterritorialization, possible lines of flight, experience them, produce flow conjunctions here and there, try out continua of intensities segment by segment, have a small plot of new land at all times. It is through a meticulous relation with the strata that one succeeds in freeing lines of flight, causing conjugated flows to pass and escape and bringing forth continuous intensities for a BwO. (p. 178)

Constantly finding a small new plot of land and freeing lines of flight, allows for resistance to stasis and the associated essentialised conceptions of the 'category boundaries' of being academic (Peterson, 2007). Ahmed (2010) provides insightful articulation of how losing the capacity to flow with the world can construct stabilized misery. We quote her at length on this point.

> When the subjects are not "in flow" they encounter the world as resistant, as blocking rather than enabling an action. Unhappy subjects hence feel alienated from the world as they experience the world as alien. … What if to flow into the world is not simply understood as a psychological attribute? What if the world 'houses' some bodies more than others, such that some bodies do not experience that world as resistant? … Perhaps the experiences of not following, of being stressed, of not being extended by the spaces in which we reside, can teach us more about happiness. (Ahmed, 2010a, pp. 11–12)

Like Keats, Ahmed emphasizes the value of affective flows, of BoW, rather than becoming stuck in a sense of lack and alienation. Having brought together these notions of jouissance, killjoys and BwO, we now consider 'happiness' in higher education.

HAPPINESS IN THE HIGHER EDUCATION MILIEU

Much has been written about the pressure in higher education institutions on academics to intensify teaching load, to ensure mappable scholarly outputs and measurable research outcomes (Green, 2011). Gannon et al. (2015) frame the notion of the neoliberal university through the lens of economic rationalities.

> The managerial practices of contemporary universities tend to elevate disembodied reason over emotion; to repress, commodify, or co-opt emotional and affective labor; to increase individualization and competition among academic workers; and to disregard the relational work that … is essential for well-being at work. (Gannon et al., 2015, p. 189)

The all-pervasive discourse of neoliberalism enshrines academics in a veil of necessity. Academics are shaped and produced in academy assemblages through processes of advanced capitalism. In a 2014 lecture, available online, Braidotti illustrates how we are complicit in the production of striated spaces in the academy that serve to capture us in conceptual structures.

New conditions are being shaped under our eyes. Advanced capitalism is mutating ... Capitalism bends, capitalism adapts, capitalism mutates. These mutations are pernicious, opportunistic and pretty lethal in their efficiency because they capture us. They capture our desires. They shape our imaginary. They make us function. Guess what we are the system. We are not external.

'Happiness' in the academy can be a disciplinary technique associated with a discourse of responsibilization (Rose, 2003) where individuals 'work on themselves' (Ahmed, 2010a). In a social interrogation of happiness, Arvanitakis (2015) makes three broad and rather astute observations. Firstly, happiness is often conceived as an 'end point': a place to which we travel. The second is focused "hyper-individuality" (p. 134) where community bonds are ignored. Thirdly, happiness is presented as a list of exercises or checklists, as in evidence in the proliferation of self-help literature (p. 134). In a further critique of happiness discourse, we observe that positive psychology (Seligman & Csikszentmihalyi, 2000) can be appropriated to support the governing of the soul (Rose, 1999). Positive psychology as a 'collective assemblage of enunciation' facilitates incorporal transformations (Deleuze & Guattari, 1987) that promote a binary of health and pathology in the construction 'happy subjects'. This is a very formulaic view of happiness. Likewise, Ahmed (2010) notes, "positive psychology involves the instrumentalization of happiness as a technique" (pp. 9-10). Thus our imaginaries are shaped through processes like positive psychology that serve as an opiate so we can function as 'the system'. Berlant (2011) frames this relation as "cruel optimism" where "something you desire is actually an obstacle to your flourishing" (p. 1). Within this milieu, Stephen Ball's (2013) point that "things are not as necessary as all that" in higher education is worth noting. In a more dramatic vein, Braidotti (2014) advocates that we "spit in the face of the manic depressive logic of advanced capitalism." She defines freedom as the adequate understanding of the conditions of our bondage and highlights that there is too much critique, and a sense of sterility in the repetitive formula of revolutionary praxis. There is not enough creativity as it is always the same metadiscourse. It is for this reason that we rethink the lack and desire of advanced capitalism ("the organ-machine") that Delezue and Guattari (1983) describe as reducing the multiple forms of desire to an Oedipal triangle.

> In order to resist organ-machines, the body without organs presents its smooth, slippery, opaque, taut surface as a barrier. In order to resist linked, connected, and interrupted flows, it sets up a counterflow of amorphous, undifferentiated fluid. In order to resist using words composed of articulated phonetic units, it utters only gasps and cries that are sheer unarticulated blocks of sound. (Deleuze & Guattari, 1983, p. 9)

For us these gasps and cries are stutters of laughter in our ecstatic engagement with 'and and and' of the break down and deterritorialization of stultifying structure.

COLLECTIVE BIOGRAPHY

Collective biography is a poststructural and feminist method (Davies & Gannon, 2006) that subverts the biopolitics of academicity (Petersen, 2007). With its origins in Friga Haug's memory work, collective biography provides shared opportunities to deterritorialize practices of governmentality. Haug (2008) writes: "[i]f increases in self-recognition, knowledge about socialization processes, competence about language and meaning, and critique of theory are fundamental and prerequisites for the growing ability to act, memory-work aims at such an outcome" (p. 38). Collective biography is appealing since it provides a connective experience where moments in the academy can be shared in such a way that it is "vividly imaginable by others ... [and] others [can] extend their own imaginable experience of being in the world through knowing the particularity of another" (Davies & Gannon, 2006, p. 12). It provides the means of unravelling emotions, ambiguities and experiences of being academics.Collective biography as a research method, supports collaboration at a pre-ideational "level of bodily knowledge and of affect, ... moving beyond individualized versions of the subject, toward subjects-in-relation, subjects-in-process" (Gannon & Davies, 2009, p. 8). Affect theory, with its origins in the Spinozan legacy of affectus, provides a conceptual tool that enables us to engage with people's "emotional cultural biographies" (Skattebol, 2010, p. 79). Our assemblage of bodies and stories generated an affective intensity. Conceived as a "force" or "active relation" with "influence, intensity and impact", affect has generated an immense surge of interest over recent years (Wetherell, 2012, p. 2). Unlike emotion that operates at a physiological level, affect transcends consciousness and disputes "separations between mind and body; and between the individual, their communities and political contexts" (Skattebol, 2010, p. 78). Affect is generative and the interrelationships between people can cause the original affect to transform (through sharing the biographies in this case).

> [W]hen people transmit affects fear, distress, anger, shame and so on the affective force is unruly and unpredictable because other people's affective responses and patterns transform the original affect. In one situation shame might be socialised as humiliation and lead to anger, yet in another situation shame might lead to surprise ... Importantly, affect theories also disrupt the notion of unmediated knowledges ... and insist on a politicised understanding of professional and personal trajectories. (Skattebol, 2010, p. 79)

In our analysis we use affect theory to explore the immersive affective "feelings of varying intensity that register a body's social relational becoming as it transitions between experiential states and between capacities for action" (Sellar, 2014, p. 6). The writing practices that contributed to this chapter arose organically as we explored the stories and material recorded from our conversations. As an extension to our initial collaborative storying, we elected to construct poems of our experience. The poems are rhizomatic encounters between the researcher/authors.

PRODUCING A BWO THROUGH A RHIZO-TEXTUAL CHOREOGRAPHY OF JOUISSANCE

We commenced by reading about joy in the academy (Kern, Hawkins, Falconer Al-Hindi & Moss, 2014), Ahmed's (2010a; 2014) text on the promise of happiness and how she theorized feminist killjoys. We discussed our experiences and then progressed to re-storying our experiences in writing. The free flow of biographical writing of collective biography (Davies & Gannon, 2006) enabled us to dwell on our emotions and loose them on the page. We strove to remove clichés and explanatory writing in order to connect with our experience in the collective space (Gonick, 2015). We were mindful of Gannon's description of the life bleeding out texts when they 'babble' in clichés.

> This is the nature of clichés: they do "just flow." Their very ease and familiarity can blunt the edges of our writing and our thinking. Metaphors that have become clichés are empty, drained of their descriptive, creative, disruptive potential. The lack of access to fresh language can leave us to choose between remaining mute with grief or babbling in clichés. (Gannon, 2002, p. 674)

The collective biography approach in this paper is deterritorialized (Gannon, Walsh, Byers & Rajiva, 2014) in such a way that it takes the form of rhizo-textual choreography, a departure from the work of Honan (2004) and De Carteret and Nye (2004). Honan and Sellers (2006) describe how their conception of rhizo-textual analysis "involves mapping ... discursive lines, following pathways, identifying the intersections and connections, finding the moments where the assemblages of discourses merge to make plausible and reason(able) sense to the reader" (p. 3). Our rhizo-textual choreography is an embodied performance of material and non-material affective flows that emanate from our collective biography texts. Storying our memories in long unrestricted conversation pieces allow for the ebbs and flow of memories. There is no concern that the content is right or correct or worthy. These are just loose collections of ideas and memories that replicated a method previously used for building ideas around theory in academia (De Carteret & Nye, 2004). The initial stories were about working with the academy at different levels. We brought together, stories of writing – a thesis, authoring a teaching unit and the academic scholarship of writing for peer-reviewed journals. Sitting together in a large remodelled School of Education meeting room, we took turns to share our stories of jouissance in the academy, inviting each other to expand on point and elaborate on particular affective entanglements of dynamics knowledge and politics. In this large room we experienced skin-prickling empathetic passion, moved by the political pathos of the stories. We giggled and laughed in our mischievous and even subversive choreography – the naughty girls – feminist killjoys.

The stories were then printed in large bold print, cut and scattered across the table. When one of us took scissors haphazardly to the manicured text and commenced shearing up her neatly constructed narrative, the other two drew breath. There was a pause. It seemed sacrilegious to dissolve the rational knowing academic subject. Then embracing the possibilities of our physical BwO, we all commenced slicing up the texts in a wild affective embodied choreography. The bodies, table, paper, thoughts, ideas, sticky tape, cough lozenges (one of us had a coughing attack) became intertwined as a "nonstratified unformed, intense matter" (Deleuze & Guattari, 1987, p. 153), full of intensity and energy as 'becomings' (see Figure 1).

With papers strewn about in a haphazard assemblage, we commenced reading fragments to each other and in doing so determined to draws lines of flight between existential angst in the text fragments. All semblance of order was removed momentarily as we scanned the text for emergent and connected threads. These scripts emerged as foreseen and unforeseen; imagined and unimagined. We scanned the textual fragments noting existential agitation, cruel optimism,

Figure 1. Textual assemblage

contentious ecstasies and affective lines that "kicked a hole in the wall". The reassemblage risked being laborious and challenging but we rejoiced in garnering a space for rigour in creative scholarship. Through juxtaposing our accounts of the academy in embodied flows, a BwO is choreographed. It seemed to us that, as we map the affective flows, joy is emergent, heralded through threshold moments. Our approach eschews asking foundationalist questions about what something means (Masny, 2013), in favour of focusing on the dynamic element of 'becoming'. Although the analysis did engage with textual interpretation, we make the caveat that by "making the language system stutter" (Deleuze, 1994, p. 24), we illustrate the affective force of the assemblage. This liminal chaotic space of suspended scholarship is both absurd and infantile, but offers an emergent and rhizomatic opportunity for scholarly collaboration on academic jouissance. The academic play is reminiscent of Cixous, Cohen and Cohen's (1976) *L'Ecriture or* feminine writing; an inscribing of a feminine practice in text and interpretation; a practice that sits outside and on the periphery of the formal and regulated academy.

In a playful move the cartography was hung up in an office, like a curtain for translation into electronic text (see Figure 2). The rhizomatic text of 'the curtain' poem follows.

JOUISSANCE IN THE ACADEMY

Summer lingers. Warmth effuses the cubicle;
Glare radiates and she draws breath.
Disappointment spreads visibly through her body.
She compartmentalises and is compartmentalised.
She ruminates – how else can she run this race?
The email pings. Is she rejected outright?
Curtly dismissed with a perfunctory email?
Drowned in well-intentioned advice?
Perhaps offered useful and respectful suggestions?

Where am I up to? Where am I going?
Where have I been? Where do I search?
This self-same footage is replayed each week
As she finds herself unwittingly in the running of the bulls!
It claims to be innovative. So boldly and impulsively
Conceived with back slapping adulation
Hailed with patriarchal bravado.
And here, she is left holding the mewling, puking baby.

She sits with it, dread in the pit of her stomach
Contemplating the tyranny of linearity – of setting a course
And sticking to it, the track record, the research profile.
Constructing the … able scholarly self. Heart beating she
Allows herself a cursory glance, she scrolls quickly down
To glimpse the substance. Going through the minutae

Figure 2. Curtain

She senses a sinking feeling, acute indignation
The mortification of peer ostracism
The jibes, the shame, the vitriol.
She remembers.

To do this she needs to dig at her own past.
Silence, she uses it, celebrates it and hides behind it.
Silence is the false protector – oppression and silence as revolt
'Rowdy silences' without constraint, new ground, privileged
In creation yet excruciating, exhausting –
No escaping.
Breathing sharply she takes in the apricot walls
Stained and ripped with the transitioning academics
Removing keepsakes and pictures, or work reminders from the walls.

She is so privileged, intensely passionate yet
Emotional and teary … comfort, once a memory
Is now a joyous series of days where she simply
Immerses herself in this task – she now knows
The theories. Free for nomadic exploration,
The visiting of every post is a delight in itself:
A revelation.

Slowly she straightens – her head erect. She muses,
'Things are not as necessary as all that.'[1]
Catching her breath she tilts her head back and laughs.
A deep laugh, bitter, yet mischievous.
She does not feel so lost, captured or constrained;
A shift from criticism to critique.

'How liberating!' She writes in her learning journal. 'Magic!'
She finds herself in the maze of theory. '
Yes, yes, yes! Use this!'
Her diaries fill quickly, they are tagged,
Coloured with theories and quotes.

She feels the effervescence of her stomach
Her skin prickles with renewed vigour.
'Too right,' she squawks with determination.
'It's a bloody game! Let's see it for what it is.'

Joy comes from the privilege of building.
Writing the seed into being and germinating thoughts.
Her eyes glint and a smile spreads across her lips.
'Absolutely', she muses, 'this is not an investment in her identity.
How very little matters.'
Falling into places not pieces. 'Gotta fly!'
A mystery to be imagined. Wonderful that her life is ….

To Stutter and Laugh

Affective flows in the academy which subvert the categories that contain and propagate mechanisms of biopower can be seen here as a wild choreography. Writing and performing our rhizome, we see our word thoughts play into the embodied assemblage as a BWO. They take flight, connecting with multiple possibilities. The embodied actions of collaborating and sharing leverage the existential agitation, the threshold moments of transition and the emergence of jouissance. Davies (2011) observes, "under neoliberal regimes academics are at risk of being frozen inside knowledges that are regular, predictable and knowable, leaving no room for the joyous, the not-yet-knowable, the unuseful, the irrational" (p. 28). Our affective choreography is part of the latter category that transcends the stasis of producing just a poem product. It is an embodied, temporal and spatial creation – a line of flight, deterritorializing the frozen knowledges of the neoliberal academy economy.

The poem ends with an ellipsis, an "and … and … and" (Deleuze & Guattari, 1987, p. 26) erasure of 'order-words'. Its motion an intervention in the "collective assemblages of enunciation" (Deleuze & Guattari, 1987, p. 6) that frame academics in a melancholic arborescent holding pattern (Braidotti, 2011). Although our bodies in the academy remain unchanged by the performance of this affective choreography, we resist the "incorporeal transformation" (Deleuze & Guattari, 1987, p. 93), taking scissors to the subject stories. We challenge the subjectifications that locate us as academic labourers who focus solely on advancing the interests of the capitalist academy.

The poetry, in celebrating what language does rather than what it represents, is a "creative stuttering" (ref) that "grow[s] out from the middle" – a body without organs (Deleuze, 1997, p. 111). Thus, rather than becoming paralysed stutterers in the academy, the act of embarking on this collective choreography produces a generative stuttering. Deleuze writes:

> It is no longer the character who stutters in speech; it is the writer who becomes a stutterer in language. [S]he makes the language as such stutter: an affective and intensive language, and no longer an affectation of the one who speaks. (Deleuze, 1997, p. 107)

As an assemblage that plugs into others, the poetry above does not have neat stanzas or tidy endings that resolve matters. In Keats' 'Ode', joy is fleeting and only those who "burst Joy's grape" pass on to other intensities of affect. For us, jouissance is an embodied enactment of agency that is characterized by affective flows between bodies, objects and words as they come together in a wild choreography.

Unplugging from questions of identity, we destabilize the verb 'to be' through offering a choreography of conjunctions. These conjunctions challenge what it means to work in the academy with questions that spontaneously emerge from the poetry assemblage. The poetic form "carr[ies] enough force to shake and uproot the verb 'to be.' Where are you going? Where are you coming from? What are you heading for? These are totally useless questions" (Deleuze & Guattari, 1987, p. 26). The questions that meant something in the context of a collective biography story become deliberately destabilized and disembodied. Thus the deterritorializing force of collective biography enables a joyful stuttering of affective intensities in the academy BwO. Through collective biography intensities are produced, transmitted, both converging and circulating.

CONCLUSION

When we conceptualize higher education settings as 'bodies without organs' (Deleuze & Guattari, 1987) that are free from identification, stratification and unification (Holland, 2013), we are open to the emergence of jouissance as an embodied affective intensity. Through these affective evocations, we circumvent the entrapment of binary conceptions that pit jouissance against despair or other similar humanist conceptions of emotion. Jouissance in the academy is leveraged on rejecting the notion of desire as a lack that projects joy forward into a hopeful future. Through acts of the moment we transcend "incorporeal transformations" (Deleuze & Guattari, 1987, p. 93) that subject us to a social order in the academy.

There is merit in openness to the emergence of affective flows of finding possibilities for deterritorialization, and lines of flight. The mobilization and juxtaposition of BwO and Jouissance as concepts together allow for joyful mappings across the academy, rather than readings that ensnare subjectivities in a malaise of powerlessness or lack. Through these becomings, we locate "small plot[s] of new land" (Deleuze & Guattari, 1988, p. 161) and deterritorialize practices to evade invasion and claim scholarship as an innovation, (if but for a moment). Whether the plot of land is collecting data, drawing from theories that help us to be fearless and courageous, forging rich relational connections with others, or engaging in exciting subversion, the affective intensities of jouissance offer an ecstasy of escape in the academy.

NOTE

[1] Refer to Ball (2013).

REFERENCES

Ahmed, S. (2010a). *The promise of happiness.* Durham: Duke University Press.
Ahmed, S. (2010b). Feminist killjoys (And Other Willful Subjects). *The Scholar and Feminist Online, 8*(3). Retrieved from http://sfonline.barnard.edu/polyphonic/print_ahmed.htm
Ahmed, S. (2014). *Willful subjects.* Durham: Duke University Press.
Anderson, B. (2011). Affect and biopower: Towards a politics of life. *Transactions of the Institute of British Geographers, 37*(1), 28–43.
Anzaldúa, G. (1987). *Borderlands/La frontera.* San Francisco: Aunt Lute Books.
Arvanitakis, J. (2015). #100 happy days. In C. Nelson, D. Pike, & G. Ledvinka (Eds.), *On happiness. New ideas or the 21st century.* Crawley, Australia: The University of Western Australia Publishing.
Ball, S. (2013). *Things are not as necessary as all that: Re-making educational research as useful and relevant.* Paper presented at the Kaleidoscope Annual Graduate Student Research Conference, 30–31 May, at the University of Cambridge, UK. Retrieved from http://sms.cam.ac.uk/media/1496842
Berlant, L. (2011). *Cruel optimism.* Durham: Duke University Press.
Braidotti, R. (2002). *Metamorphoses: Towards a materialist theory of becoming.* Cambridge: Polity Press.
Braidotti, R. (2011). *Nomadic theory: The portable Rosi Braidotti.* Columbia, NY: Columbia University Press.
Braidotti, R. (2014). *Thinking as a nomadic subject.* Germany: Berlin ICI Lecture series. Retrieved from www.ici-berlin.org/event/620
Cixous, H., Cohen, K., & Cohen, P. (1976). The laugh of the medusa. *Signs, 1*(4), 875–893.
Charteris, J., Gannon, S., Mayes, E., Nye, A., & Stephenson, L. (2016). The emotional knots of academicity: A collective biography of academic subjectivities and spaces. *Higher Education Research & Development, 35*(1), 31–44. doi: 10.1080/07294360.2015.1121209
Coleman, F. (2005) Affect. In A. Parr (Ed.), *The Deleuze dictionary* (pp. 11–12). Edinburgh: Edinburgh University Press.

Coole, D., & Frost, S. (2010). *New materialisms: Ontology, agency, and politics.* Durham: Duke University Press.

Davies, B. (2011). Intersections between Zen Buddhism and Deleuzian philosophy. *Psyke and Logos, 32*(1), 28–45.

Davies, B., & Gannon, S. (2006). *Doing collective biography: Investigating the production of subjectivity.* New York, NY: Open University Press.

De Carteret, P., & Nye, A. (2004). *What is feminism today?* Paper presented at the Australian and International Feminisms: An International Conference, Boston University, Sydney, 12–14 December 2004.

Deleuze, G. (1994). He stuttered. In C. Boundas & D. Olkowski (Eds.), *Gilles Deleuze and the theater of philosophy* (pp. 23–29). New York, NY: Routledge.

Deleuze, G. (1997). *Essays critical and clinical* (D. W. Smith & M. A. Greco. Trans.). Minneapolis, MN: University of Minnesota Press.

Deleuze, G., & Guattari, F. (1983). *Anti-Oedipus: Capitalism and schizophrenia* (R. Hurley, M. Seem, & H. R. Lane, Trans.). Minneapolis, MN: University of Minnesota Press.

Deleuze, G., & Guattari, F. (1987). *A thousand plateaus: Capitalism and schizophrenia* (B. Massumi, Trans.). Minneapolis, MN: University of Minnesota Press.

Gannon, S. (2002). "Picking at the scabs": A poststructural feminist writing project. *Qualitative Inquiry, 8*(5), 670–682. doi: 10.1177/107780002237021

Gannon, S. & Davies, B. (2009). *Pedagogical encounters.* New York, NY: Peter Lang.

Gannon, S., Kligyte, G., McLean, J., Perrier, M., Swan, E., Vanni, I., & van Rijswijk, H. (2015). Uneven relationalities, collective biography, and sisterly affect in neoliberal universities. *Feminist Formations, 27*(3), 189–216. doi: 10.1353/ff.2016.0007

Gannon, S., Walsh, S., Byers, M., & Rajiva, M. (2014). Deterritorializing collective biography. *International Journal of Qualitative Studies in Education, 27,* 181–195. doi: 10.1080/09518398.2012.737044.

Gonick, M. (2015). Producing neoliberal subjectivities: Literacy, girlhood, and collective biography. *Cultural Studies ↔ Critical Methodologies, 15*(1), 64–71. doi: 10.1177/ 1532708614557322

Green, J. (2011). *Education, professionalism, and the quest for accountability: Hitting the target but missing the point.* New York: Routledge.

Haug, F. (2008). Memory-work: A detailed rendering of the method for social science research. In A. E. Hyle, M. Ewing, D. Montgomery, & J. S. Kaufman (Eds.), *Dissecting the mundane: International perspectives on memory-work* (pp. 21–44). New York: University Press of America.

Hemmings, C. (2012). Affective solidarity: Feminist reflexivity and political transformation. *Feminist Theory, 13*(2), 147–161. doi: 10.1177/1464700112442643

Holland, E. W. (2013). *Deleuze and Guattari's A thousand plateaus.* London: Bloomsbury.

Honan, E. (2004). (Im)plausibilities: A rhizo-textual analysis of policy texts and teachers "work". *Educational Philosophy and Theory, 36*(3), 267–281. doi: 10.1111/j.1469-5812.2004.00067.x

Honan, E., & Sellers, M. (2006, November). *So how does it work? – Rhizomatic methodologies.* Paper presented at the Australian Association for Research in Education Conference. Retrieved from http://espace.library.uq.edu.au/view/UQ:136704

Ibrahim, A. (2015). Body without organs: Notes on Deleuze & Guattari, critical race theory and the socius of anti-racism. *Journal of Multilingual and Multicultural Development, 36*(1), 13–26. doi: 10.1080/01434632.2014.892498

Irigaray, L. (1985). *This sex which is not one* (C. Porter, Trans.). Ithaca, NY: Cornell University Press.

Kern, L., Hawkins, R., Falconer Al-Hindi, K., & Moss, P. (2014). A collective biography of joy in academic practice. *Social & Cultural Geography, 15*(7), 834–851. doi: 10.1080/ 14649365.2014.929729

Khasnabish, A. (2006). *Jouissance as Ananda: Indian philosophy, feminist theory, and literature.* Lanham, MD: Lexington Books.

Kroker, A. (1992). *The possessed individual: Technology and the French Postmodern.* Montreal: World Perspectives.

Masny, D. (2013). Rhizoanalytic pathways in qualitative research. *Qualitative Inquiry, 19(*5), 339–348. doi: 10.1177/1077800413479559

Massumi, B. (1987). Foreword. In G. Deleuze & F. Guattari, *A thousand plateaus: Capitalism and schizophrenia* (B. Massumi, Trans.) (pp. ix–xvi). Minneapolis, MN: University of Minnesota Press.

Massumi, B. (2015). *The politics of affect.* Cambridge, UK: Polity Press.

Mayes, E. (2016). Shifting research methods with a becoming-child ontology: Co-theorising puppet production with high school students. *Childhood, 23*(1), 105–122. doi: 10.1177/ 0907568215576526

McLaren, P. (1995). *Critical pedagogy and predatory culture: Oppositional politics in a postmodern era.* London: Routledge.

Petersen, E. (2007). Negotiating academicity: Postgraduate research supervision as category boundary work. *Studies in Higher Education, 32*(4), 475–487. doi: 10.1080/ 03075070701476167

Rabinow, P., & Rose, N. (2006). Biopower today. *BioSocieties, 1,* 195–217. doi: 10.1017/ S1745855206040014

Ringrose, J. (2014). "F**k rape!": Exploring affective intensities in a feminist research assemblage. *Qualitative Inquiry, 20*(6), 772–778. doi: 10.1177/1077800414530261

Rose, N. (1999). *Governing* the *soul: Shaping of the private self.* London: Free Association Books.

Rose, N. (2003). *Powers of freedom: Reframing political thought.* Cambridge UK: Cambridge University Press.

Russell, H. (2009). *Irigaray and Kierkegaard: On the construction of the self.* Macon, GA: Mercer University Press.

Sellar, S. (2014). A feel for numbers: Affect, data and education policy. *Critical Studies in Education.* doi: 10.1080/17508487.2015.981198

Skattebol, J. (2010). Affect: A tool to support pedagogical change. *Discourse: Studies in the Cultural Politics of Education, 31*(1), 75–91. doi: 10.1080/01596300903465435

Slaughter, S., & Leslie, L. (2001). Expanding and elaborating the concept of academic capitalism. *Organization, 8*(2), 154–161. doi: 10.1177/1350508401082003

Seligman, M. E. P., & Csikszentmihalyi, M. (2000). Positive psychology: An introduction. *American Psychologist, 55*(1), 5–14. http://dx.doi.org/10.1037/0003-066X.55.1.5

Wetherell, M. (2012). *Affect and emotion: A new social science understanding.* Thousand Oaks, CA: Sage.

Jennifer Charteris
Institute of Higher Education
University of New England, Australia

Adele Nye
Institute of Higher Education
University of New England, Australia

Marguerite Jones
Institute of Higher Education
University of New England, Australia

SARAH LOCH, LINDA HENDERSON, AND
EILEEN HONAN

6. THE JOY IN WRITINGASSEMBLAGE

INTRODUCTION

This chapter unpicks a writing-assemblage: sarahlindaeileen, lindaeileensarah, eileenlindasarah. We seek to write in playful ways. Playful writing. Writing that brings pleasure, encourages rhizomatic thought. Here lies the purpose of this chapter as us-three together make sense of how our writing-assemblage is created and how we can write playfully to produce more than just lines of writing that count within the 21st century university.

Through publishing, conferencing and connecting we claim space for lines to "conjugate with other lines, life lines, lines of luck or misfortune, lines productive of the variation of the line of writing itself, lines that are between the lines of writing" (Deleuze & Guattari, 1987, p. 215). Our collaborations bring pleasure into our work and engage us with making sustainable, life enhancing spaces instead of deadening ones.

But is this enough to satisfy 'academic' 'requirements'? Are we enough, and do we offer enough, to be counted 'academically'? Have we crocheted careers that will be firm and useful? To answer these questions our chapter seeks to break things apart: career-crochet is for academics to create, get crotchety, crossover, go crazy … to work against the quantifiable, accountable, countable, work-at-a-table, work alcoholic (Johnson & Mullen, 2007). Crocheting brings thinkers to the "open space … that is prolongable in all directions [yet which] still has a center" (Deleuze and Guattari, 1987, p. 476). It's what happens when the 'small hook' moves yarn into stitches then opens stitches apart and sets them off onto lines of luck – lines that are between the lines of writing in order "to do good work" (Somerville & Davies, 2015). Work that is political within the deadening spaces of the 21st century university.

In seeking to do good work we actively create a writing-in-assemblage that is different. We look for ways to write that are joyful, funny and pleasure filled. We throw caution to the wind and write of dogs at the beach and of pain and tears. We invite others into these pieces/peaces and offer our experiences of collaboration for others to see.

MAKING SPACE FOR JOY

As many have written, and as many remind us frequently through blogs and internet memes and Facebook groups and pages, working in a 21st century university is not much fun:

> It is no longer a (thinly veiled) secret that in contemporary universities many scholars, both junior and senior, are struggling – struggling to manage their workloads; struggling to keep up with insistent institution demands to produce more, better and faster; struggling to reconcile professional demands with family responsibilities and personal interests; and struggling to maintain their physical and psychological health and emotional wellbeing. (Pereira, 2016, p. 100)

Tenured academics look into a mirror where 20 year olds tell us we are boring and irrelevant; casual and temporary researchers receive emailed dismissals, (sorry no money to employ you this year); newly minted academics have their enthusiasms stifled through constant reminders of audits and accounting mechanisms used to rank us against each other (wow my h-index is really getting big!). In Australia, success rates for research grants are below 20% (Australian Research Council, 2015), the policy directions that will determine higher education funding are in constant flux and turmoil leaving universities without enough certainty to expand departments, and one outcome of growing casualization of the academic workforce is the line of empty offices and darkened corridors. Academics often live very separate lives; we have colleagues not friends, we live within 10 kms of each other, yet only talk at international conferences in strange cities. Little wonder a "permeating feature of the university in both research and teaching is a strong academic loneliness" (Jauhiainen, Jauhiainen & Laiho, 2009, p. 424).

> ... as with every day last week, and all through the conference and study school, I get up, I wash and dress. I have breakfast – something resembling breakfast. I put on the mask and perform the competent academic and adult. Inside, though, I am dissolving. Each moment it is harder to maintain this fiction of calmness, of 'togetherness'...I am caught between anxiety and normality. Normality is increasingly unreal. Anxiety is increasingly normal. The idea of facing all my colleagues tomorrow at the staff meeting ... God, I don't know ... I MUST, I MUST ... just get through this week ... GET THROUGH THIS WEEK. (Warren, 2016, p. 105, original emphasis)

Is that what the 21st century university has become: a life sucking vampire? A string of "divided lives" (Black, 2015, p. 53)? A dead space – deadening space. Death. "... you are already dead when you receive the order-word" (Deleuze & Guattari, 1987, p.107). But let us "consider the other aspect of the order-word, flight rather than death...variables...in a new state, that of continuous variation...the broken line to become a curve, a whole operative geometry of the trait and movement, a pragmatic science of placing-in variation that operates in a different manner than the royal of major science[s]" (Deleuze and Guattari, 1987, p.108-109).

Getting crotchety is the continuous variation. It is the broken line that becomes a curve. Somehow, and unlikely as it appears, we find this movement in our scholarly work. We play with crochet and become crotchety. Career-crochet is an activity for academics to create, get crotchety, crossover, go crazy ....

Do we crochet careers in the crotchety university? Have we crocheted careers that will be firm and useful?

Hang on! Career-crochet? Now, this holds potential. Career-crochet is for academics to create, to generate. Career-crochet permits all sorts of movement that holds potential for crossing over, going crazy, breaking open the madness to work with/in/against the quantifiable, accountable, countable, work-at-a-table, discipline the academic body, the well-behaved academic body. Crocheting brings thinkers to the 'open space … that is prolongable in all directions [yet which] still has a center' (Deleuze and Guattari, 1987, p.476). It's what happens when the 'small hook' moves yarn into stitches then opens stitches apart; 'to do good work' (Somerville & Davies, 2015).

> Hat with lacy brim: TENSION 18.5dc and 23 rows to 10cm over dc fabric, using 3.5mm hook. To work a tension square, using 3.5mm hook, make 28ch. Work 34 rows dc fabric. Fasten off. Check your tension carefully. If less dc to 10cm use smaller hook, if more dc use larger hook. With correct yarn and tension, your Hat will look like our photograph. (Patons, 2015)

TENSION: Can we/dare we, use images and metaphors of a craft often viewed as women's work to describe the writing-assemblage work? Does the image of women doing needlework produce a lack of intellectual endeavour? Is there some connection to be made between our need to explain our joy in the assemblage and the use of these images? The assemblage creates, the writing is created through a multiple of threads. It sets in motion movement that seeks to:

> Transpierce the mountains instead of scaling them, excavate the land instead of striating it, bore holes in space instead of keeping it smooth, turn the earth into swiss cheese. (Deleuze & Guattari, 1987, p. 413)

Crochet, from croc or croche, the word for hook in Middle French, and *krokr*, for hook in Old Norse, has roots in Arabia, South America and China (Marks, 1997). It is hard to pin down this craft with complex historical beginnings most likely richly shaped by trade routes, adornments for puberty rites and the making of dolls for children to use (Marks, 1997). During the Irish Potato Famine in the mid-nineteenth century, whole villages in that country worked together to crochet garments for sale to scrounge some income towards survival. Crochet has a history of moving in all directions, creating a net in communities, creating ceremony, income, artistry, expression.

We open ourselves to similar movements in our academic writing lives and experience joy in writing-assemblage. We bring our own beginnings and purposes into the desire to write. We sense that the madness is not a captivating centre but rather a space of striations and smoothness. A space that is not fixed, locked into, tied up in unbreakable binaries. Rather, it is a mixture of two spaces, striated and smooth. Constantly being translated, traversed, and reversed: striated to smooth, smooth to striated, and the line of flight:

> Smooth space and striated space – nomad space and sedentary space – the space in which the war machine develops and the space instituted by the State apparatus – are not of the same nature. No sooner do we note a simple opposition between the two kinds of space than we must indicate a much more complex difference by virtue of which the successive terms of the oppositions fail to coincide entirely. And no sooner have we done that than we must remind ourselves that the two spaces in fact exist only in mixture: smooth space is constantly being translated, transversed into a striated space; striated space is constantly being reversed, returned to a smooth space. (Deleuze & Guattari, 1987, p. 475)

We place in continuous variation that which seeks to order death upon us: the order-word. We find joy; we find pleasure in our scholarly work. Is it subversive? Is it political? We want to talk about joy in writing together. Joy, friendship, trust, love, compassion and laughter through our encounters:

> …each goes about his own business while encountering others, each brings in his loot and a becoming is sketched out – a 'bloc' starts moving – which no longer belongs to anyone, but is 'between' everyone … (Deleuze & Parnet, 2007, p. 9)

> Please. Do not fear the blocking …. If it raises your comfort level to think of blocking as simply "hand wash, lay flat to dry", then that should be your mantra. Unless the pattern instructions tell you to leave any tails for whatever reason, weave in all the loose ends before blocking, so that the ends have the greatest opportunity to get locked into the fabric. (Chan, n.d.)

> As rounds are not completed with a sl st but worked in a spiral shape, mark end of round with a contrasting thread or safety pin. (Country Spinners, 2014)

Here, in this chapter, we attempt to capture what it is that we do as a writing-assemblage. We pause over why it is that this writing brings/creates/allows joyful pleasure, and how it is that this writing moves beyond the collective or collaborative or co-authored writing that we do separately and together with others.

We do know, with a kind of certainty, that part of this is about making space/creating space/understanding space or, in crochet-language; keeping a looser tension so the hook can move through the wool.

> The real difficulty for critical work is in the lack of spaces within which to explore collective interests and sustain collegiality. (Clegg, 2010, p. 32)

Our spaces are separate, but our writing is together. It is like the circle of crocheting that moves out in all directions while creating a piece. We were once three 'I's' but have become an assemblage. The 'I' dissolved into multiplicities, singularities, life-lines, lines of luck and misfortune, lines of flight. We live in different cities, in different states. We came together by accident. Eileen examined

Linda's dissertation. Eileen was on Sarah's PhD advisory panel. Sarah emailed Linda about a paper she presented at a conference. We came together; novice-expert-examiner-examined then let new stitches – new ways of being ourselves – alter previous patterns of relationship and power. Eileen emailed Linda and Sarah: "hey, want to do a symposium together?" This was the beginning, or was it something other than a beginning? A re-working of the wool?

We hold the wool differently around our fingers as the hook twists in and around to make the foundational row of chain stitches. Our hands are different, our tension, choice in wool, from whom we learned, the places we find for crochet. We meet first as this virtual assemblage becomes 'real', in the 'meatspace' (*Deriving from cyberpunk novels, meatspace is the world outside of the 'net – that is to say, the real world, where you do things with your body rather than with* …) of another university campus, at another conference, this time all three together. In the coffee shop, in the lane way, we de-briefed after the collaborative presentation we had just given. Coffee and cake. We let the stitches loosen and come off the hook to make room for new ideas. Some unravelling.

WRITING FOR AND WITH PLEASURE

We write at night when children are sleeping, we write on the writing day carved out of our careers, we write on shifting sands, we write in spare moments, in the darkness of the night. We write outside of offices, we write to each other, we write and find it sets off a line of pleasure, intensity, a line of flight. We have talked about writing days, can we get together, can we sit and write together? Three women, in three different states. The logistics are complicated. The only time we tried, the three of us, we talked, we drank coffee, we scribbled notes and typed up ideas on a computer, and then some time later went looking for these scribbled notes only to find that we had promptly lost them all.

But we do write together. In ways that allow for creative thought. For thought to creep up through the cracks and behind one's back (Davies, 2010). A shared document … no track changes, no multiple files with various versions … just one shared document in a Dropbox folder. We enter the file when the feeling takes us. Plugging into the text whatever the season, the day, the hour permits. Like with crochet, where stitches are based on pulling loops through another loop on a hook, our writing pulls one story through another and another and ….

There is an excitement in this sharing – a feeling of anticipation when opening the file – what will be there today? I wonder who added something yesterday? This is not like other collaborations, other co-authored attempts that are sometimes laced with trepidation, anxieties, and dread. Eileen has written elsewhere about her engagement with 'doing collective biography' (Davies & Gannon, 2006) and the desire to be constituted as competent academic through working within this feminist collective (Davies & Gannon, 2006, pp. 141–144). This assemblage sarahlindaeileen is more than collective, more than collaboration, there is an intensity in the forming and reforming and unforming and uniforming.

> What is the individuality of a day, a season, an event? ... A degree, an intensity, is an individual, a *Haecceity* that enters into composition with other degrees, other intensities, to form another individual. Can latitude be explained by the fact that the subject participates more or less in the accidental form? (Deleuze & Guattari, 1987, p. 253, original emphasis)

Words do not belong to Sarah, Linda or Eileen: the all knowing 'I'. We abandon phrases and words that construct the individual, that subject that exists in advance; we are not collaborators, nor a collective. The writing-assemblage represented in this text, by this text, is not three joined as one, nor is it one divided into three.

> To me, the concept collaboration assumes the humanist subject, because to think collaboration as typically described, one must assume there are separate writers who exist in advance of writing who can come together to collaborate, to write a text together. I wonder whether one can think collaboration without the humanist subject. (Wyatt et al., 2014, p. 414)

The assemblage becomes assemblage through the words on the screen and the loopy connections we make with our lives. These are not words created by one to be read by the other, but words that can only be created through the assemblage. The writing is different – we *do not* write like this separately, and we *do not* write like this with other writers. What is created is ....

Purposeful, pleasurable, warming
Holding the hook, a slip knot, a chain, a working into what we've just made
A single, a double, treble, slip stitch
Yarn over, front and back loop, yarn joined, threads loose

As well as, a tight curling purposeless bundle of wool
A learning piece, a sample
An attempt
A start
A try
A sputter

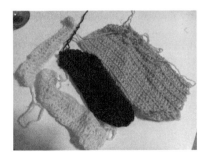

Figure 1. Early attempts

To expression, for meaning
Crochet bombing
Claiming public space, adding colour
Keeping trees and
Keeping souls warm

Figure 1. Public crochet bombing-found artefact

Writing in a writing-assemblage is not orderly; it is eventful, emerging, never finished, always in the moment; becoming. Becoming writing-assemblage. It brings joy, pleasure, it decentres until there is no longer an 'I', only multiplicities. Who wrote what does not matter, it is not important. Words flow with intensity, they leak, and they cry out, they refuse to be captured. Becoming-intensive. They create spaces to do things differently, to produce academic work that is without fear – words that know no boundaries, yet they care deeply about their effects/affects (Davies, 2005). They produce joy. They enable joy – joyousness. The joy in writing-assemblage.

Collaborative writing through a Deleuzian lens seeks to cultivate the grass that grows between. It is concerned not with the paving slabs of our exchanged writing but with the resilient weed that forces its way through the

> cement that we lay between them; the shapes we create around and between us, as we sit back and admire the careful crafting of our landscape. Rocks, flowers, pond, trees...each set out to complement, echo or contrast with the other, to form our free-flowing, wild but thoughtfully-designed garden. But, it seems, for Deleuze, it is in the spaces, the middles, that muddled flows that the unexpected opens up between us, taking us into the not-yet-known. (Wyatt, et al., 2011, p. 32)

Joy in writing? Where is that to be found in the contemporary university with its mad need to count – count everything – do not let it escape without being counted. No you don't count; you are not good enough! But; hey, you over there, yes we can count you. You are a good disciplined subject! We can count on you to produce, to behave, to join us in our A star journal metrics that count. A captured machine tied to counting.

JOYFUL WRITINGASSEMBLAGES

Stop! Stop the madness. Do not be fooled by it. There is joy to be found in a writing-assemblage, for the 21st century university is really like the textile that Deleuze and Guattari (1987) discuss in 'A Thousand Plateaus', referring to felt and patchwork and crocheting;

> There are many interfacings, mixes between felt and fabric. Can we not displace the opposition yet again? In knitting, for example, the needles produce a striated space; one of them plays the role of warp, the other woof, but by turns. Crochet, on the other hand, draws an open space in all directions, a space that is prolongable in all directions – but still has a centre. (Deleuze & Guattari, 1987, p. 476)

Our writingassemblage starts with a stitch, a centre, a concept to think with, on, and through. A few words and phrases on a page. But the page has no edges, no borders, no border patrol. Centres fall away. The movement becomes an outward movement. Experimentation. Open and creative. It is always on the move, moving outward, sideways – a continual movement in all directions. Plugging in ... plugging out ... good days ... bad days ... shitty days ... days where the wind just blows the cobwebs away. We open ourselves up to this movement ... we feel it ... sense it ... experience it ... experiment with it ...

> ... experiment with the opportunities it offers, find an advantageous place on it, find potential movements of deterritorialisation, possible lines of flight, experience them, produce flow conjunctions here and there, try out continuums of intensities segment by segment, have a small plot of new land at all times. (Deleuze & Guattari, 1987, p. 161)

> Experience is that milieu which provides the capacity to affect and be affected; it is a-subjective and impersonal. Experience is not an individual

property; rather subjects are constituted in relations with experience itself, that is, by means of individuation via *haecceity*. (Semetsky, 2010, p. 91)

We laugh, and cry, we throw images at each other, we drop papers we have read in our communal folder, days of silence, days of emails crossing over each other. We provoke each other into action of varying sorts. We have deadlines, yes, but these somehow do not matter; we are not writing to a 'dead'-'line', we are writing to each other, with each other, and usually, somehow, without intention even, the writing is completed before the deadline approaches.

This is good work that nurtures open spaces. A centre that is always moving outwards in all directions. Directions that nourish … that feed the soul as it lives within the soulless and deadening spaces of the 21st century university. An indefinite outward movement that fosters pleasure. Pleasure is possible in this movement. Holes can be found, located, broken open, unravelled and explored.

My mum tells stories, has always turned our childhoods into stories. She tells us her mother crocheted granny square rugs for us all, but gave up in frustration when they, mother and grandmother, have to spend their nights sewing the squares back together – we delight in finding the spaces, the holes and pushing our fingers through, making the holes wider and wider until the crochet wool snaps.

Deterritorialisation. Pleasure within holes, within cracks – the in-between. In-between smooth and striated. Possible lines of flight …

Crocheting is
learning from my mother as a 40 year old
How to hold the wool
Make a chain
Hold the hook
Pull it through
Then a double with a chain on the end. Repeat.

Figure 3. Mother's Blanket 1

Crocheting is:
Learning from my mother as a teenager, something to do, keeping idle hands busy, hopeless at sewing, can't cut a straight line, knitting never straight, too many dropped stitches, but yes I can crochet. She teaches me to crochet, just as she teaches me to cook, and not to marry, just as she teaches me not to obey, to open a 'running away' account. I have academic mothers, who teach me to write and to think, I have feminist mothers, who teach me to demand equality, love, compassion, and an ethics of care.

But my mum, she taught me to crochet.

>My hands and fingers want to switch to knitting
>The other thing she taught me
>Years ago
>My mother speaks in woolly tongues
>In language learned from her mother
>While needles and hooks softly click
>As I make us dinner and put my own child to bed.
>I 'mother' and fuss and she unpicks, recounts
>Re-does, and fixes my mistakes.
>Still.

Figure 4. Mother's Blanket 2

Repeat

>In crochet, my mother writes in lines
>Which loop and bauble along a metal stick
>Being useful, giving warmth
>Bringing colour, giving pleasure.
>For many Christmases, my mother has been giving
>Blankets to family as gifts.

It's night-time. I play with lines on a screen
Looping back, opening files, writing in
Opening a new ball of wool; read more Deleuze
Remembering where I was up to; email lindaeileensarah
The smooth, the striated
'the two spaces in fact exist only in mixture' (Deleuze & Guattari, 1987, p. 474) –
Deleuze and Guattari, I like to think, sound slightly pleased with crochet.

As my mother crochets at night
With movement of fingers-hands-wrists learned from her mother
As I try to move with her
In stops and starts, with high tension, with invention,
Is this university?
We write together
We crochet together
1ch, 1dc in first dc, 3ch, miss 3dc, * 1dc in next dc, 3ch, miss 2dc, 1dc in next dc, 3ch, miss 3dc, rep from * to last 3dc

Crocheted lines with multiple thread patterning into one.

It's warm.

4ch, (1tr, 1ch) 3 times in same 3ch sp, 1dc in next 3ch sp, 1ch, * (1tr, 1ch) 4 times in next 3ch sp, 1dc in next 3ch sp,

Early in the piece on pleasure in university life
(The pleasure in peace) on life in this 'verse'
We choose our colours
Make our chains
Work some rows
They might be undone and redone

Over and over
Repeat

1ch, rep from * to end, sl st in 3rd of 4ch at beg, sl st in next ch sp.
We head towards
a crocheted flower.

Figure 5. Knitted flower on A Thousand Plateaus

A flower has a centre but no edges. Its design opens to the wind, rain, sun, water, soil, nutrients, all play their part. It does not count, but rather opens up to life to shine in all its glory. It opens to connect to bee, to insect, to bird, fertile territory. Smooth territory of cross fertilisation. It is an assemblage – a fertile assemblage. A fertile joyous writing-assemblage. To write like the flower – open to connect to bee, to insect, to bird, to fertile cross fertilisation. To life. Intensive life:

> If everything is alive, it is not because everything is organic or organized but, on the contrary, because the organism is a diversion of life. In short, the life in question is inorganic, germinal, and intensive, a powerful life without organs, a Body that is all the more alive for having no organs, everything that passes between organisms. (Deleuze & Guattari, 1987, p. 499)

Life creates. It creates joy in writing-assemblage. Joy that cannot be measured, nor captured by the 21st century university. It cannot be pinned down to moments, but rather only ever exists in the in-between spaces … in-between moments; "it doesn't just come about or come after but offers the immensity of an empty time where one sees the event yet to come and already happened" (Deleuze, 2001, p.29). Joy in seeking out the in-between. Joy in producing/making for "making produces new thought, but such thought is often disavowed and devalued through processes of feminization and abjection" (Hickey-Moody, Palmer, & Sayers, 2016, p.218).

PLEASURE – THE ABSTRACT LINE

Crocheting is more than 'just' a craft; it is the abstract line – the 'pure feminine line', lifelines', or 'lines of flesh' (Deleuze & Guattari, 1987). Life is not a straight line that has a beginning and an end. We are all made up of lines – several lines that seek out and explore potential variations. Just like the crochet hook that seeks out the in-between spaces to sets of new lines. These lines are not lines that delineate subject and object, author and text. Rather pleasure in the writing-assemblage is the abstract line that is released from such binaries and hierarchies. It is not pleasure from the point of view of an organised body. It is not a straight line that takes the form of an organised writing formula or joint authoring of a paper with divisions of labour. Such lines are like leeches sucking all pleasure from the writing-assemblage.

Instead pleasure in the writing-assemblage always begins in the middle. A middle that holds a deep ethical-emotive response/ability that seeks to generate affectivity and joy permitting bodies to pursue lines that open up capacity to affect and be affected both with pain and extreme pleasure. As a space it affirms the positivity of the intensive subject and their potential to endure and transform the negativity of the 21st century university into positive action – collective action. Collective activism (Braidotti, 2006).

This collective activism requires an active and explicit resistance to the "twin pillars" of the neoliberal performativity regime, "the extensification and elasticisation of academic labour" (Pereira, 2016, p. 104). At the same time however, such 'resistance' must "acknowledge that where resistance to oppression emerges, it exists in relation to oppression. Only by attending to the ways in which these two structures co-exist in the same discursive spaces can one effectively create possibilities or solidarities of praxis" (Bhattacharya, 2016, p. 314). We acknowledge the complex co-existence of the creation of this writing-assemblage that explicitly rejects neoliberal accountability measures, with the purpose and intention of this writing, to be published in a format that will in itself create a response to those measures.

B1. Book Chapters *Weighting: 1**

Eligibility
This category refers to a contribution, consisting substantially of new material, to an edited compilation in which the material is subject to editorial scrutiny. To be included in this category the book chapter must meet the definition of research

There are no rules, no steps to follow in the creation of joyful, pleasurable writing. We do not offer this as some earth shattering new approach to academic writing.

Therefore, we offer no straight line that takes the form of recommendations or steps or formulas. It is impossible to advise others on how to create joy in writing-assemblage. Instead, in vague abstract terms we encourage others to make space, create, communicate, experiment – become unravelled. There is, *we affirm*, an ethical responsibility to share accounts of joyful writing-assemblages, to celebrate emotion rather than stifle it (Zipin & Nuttall, 2016). We provide here a writing-assemblage that illustrates and illuminates a way of being-academic, a way of becoming academic*writing*machine that is filled with pleasure, rather than pain. That is generated through compassionate collaboration, rather than selfish, cruel, harsh and competitive individualism. Academic writing that is joyful and pleasurable, rather than "academic writing [that] is bullshit", "important" and mere "process and product". Our offering is a writing-assemblage that has sought an ethical commitment to generating lines of pleasure with/in the academic*writing*machine (Henderson, Honan, & Loch, 2016).

REFERENCES

Australian Research Council (ARC). (2015). *ARC's 2015 major grants announced.* Retrieved 8 September 2016 from: http://www.arc.gov.au/news-media/news/arcs-major-grants-announced

Bhattacharya, K. (2016) The vulnerable academic: Personal narratives and strategic de/colonizing of academic structures. *Qualitative Inquiry, 22*(5), 309–321.

Black, A. L. (2015). Authoring a life: Writing ourselves in/out of our work in education. In M. Baguley, Y. Findlay, & M. Kerby (Eds.), *Meanings and motivation in education research* (pp. 50–71). UK: Routledge.

Braidotti, R. (2006). The ethics of becoming imperceptible. In C. Boundas (Ed.), *Deleuze and philosophy* (pp. 133–159). Edinburgh: Edinburgh University Press.

Chan, D. (n.d.). *Blocking is your friend.* Retrieved 2 May, 2016 from: https://dorischancrochet.com/blocking-is-your-friend/

Clegg, S. (2010). The possibilities of sustaining critical intellectual work under regimes of evidence, audit, and ethical governance. *Journal of Curriculum Theorizing, 26*(3), 21-35.

Country Spinners. (2014). Free crochet patterns. Retrieved 26 May 2016 from: http://www.auspinners.com.au/free-crochet-patterns-download/default.aspx

Davies, B. (2005). The (im)possibility of intellectual work in neoliberal regimes. *Discourse: Studies in the Cultural Politics of Education, 26*(1), 1–14.

Davies, B. (2010). The implications for qualitative research methodology of the struggle between the individualised subject of phenomenology and the emergent multiplicities of the poststructuralist subject: The problem of agency. *Reconceptualizing Educational Research Methodology, 1*(1), 54–68.

Davies, B., & Gannon, S. (2006). A conversation about the struggles of collaborative writing. In B. Davies & S. Gannon (Eds.), *Doing collective biography* (pp. 114–144). Maidenhead, Berkshire: Open University Press.

Deleuze, G. (2001). *Pure immanence: Essays on a life* (A. Boyman, Trans.). New York: Urzone.

Deleuze, G., & Guattari, F. (1987). *A thousand plateaus: Capitalism and schizophrenia* (B. Massumi, Trans.). Minneapolis: University of Minnesota Press.

Deleuze, G., & Parnet, C. (2007). *Dialogues II* (2nd ed.). New York, NY: Columbia University Press.

Henderson, L., Honan, E., & Loch, S. (2016). The production of the academic*writing*machine. *Reconceptualizing Educational Research Methodology, 7*(2), 4–18

Hickey-Moody, A., Palmer, H., & Sayers, E. (2016). Diffractive pedagogies: Dancing across new materialist imaginaries. *Gender and Education, 28*(2), 213–229.

Jauhiainen, A., Jauhiainen, A., & Laiho, A. (2009). The dilemmas of the 'efficiency university' policy and the everyday life of university teachers. *Teaching in Higher Education, 14*(4), 417–428.

Johnson, W. B., & Mullen, C. A. (2007). *Write to the top: How to become a prolific academic writer*. New York, NY: Palgrave Macmillian.

Marks, R. (1997). History of crochet. Retrieved 2 May, 2016 from http://c.ymcdn.com/sites/www.crochet.org/resource/resmgr/pdf/history-of-crochet-rm.pdf

Patons. (2015). *Hat with lacy brim*. Retrieved 3 June, 2016 from http://www.auspinners.com.au/sites/auspinnerscomau/assets/public/File/Free%20Crochet%20Patterns/Patons/Patons_Z676_Cotton_Blend_Hat.pdf

Pereira, M. (2016). Struggling within and beyond the performative university: Articulating activism and work in an 'academic without walls'. *Women's Studies International Forum, 54*, 100–110.

Semetsky, I. (2010). Experience. In A. Parr (Ed.), *The Deleuze dictionary* (rev. ed., pp. 91–92). Edinburgh: Edinburgh University Press.

Somerville, M. J., & Davies, B. (2015, 2 December). *Third education and theory dialogue: "New feminist poststructuralisms and the neoliberal university"*. Paper presented at the Australian Association for Research in Education. University of Notre Dame Australia, Fremantle.

Warren, S. (2016). Writing of the heart: Auto-ethnographic writing as subversive storytelling – A song of pain and liberation. In J. Smith, J. Rattray, T. Peseta, & D. Loads (Eds.), *Identity work in the contemporary university: Exploring an uneasy profession* (pp. 105–116). Rotterdam: Sense Publishers.

Wyatt, J., Gale, K., Gannon, S., & Davies, B. (2011). *Deleuze and collaborative writing: An immanent plane of composition*. New York: Peter Lang.

Wyatt, J., Gale, K., Gannon, S., Davies, B., Denzin, N. K., & St. Pierre, E.A. (2014) Deleuze and Collaborative writing: Responding to/with "JKSB". *Cultural Studies ↔ Critical Methodologies, 14*(4), 407–416.

Zipin, L. & Nuttall, J. (2016). Embodying pre-tense conditions for research among teacher educators in the Australian university sector: A Bourdieusian analysis of ethico-emotive suffering. *Asia-Pacific Journal of Teacher Education*, doi: 10.1080/1359866X.2016.1177164

Sarah Loch
International Research Centre for Youth Futures
University of Technology Sydney, Australia

Linda Henderson
Faculty of Education
Monash University, Australia

Eileen Honan
School of Education
The University of Queensland, Australia

CECILY JENSEN-CLAYTON AND RENA MACLEOD

7. FEMALE PLEASURE IN THE ACADEMY THROUGH EROTIC POWER

INTRODUCTION: THE CHALLENGES FOR WOMEN

Women entering the academy is a recent historical phenomenon. Subsequently, women have had to take on the historical legacy of androcentric/masculinist ways of thinking of the institution in order to pursue an academic life. More recently, neoliberalism in the academy has increased the complexity of the experience of women academics. Therefore taking pleasure in the academy holds even greater challenges for women as academic life and women themselves are shaped by neoliberalism to support the (androcentric/ masculinist) status quo. On the other hand, feminist scholarship resources female academics with alternate ways of knowledge production, beyond androcentric frameworks and beyond neoliberal constructions and mystifications. These alternate ways of working present women with avenues to journey out of androcentric modes of thinking, journeying towards being able to work with an increasing authentic female self. One of these ways is through encountering and reengaging with the eroticism of the human life force. Thus, embracing eros within the constructions of a neoliberal academy means new questions can be given voice and new imaginings made possible. In addressing women's experience in the neoliberal academy, this chapter provides a model that gives expression to an increasingly authentic female self through engaging intellectual virtues, thereby increasing the possibilities for pleasure through the co-optation of an entrepreneurial self.

This chapter focuses on increasing pleasure for women scholars through engagement with the liberating potential of pleasure. We authors believe it is necessary to give life to the liberating potential of pleasure for female academics as women face two major challenges in working within the academy. One challenge is that of working within the historical legacy of masculinized frameworks and all that this means in terms of gender bias (Howes, 2012), especially the single (male) subject of Western culture (Khader, 2011), and thus the compromise of femaleness.[1] The second challenge is an even more insidious one. This challenge comes from the influence of neoliberalism, which for female academics means working within institutionalized frameworks that are built on the assumption of a single entrepreneurial subject (this aspect is developed later in the chapter). According to this ordering, women scholars work within masculinized and corporatized institutional frameworks as pseudo men. Thus, this social construction doubles the negative effects for female academics. As this chapter will reveal, androcentric frameworks and thinking, as well as the discursivity of neoliberalism as a global and local force, renders women unable to address directly the coercive and homogenizing force of neoliberalism (Chatterjee, 2012; Jensen-Clayton & Murray, 2016a, 2016b; Springer, 2015b): women's personal power and subsequent pleasure is reduced in their structurally induced uncritical appropriation of a neoliberal entrepreneurial self. To engage these two challenges, we begin addressing women's struggle of working within masculinized frameworks by recognizing that women entering academic life is a recent historical phenomenon. This phenomenon, however, does not lend itself to transparency given that the constraints upon women's experience are not immediately visible (Valian, 2005). Masculinized frameworks sustain a worldview where women's experience is mystified even to themselves (Bartky, 1990). This mystification that hides the particularities of women's experience, means that women's experience has been and continues to be subsumed by male interpretations of human experience as universal; in this way male experience continues to be conceptualized as the norm. This chapter, then, draws on the thinking of feminist scholars who lay bare some of the masculinized structures and subsequent exclusions that set conditions for women's experience of work and pleasure in the academy (Bell & Sinclair, 2014; Valian, 2005). This engagement also uncovers an even greater challenge for the experience of women within the academy, that of working within a corporatized context shaped by neoliberalism. Honan, Henderson and Loch (2015, p. 47) note that "the neoliberal apparatuses of the university work to construct our selves as lacking". In a further regressive move, women and their experiences of being human are once again made invisible, this time due to the functional agenda of serving corporate ends (Cox, 2016). Thus the route that this chapter takes commences by addressing both these challenges; firstly by outlining masculinized frameworks as a product of androcentric thinking, and, secondly, by outlining neoliberalism as an epistemology that women internalize. In outlining androcentricity and androcentric thinking and the ways these serve neoliberal purposes, we show that these two forces construct women's academic subjectivity. Women academics are shaped by their neoliberal epistemology to act as neoliberal selves. Following a description of some implications of the dual construct, the chapter then explores the liberating potential of pleasure as a result of erotic power. Eros is examined as a life-giving force with the potential to be harnessed in dynamic and empowering ways; however, harnessing this life-giving force needs a new identification with eros. The power of the female expression of eros is described as increasing pleasure in forging new ways of being more authentically female within the academy free from the constructs of binary thinking.

In addressing the two challenges that women face in working within the academy, we authors acknowledge the ambitious nature of this chapter as the chapter brings together four major interrelated concepts, the dynamics of which have been conveyed in the diagram in Figure 1.

In sum, this chapter engages with two significant challenges that women experience working within the academy, androcentricity and neoliberalism. From this engagement, the chapter also offers women scholars a way to meet and move beyond these challenges by an imaginative reclamation of erotic power as women's

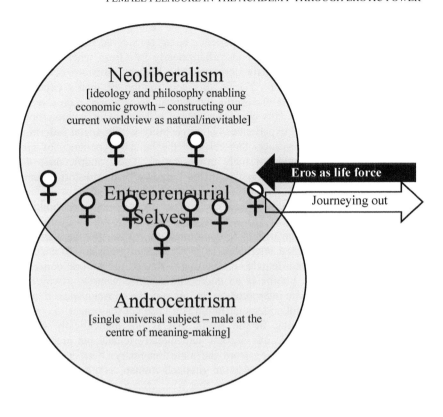

Figure 1. Relationships between four major concepts

life force and subsequently a more authentic expression of female selves within the academy. This chapter in providing a conceptual tool/model that enables greater pleasure for women within the academe, concludes with the provision of a model that draws on eros, the concept of intellectual virtues, and the co-optation of an entrepreneurial self, to perform transformative tasks in women's intellectual life within the academy.

ANDROCENTRIC THINKING, MASCULINIZED FRAMEWORKS, AND WOMEN

Addressing the first challenge for women scholars necessitates understanding the source and nature of masculinized frameworks. These historically problematic frameworks are a consequence of androcentric (male centred) thinking, the same type of thinking that has constructed and continues to construct western culture and experience (Meyers, 2002). Androcentric thinking also underpins patriarchal constructs and in this way can be seen as a form of thinking that privileges the interests, benefits, and experience of men. At the same time, androcentricity acts as a hegemonic force, with men's experience being considered the norm for human experience. This problematic is identified clearly by Gross when she says: "in androcentric thinking, the male norm and the human norm are collapsed, and become identical" (2009, p. 57). In this construction of men's experience as synonymous with, and as the norm for, human experience, men's experience becomes universalized.[2] This conceptual move effects covert repercussions as it renders invisible female experience. This invisibility within social ordering stems from gender binary constructs that relegate the human experience of girls and women within the bounds of male interpretation. Thus, androcentric thinking creates and sustains dominant masculinized frameworks that distort potentialities for other ways of being.

Females are born into a world constructed by androcentric thinking. The significance of this is that women are born into a world of institutionalized meanings that are foreign to female consciousness. To say this another way: the consciousness that women internalize as girls, through processes of enculturation and socialization, is not a female consciousness. Rather, the cultural consciousness that girls and women imbibe is an androcentric consciousness, a way of being female according to male interpretation. In this way the consciousness that women internalize through childhood socialization is a false consciousness; a conditioned way of seeing and being in the world that is not authentically their own. Subsequently, women's desires are not authentically female but are conditioned desires and imaginings arising from the male imaginary. Further, this acquired androcentric consciousness is hidden to girls and women, as they are mired in and subject to the male cultural conditions that have created the parameters for their experience. This hiddenness of androcentricity, a hiddenness that results from being the dominant discourse, is also due to androcentric thinking not having ideological drives of its own, but nevertheless functions to serve the legitimation of unjust structures and social inequalities women observe and experience.

False Consciousness for Women

As has been outlined, women's socialization and enculturation within an androcentric world creates a false consciousness in girls and women (Bartky, 1990; Meyers, 2002; Miller, 2012). From birth they are "locked into a routinized pattern of cognition that disables critical cognitive and epistemic capacities and naturalizes the dominant ideas and values that legitimate prevailing power relations and interests" (Thompson, 2015, p. 250). Androcentricity as the dominant discourse constructs a stereotypical framing of 'female' and 'femininity', making these all-encompassing of what it means to be female; this constant pressure of conditioning to the cultural gender narrative in turn makes women's experience mystified even to themselves (Bartky, 1990; Miller, 2012). On the other hand, women, and even girls, become cognisant of their androcentric consciousness as they become aware of ambiguities in their experience of the world (Meyers, 2002). These experiences of dissonance between their human experience and the cultural narratives forming their subjectivity, signals a movement from being subject to their own culturally constrained thinking, while at the same time moving towards the journey out of an androcentric consciousness to a female consciousness. In this journey of liberation, women face many barriers, one of which is a belief in a just world. This belief is often held firmly in spite of their experience of injustice and even when their experience is being constrained by oppressive structures, such as being systematically subordinated to male experience and interests. Women's experience of an androcentric consciousness becomes that of subordination as women's interests and agendas become attuned to the dominant discourse of androcentricity. Jean Baker-Miller (2012) addresses this aspect of subordination in women's experience as one of distorted desire. Those who are in a position of subordination become highly attuned to the dominants, able to predict the dominants' reactions of pleasure and displeasure. Subordinates then adjust their desires to predicted outcomes.[3] Women's need to control their fate within masculinized frameworks means that their experience of desire and pleasure is largely influenced and even derived from male inspired cultural narratives and/or discursive conditioning rather than from an authentic sense of femaleness. Discovering a more authentic expression of being female leads to greater genuine pleasure while greater authenticity in being female leads to moving beyond the constraints of masculinized frameworks.

The work of feminist scholarship recognizes well this need to journey out of an androcentric consciousness, a difficult journey that requires confronting the psychic alienation that has occurred at birth. Rather than only being "an inherent flaw from birth" (Bartky, 1990, p. 31), this psychic alienation is the estrangement from attributes of their personhood. Leaving behind the familiar psychic alienation that has occurred at birth, is a painful task of moving beyond the false woman of androcentricity in order to define our own femaleness (Cixous, 1976). "We must kill the false woman who is preventing the live one from breathing. Inscribe the breath of the whole woman" (Cixous, 1976, p. 880). This journey to greater consciousness and pleasure that women face within the corporatized academy cannot be held in isolation from the need to also address the challenge of their construction by the constraining forces of neoliberalism.

NEOLIBERALISM AND THE NEOLIBERAL SELF

The second challenge that women face is a new phenomenon. Female academics in the 21st century work differently to those in the previous century. The difference is that now women scholars work within a masculinized context that has become corporatized by neoliberalism (Bansel & Davies, 2005; Davies, Browne, Gannon, Honan, & Somerville, 2005; Mountz et al., 2015). In this chapter, neoliberalism is considered both as a political philosophy and as an epistemology (Harvey, 2005). As a political philosophy, neoliberalism has been co-opted by governments and interested stakeholders across the globe to serve economic ends (Jensen-Clayton & Murray, 2016a, 2016b). Through public education, neoliberalism has gained a ubiquitousness that has created a sense of normality (Giroux, 2004), a way of thinking and being within society that is imbued with a sense of inevitability (Springer, 2015a, 2015b).

Within the academy, a neoliberal epistemology shapes both female and male academics as neoliberal selves to work within neoliberal time (Bansel & Davies, 2005). No longer do researchers have enough time to think and reflect to produce new knowledge as in times past, but are forced to work at an accelerated pace to produce work within systems of surveillance and control that have been applied both locally and globally (Bansel & Davies, 2005). In this accelerated time, researchers and academics are accounted for as quantifiable and quantified selves (Honan et al., 2015). This situation has extraordinary implications for female academics working within masculinized frameworks as women's experiences of pay discrepancies, job loading discrepancies, bullying, and blatant sexism are further exacerbated by their living out a neoliberal self (Bell & Sinclair, 2014; Blackmore, 2013). A neoliberal self is also a market self, an institutionalized self that must act in entrepreneurial ways, in that agency for the neoliberal self is a task of "reflexively manag(es)ing oneself as though the self was a business" (Gershon, 2011, p. 537). This entrepreneurial self that women embody as female academics, requires a personal governance, one that is synonymous with as well as reflecting state governance, both serving national and corporate interests (Bell & Sinclair, 2014; Honan et al., 2015). Thus the interests and pleasures of female academics as entrepreneurial selves are aligned with and are derived from meeting masculinized institutional demands. What can be known about the entrepreneurial self within the context of neoliberalism is that it engenders a regressive motion as women scholars are also constructed to work as androcentric selves, institutionalized selves constructed to work as pseudo men.

The exceeding problematic for women's experience of pleasure in working within the academy is the assumption that underlies their neoliberal self, an assumption of human experience as universal (Cox, 2016). In this way, neoliberalism subsumes the huge gains made by feminist scholarship, gains around women's visibility and recognition of women's experience as different to men's experience. Cox (2016) makes clear this threat to the work of feminism in the return to the single subject of history. Cox sees this regressive move as a failure of feminism (2016, p. 1):

> early support for increasing the proportion of women in positions of power was not driven by wanting more women sharing male privilege, but a belief that feminists could infiltrate and make the social and cultural changes we wanted. Now, the increasing numbers of women allowed to join men in positions of power and influence are mostly prepared to support the status quo, not to seriously increase gender equity.

Female scholars, as women in positions of power and influence, enact their entrepreneurial neoliberal self as a single subject self. In this way, female scholars inadvertently draw on an androcentric self that functions to serve the interests and benefits of male subjectivity, with an experience of pleasure that is largely influenced and even derived from masculine values, discourses and practices, working in these masculinized conditions that continue to constitute academic culture.

Reclamation of Erotic Power as Increasing Pleasure

Having problematized women's experience of pleasure within the academy, this chapter now proposes a process whereby women's experience of pleasure can be sourced from a greater sense of what it means to be more authentically female. In a radical move, we authors co-opt the entrepreneurial self of neoliberalism for the purposes of journeying out of the construction and negative effects of an androcentric consciousness. What we offer in this model (Figure 2) is a process whereby women can embrace their entrepreneurial self, not as single subject self of androcentricity and neoliberalism but as an entrepreneurial self that is journeying with others out of an androcentric consciousness. The process we propose is unfolded throughout the rest of this chapter. This process involves a reclamation of eros as the human life force, together with a focus on intellectual virtues, forces that create a dynamic of increasing pleasure that comes into play through an entrepreneurial self as shown in Figure 2.

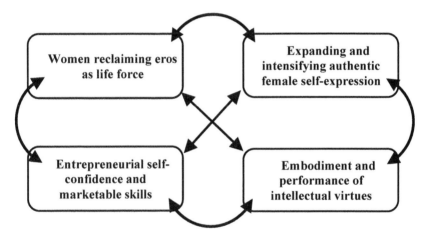

Figure 2. Dynamic model of interactivity for increasing pleasure

The chapter concludes with the provision of some tools to enhance the means whereby pleasure can be increased through a focus on the relationship between erotic power and intellectual virtues.

PLEASURE AND EROTIC POWER

This section is an intentional reclamation of women's erotic power as both pleasure giving and life-giving through the feminist heuristic of novelty used in this chapter. That is, novelty is valued as a virtue that buttresses the quality of our model

(Longino, 2008).[4] The aim in providing this model (Figure 2) is to provide a conceptual bridge to reconnect women's imagination to their childhood memory of eros as playfulness, providing access to their life force that has been historically denied to them by androcentric socialization and prohibitions. Furthermore, as adult persons, women's institutional selves have become estranged from the vast dynamics of eros as female desire, in turn becoming estranged from the intuitive source from which experiences of deep and robust pleasure are generated (Lorde, 1984). We authors claim that eros as female desire has the capacity to counter, ameliorate and perhaps even annihilate the negative effects of androcentrism and neoliberalism, so that women scholars are able to harness the power and pleasure that comes from engaging their genuine erotic dimension. In other words, as women come to be transformed through eros' capacity to cultivate more authentic selves and experiences of pleasure, so a counter-force becomes innately operative against the stifling discursivity of androcentricity and neoliberalism.

Essential to harnessing this transformative power of eros, is broadening our consciousness with regard to what eros truly encompasses. Eros is much more than the connotations of sex to which historically and basely eros has been bound. The reduction of eros to sexual connotations can be seen as motivated by commercial/capitalist interests: "the idea of eros as sensuality, connection and love has been lost within the dominance of a capitalized market discourse that defines eroticism as sex, and erotic as sexy" (Bell & Sinclair, 2014, p. 269). Eros has been co-opted and distorted so as to be exploited for its market commodity value. This entrapment and diminishment of eros to merely its dimension of sex has had particularly debilitating effects for women, who have long been subject to sexual objectification (Bell & Sinclair, 2014). What this emphasis on sex for commercial purposes has meant is that eros has become associated with feelings of shame and degradation, with significant impact for girls and women. In the process of girls becoming women, in the growing realisation of their femaleness, girls and women have been socialized away from cognisance of eros as the wellspring of their vitality (Whitehead & Whitehead, 2008). Subsequently, there is a need for women to reclaim eros from its diminished and compromised state, to be able to access all the power of its fuller dimensions as a life-giving force.

The reclamation of eros in feminist scholarship is a work of disconnection with gender with eros being understood as a gender neutral force. In freeing eros from its commercialization, eros can be experienced as a life-giving force, as the vital energy animating creation (Whitehead & Whitehead, 2008). As an ebullient and eager energy, that is sometimes disruptive (Lorde, 1984) as it moves us again and again toward more life, eros can be recognized in the surge of delight, the arousal of passion, the stirring of compassion, and the rush of pleasure (Whitehead & Whitehead, 2008). Audre Lorde articulates her experience of eros as "the power which comes from sharing deeply any pursuit with another person. The sharing of joy, whether physical, emotional, psychic, or intellectual, forms a bridge between the sharers which can be the basis for understanding much of what is not shared between them, and lessens the threat of their difference" (Lorde, 1984, p. 341). In this reclaiming of eros from its reduction through commercialization, women are harnessing the capacity of eros as pleasure to make us present to ourselves, a capacity to bring us back into the here-and-now, making us present again to our lives and within our lives (Whitehead & Whitehead, 2008).

Bell identifies the conflict between eros and cultural and societal factors for women working in universities, when she says universities are "a place where a love of learning and pleasure is possible. Yet a range of cultural and societal factors have rendered academic life on the one hand disembodied, and on the other, commodified and sexualized, especially for women" (Bell & Sinclair, 2014, p. 268). Further to this, Bell highlights the loss of the erotic from academic life in the institutional denial of the erotic. This is made systemically manifest in the academy, where the culture emphasizes the life of the mind while suppressing bodies (Bell & Sinclair, 2014, p. 269). In highlighting a need to reclaim eroticism, and the role of the body, in acquiring knowledge, Bell also stresses a need to acknowledge that meaningful academic work is an embodied practice (Bell & Sinclair, 2014). As Lorde acutely summates: 'The erotic is the nurturer or nursemaid of all our deepest knowledge' (Lorde, 1984, p. 341). Yet it generates a knowledge that is also Other-directed as it is informed by eros' want to pursue generous *jouissance* and love (Whitehead & Whitehead, 2008). Eros, therefore, enables a gleaning of a profound knowledge in relation to "creating and experiencing our bodies, careers, lives through embodied participation with others" (Bell & Sinclair, 2014, p. 270). The term 'erotic' from the Greek 'Eros', as Lorde reminds us, is "the personification of love in all its aspects" (Lorde, 1984, p. 341). It steers our desires beyond self-absorption towards self-transcendence, and a yearning for expressing to others love, compassion and generosity (Whitehead & Whitehead, 2008).

In being a vital energy oriented to love and understanding that is self and other directed, eros is fundamentally our life force. It is the vital energy through which all of creation becomes animated (Whitehead & Whitehead, 2008). Eros is the energy of ebullience and eagerness that moves us towards a richer plumbing of life (Whitehead & Whitehead, 2008). As a disruptive energy (referred to earlier) eros upsets the structures we have become conditioned to and feel secure in (Lorde, 1984). Yet, through this discomfort we are propelled towards new growth and liberating consequences. Eros can be recognized in the blissful sense of freedom; surges of delight, arousals of passion, stirrings of compassion, and the rush of pleasure. The French term for pleasure – *jouissance* – encapsulates the rich emotional outworking of eros: "a state of blissful freedom and pleasure that arises when sexual activity is no longer centred on the genitals. Eroticism is not sexuality according to this view – far from it" (Bell & Sinclair, 2014, p. 269). *Jouissance* speaks to eros as that which drives our desires to 'touch', 'taste', and 'consume' as we seek to engage with vivid sensitivity the fabric of life (Whitehead & Whitehead, 2008). It encompasses the intensities of physical, emotional, and intellectual pleasure. *Jouissance* emphasizes in eros "potential, playfulness, unpredictability, and danger" (Bell & Sinclair, 2014, p. 269).

What is clear in these descriptions is that eros has ontological effects, that is to say eros has power to affect the whole of our being. And not only for our own sake, for our own pleasure. Eros is also a mutually enhancing power. Authentic engagement with the dynamism of eros then, moves the ego beyond a self-serving quality to a positively relational/sensual/embodied self: that is communal, relational, 'other' directed (Alexander, 2013; Bell & Sinclair, 2014; Jones, 1981; Lorde, 1984; Whitehead & Whitehead, 2008). Eros shifts consciousness to a higher level through the transformative power that stems from the positive interplay between the individual erotic self and its communal engagement with others. Hence its capacity to generate new experiences and knowledge within a frame of embodied sensual pleasure. As we have endeavoured to present here, nurturing authentic female expression and experience of *jouissance* and eros promises new vistas of knowledge and generative dialogue. As women continue to push against the institutional censoring of the erotic (Bell & Sinclair, 2014) it is worth remembering that eros draws and calls us to remember our life-giving source: 'eros stirs in absence' also, 'in the pangs of solitude, in our lament for desires unfulfilled' (Whitehead & Whitehead, 2008, p. 16).

In summarizing and promoting the reclamation of erotic power as a means to increasing authentic femaleness and so pleasure, this section has evoked the feminist heuristic of novelty. Deploying novelty has allowed the development of a new model that honours erotic power as our life force while at the same time new ways of being provide "protection against unconscious perpetuation of the sexism and androcentrism of traditional theorizing" (Longino 2008b, 70). Embracing novelty allows intellectual virtues such as intellectual courage, curiosity, and creativity to become the means of increasing pleasure as individual women interpret their unique journey in pursuit of more authentic expressions of their femaleness within the academy. An increased focus on intellectual virtues within the academy means an increase in the explicit recognition of intellectual virtues within society to the betterment of our social environment. "The more intellectual virtues become an explicit part of our social environment, the more we can use them to manage the "complex antecedents of interest", including consciously and unconsciously held emotions, attitudes, evaluations, self-concepts, goals, and motives" (Howes, 2012, p. 745). In this way, developing intellectual virtues acts to identify sources of masculinist interests as well as acting as an antidote to masculinist androcentric frameworks. Further to this, intellectual virtues in their personal and communal embodiment have the power to transform existing social ordering.

EROTIC POWER, INTELLECTUAL VIRTUES, AND PLEASURE

Outlining a feminist understanding of eros as a communal engagement with others as we have done in the previous section has formed a link between erotic power and intellectual virtues as tools within communities of practice. Howes (2012, p. 737) elaborates on the use of these tools as praxis when she says: "intellectual virtues are not merely personal qualities, and the development of intellectual character is not simply a subjective matter. Intellectual virtues develop in epistemic communities and are exercised in relation to those communities". These personal and communal attributes of intellectual virtues need first to be embodied as personal qualities in order that these intellectual qualities affect epistemic goods, and these as they extend into epistemic communities and the social environment in general. Intellectual virtues[5] provide an inherent epistemic orientation towards "a firm and intelligent love of epistemic goods" (Baehr, 2013, p. 250), a love of and desire for knowledge, truth and understanding. These qualities that refer to both personal and communal aspects further highlight the scope of erotic power as well as the scope of the model proposed in this chapter.

We authors in final explication of our model, purposively select the virtue of intellectual playfulness as a critical scholarly virtue. Considerable research validates the importance of playful behaviours both for creativity and academic success (Boyer, 1997). Maier (1980) explains that to be playful is to invent and construct alternate, separate realities. It is to frolic in the space between what is known and what is not. Playfulness enables the fruitful disruption of what is familiar; initiating an opening up to assimilating new content onto/into the old and familiar (Maier, 1980). To be playful is to operate outside otherwise rigid modes of mental conduct. Playfulness also evidences the presence of erotic power, playfulness as part of the creative energy that seeks human expression, the power that this chapter has adopted as the energy that empowers the entrepreneurial self of female academics. For women this comprises engaging with their embodied ways of knowing; their senses and intuition; and nurturing their capacity to remember, invent, visualize, speak and write liberated and more authentic selves. The intellectual virtue of playfulness provides such a space for this to occur.

Specifically, the intellectual virtue of playfulness provides a location for women to allow more authentic experiences of *jouissance* to surface, where they can explore dimensions of eros in their lives. In play, our imagination is given flight; our emotions are unrestrained; our senses are heightened; our intuitions are present to us; our body feels good as we feel more free; social boundaries are scaled back as we move towards intimacy and share laughter and creativity with others. To be intellectually playful in the academic forum is therefore ripe with the potential for considerable pleasure to be garnered through innovatory engagement with academic work and its generative power. In sum, erotic power can be generated for women as embodied joy that becomes manifested in and through intellectual virtues.

Pleasure as a Liberating Force

What we have presented here in women's reclamation of their life force is that women, in moving towards a more authentic erotic female self, can both empower and liberate their experience within the academy. And this has been the aim of our model, the provision of a conceptual framework which encourages women to journey beyond masculinist androcentric frameworks, and move towards increasing pleasure within the academy. We have proposed that erotic power as our human life force together with intellectual virtues offers women scholars more opportunities to work in ways that manifest pleasure, self-worth, and a commanding entrepreneurial profile within the academic neoliberal marketplace.

NOTES

[1] The effect of the single male subject of western culture is at the heart of western feminist theory. While western feminist theory is inclusive of the many diverse groups of women within western culture, our work is beyond white feminism, and feminism generally. We understand this chapter could have issues and concepts useful to all marginalized groups who are affected by androcentric constructs, e.g., transgender and nonbinary gendered identities.

[2] We authors recognize men as a group are also impoverished by androcentric thinking, a form of thinking in which men's experience is also homogenized. Kegan-Gardner notes that human experience conceptualized as universal has a cost for men, "the price men pay for representing the universal is disembodiment, or loss of gendered specificity into the abstraction of phallic masculinity" (Braidiotti, as cited in Kegan Gardiner, 2002, p. 37).

[3] Predicting another's abusive behaviour in order to construct a response that needs rationalization by a subordinate signals the presence of the abuse. Predicting is a strategy that many abused women use as a way of giving themselves some control of the violence that is to come. For example in knowing some of the things that trigger the violence of the abuser, the woman understands herself as having some power in the situation. Yet this is, in fact, an illusion, for she is functioning within the parameters of his discourse, logic and power, and each time she exercises this strategy she further internalizes the abuse that is being done to her by allowing his power to reign in the situation.

[4] "Feminists endorse the virtue of novelty of theoretical or explanatory principle as protection against unconscious perpetuation of the sexism and androcentrism of traditional theorizing, or of theorizing constrained by a desire for consistency with accepted explanatory models. The novelty envisioned is not the novelty of discovery of new entities (like the top quark) predicted by theory but rather of frameworks of understanding" (Longino, 2008, p. 91).

[5] Intellectual virtues are described differently by different scholars. Baehr (2011, p. 21) provides a taxonomy including: "intellectual autonomy, carefulness and thoroughness; intellectual humility, honesty, tenacity, adaptability, patience, perseverance and courage; intellectual curiosity, wonder, contemplativeness, open-mindedness, creativity and imagination".

REFERENCES

Alexander, L. (2013). Hélène Cixous and the rhetoric of feminine desire: Re-writing the medusa. *Mode Journal*. Retrieved from http://www.english.arts.cornell.edu/publications/mode/documents/alexander.doc

Baehr, J. (2011). *The inquiring mind: On intellectual virtues and virtue epistemology*. Oxford: Oxford University Press.

Bansel, P., & Davies, B. (2005). The time of their lives? Academic workers in neoliberal time(s). *Health Sociology Review, 14*, 47–58.

Bartky, S. L. (1990). *Femininity and domination: Studies in the phenomenology of oppression*. New York, NY: Routledge.

Bell, E., & Sinclair, A. (2014). Reclaiming eroticism in the academy. *Organization, 21*(2), 268–280. doi: 10.1177/1350508413493084

Blackmore, J. (2013). Within/against: feminist theory as praxis in higher education research. In J. Huisman & M. Tight (Eds.), *Theory and method in higher education research* (Vol. 9, pp. 175–198). London, UK: Emerald Group Publishing.

Boyer, W. A. (1997). Enhancing playfulness with sensorial stimulation. *Journal of Research in Childhood Education, 12*(1), 78–87.

Chatterjee, I. (2012). Feminism, the false consciousness of neoliberal capitalism? Informalization, fundamentalism, and women in an Indian city. *Gender, Place & Culture, 19*(6), 790–809. doi: 10.1080/0966369X.2011.649349

Cixous, H. (1976). The laugh of the Medusa. *Signs, 1*(4), 875–893.
Cox, E. (2016). Feminism has failed and needs a radical rethink. *The Conversation*. Retrieved from http://theconversation.com/feminism-has-failed-and-needs-a-radical-rethink-55441
Davies, B., Browne, J., Gannon, S., Honan, E., & Somerville, M. (2005). Embodied women at work in neoliberal times and places. *Gender, Work & Organization, 12*(4), 343–362. doi: 10.1111/j.1468-0432.2005.00277.x
Gershon, I. (2011). Neoliberal agency. *Current Anthropology, 52*, 537–555.
Giroux, H. (2004). Public pedagogy and the politics of neo-liberalism: Making the political more pedagogical. *Policy Futures in Education, 2*, 494–503.
Gross, R. M. (2009). *A garland of feminist reflections: Forty years of religious exploration*. University of California Press.
Harvey, D. (2005). *A brief history of neoliberalism*. New York, NY: Oxford University Press.
Honan, E., Henderson, L., & Loch, S. (2015). Producing moments of pleasure within the confines of an academic quantified self. *Creative Approaches to Research, 8*(3), 44–62.
Howes, M. (2012). Managing salience: The importance of intellectual virtue in analyses of biased scientific reasoning. *Hypatia, 27*(4), 736–754. doi: 10.1111/j.1527-2001.2011.01237.x
Jensen-Clayton, C., & Murray, A. (2016a). Working beyond the research maze. In D. Rossi, F. Gacenga, & P. A. Danaher (Eds.), *Navigating the education research maze: Contextual, conceptual, methodological and transformational challenges and opportunities for researchers* (pp. 253–273). Cham: Springer.
Jensen-Clayton, C., & Murray, A. (2016b). Working in the research maze: At what price? In D. Rossi, F. Gacenga, & P. A. Danaher (Eds.), *Navigating the education research maze: Contextual, conceptual, methodological and transformational challenges and opportunities for researchers* (pp. 21–45). Cham: Springer.
Jones, A. R. (1981). Writing the body: Toward an understanding of "L'Ecriture Feminine". *Feminist Studies, 7*(2), 247–263.
Kegan Gardiner, J. (2002). Men, masculinities and feminist theory. In J. K. Gardiner (Ed.), *Masculinity studies and feminist theory*. New York: Columbia University Press.
Khader, S. (2011). The work of sexual difference. In M. C. Rawlinson, S. L. Horn, & S. J. Khader (Eds.), *Thinking with Irigaray*. Albany, NY: State University of New York Press.
Longino, H. E. (2008). Values, heuristics, and the politics of knowledge. In M. Carrier, D. Howard, & K. Janet (Eds.), *The challenge of the social and the pressure of practice: Science and values revisited* (pp. 68–86). Pittsburgh, PA: University of Pittsburgh Press.
Lorde, A. (1984). The uses of the erotic: The erotic as power. *The lesbian and gay studies reader* (pp. 339–343). New York, NY: Routledge.
Maier, H. W. (1980). Play in the university classroom. *Social Work with Groups, 3*(1), 7–16.
Meyers, D. T. (2002). *Gender in the mirror: Cultural imagery and women's agency*. New York: Oxford University Press.
Miller, J. B. (2012). *Toward a new psychology of women*. Beacon Press.
Mountz, A., Bonds, A., Mansfield, B., Loyd, J., Hyndman, J., Walton-Roberts, M., ... Curran, W. (2015). For slow scholarship: A feminist politics of resistance through collective action in the neoliberal university. *ACME: An International E-Journal for Critical Geographies, 14*(4), 1235–1259.
Springer, S. (2015a). Postneoliberalism? *Review of Radical Political Economics, 47*(1), 5–17. doi: 10.1177/0486613413518724
Springer, S. (2015b). *Violent neoliberalism: Development, discourse and dispossession in Cambodia*. New York, NY: Palgrave Macmillan.
Thompson, M. J. (2015). False consciousness reconsidered: A theory of defective social cognition. *Critical Sociology, 41*(3), 449–461. doi: 10.1177/0896920514528817
Valian, V. (2005). Beyond gender schemas: Improving the advancement of women in academia. *Hypatia, 20*(3), 198–213.

Whitehead, J. D., & Whitehead, E. E. (2008). *Holy eros: Recovering the passion of God.* Maryknoll, NY: Orbis Books.

Cecily Jensen-Clayton
University of Southern Queensland, Australia

Rena MacLeod
Australian Catholic University, Brisbane, Australia

GAIL CRIMMINS

8. THE INTRINSIC PLEASURE OF BEING PRESENT WITH/IN HUMANISTIC RESEARCH

INTRODUCTION

Qualitative research is said to add flesh to the bones of quantitative data, and narrative inquiry more specifically, is described as emotionally comforting, reassuring, and validating for the participants who share their stories. But little is written on the impact of engaging in qualitative research on the researcher. This chapter therefore explores a humanistic approach to investigating the lived experience of women casual academics in Australian universities, and exposes the emotional and embodied labour and rewards involved in researching others' stories. Through reflecting in and on my practice as a narrative inquirer I discuss how I was affectively and ideologically motivated to investigate the lives of women casual academics, and demonstrate how my heart worked in conjunction with my head with/in the research process. I also explore how humanistic inquiry cannot be fully pre-planned or determined as we use our affective and logical response to each research stage to inform the next re-search action. Humanistic inquiry therefore requires emotional and cognitive presence and embodied reflection where we look outward to connect with research participants, and reflect inward to learn how we feel and think about our research journey, relationships and emerging outcomes. We then use our feelings, values and thoughts to motivate and shape subsequent steps in the investigation. Regular self-reflection allows us to connect with Others/research participants, (re)connect with ourselves, and achieve a sense of research 'flow' and unbounded and pleasure.

BACKGROUND AND CONTEXT – THE HUMAN CONDITION

Qualitative research invites researchers to inquire about the human condition and explore the meaning of human experiences (Taylor, 2013), and is often ascribed human or humanizing characteristics. For instance, Patton (2002, p. 132) suggests that 'qualitative data can put flesh on the bones of quantitative results, bringing results to life'. Similarly, particular approaches to qualitative research such as arts-informed, person-centred and narrative inquiry are afforded humanizing qualities. For example, Dewing (2002) suggests that contributing to person-centred research can affirm the humanity of participants, whilst White and Epston (1990) claim that listening attentively to research participants' accounts of lived experience can validate participants' humanity and enhance their self-efficacy. Finally, the artistic representation or performance of narrative research is considered to have a humanizing effect on an audience. In particular, Sikes and Gale (2006) claim that performed data enhances the emotional connection of humans by opening our senses to others, and Gray, Fitch, LaBrecque, and Greenberg (2003) posit that engaging with patients' lives on the stage has a "humanizing effect" by offering increased insight into, and empathy with, the experiences of patients and their families.

Yet, despite the human and humanizing qualities ascribed to qualitative research on its participants and audiences, there is currently very little discussion on how the research process impacts on us/researchers, or that the emotional and cognitive experience of research can actually shape research decisions making. That is, it is not fully understood how we as researchers *feel* and *think* during the research process, and how our experience helps to determine our practice. In order to uncover and acknowledge the human dimension of academic research (and perhaps in doing so celebrate our humanity) I share with you here a reflection in and on my process (Schön, 1983) as a humanistic narrative inquirer.

Humanism is a secular, philosophical and ethical stance that places importance on the dignity and values of human beings. It also recognizes humans' affective, emotional and rational domains of being. Humanism accepts that we engage with our environment on affective/emotional and intellectual levels and that our thoughts and feelings motivate our action in the world (Huitt, 2009). More specifically, a humanistic approach to research is described as compassionate, caring, concerned with meeting human needs; and aims to address human problems for both the individual and society (Rogers, Lyon, & Tausch, 2013). Therefore, humanistic research is undertaken by fully embodied persons (that is, persons with affect and cognition) for the good of individuals (selves and others), and for society.

RESEARCH APPROACH AND PROCESS

For the project I discuss here I adopted a self-reflexive stance of "not knowing" (Anderson & Goolishian, 1992) how my humanistic stance might impact on my research decision-making within an investigation into the lived experience of women casual academics in Australia. Self-reflexivity is understood to be an integral process in qualitative research where we/researchers reflect on how our perceptions and actions impact upon our actions (Gerrish & Lacey, 2006). It is also considered to be an important part of transparency and self-disclosure within the qualitative research process (Smith, 2008). Yet, despite the fact that self-reflexivity is usually a central characteristic of qualitative inquiry, it remains under-discussed and almost invisible in the scholarship we create about our research practices. In contrast, in this chapter I focus explicitly on my thoughts, feelings and emotions experienced during a research project, and how they inform/ed the research journey.

Selecting a Research Focus and Approach

Prior to researching the lived experience of women casual academics in Australia I had held a Senior Lectureship in the UK and enjoyed what I understand now as the dignity of ongoing academic employment. The role afforded me an office, regular salary, and a visible presence, a significant degree of academic autonomy, and a voice in the school and university in which I worked. After six years in the role I immigrated to Australia, seven months pregnant with my first child, a husband, and two suitcases. I returned to academia, this time part-time and in Australia, when my second child was eight months old and my first born was two. I was employed as an academic development coordinator three days a week. Again, in this role I was provided the dignity of an office, regular income, social/cultural integration, academic autonomy and recognition. But I missed teaching students, and so after a year I resigned from that post to work as a casual academic. Casual academics are also known as an adjuncts, sessional staff or casual teachers. Yet within my role as a casual academic I felt anonymous. I was without a regular income and paid entitlements and had very little control over what, I taught, or even how I designed the learning and teaching I offered. The feelings of invisibility and disenfranchisement were highly emotional for me. On the one hand I re-enjoyed teaching and engaging with students, but I felt lonely, undervalued and without voice. It was this emotional response to experiencing the lived experience of being a casual academic that compelled me to explore academic casualisation within a research process.

Subsequently, by examining the scholarship around casualisation, I identified that there was indeed a "gap in the literature" and that very little was known about the lived experience of casual academics (Coates et al., 2009). Yet "turning to the literature" was a *response* to my embodied self-reflexivity, not my primary impulse. Embodied cognition is considered a primal, pre-rational, non-introspective process (Wojciehowski & Gallese, 2011), where self-knowledge is contained and communicated through bodily and emotional sensations (Pagis, 2009). Embodied self-reflexivity is described as the capacity to identify and understand bodily sensations as indexes to psychological states (Pagis, 2009). For me, my emotional response to working as an adjunct motivated me to explore the lived experience of women casual academics, a motivation that was supported by engaging with the scholarship around casualisation of academia.

Second, through the feminist lens with which I view and understand the world, I observed that most casual academics in Australia are women (May et al., 2011), and as a feminist researcher I recognize "the essential importance of examining women's experience" (Hesse-Biber, Leavy, & Yaiser, 2004, p. 3). I decided therefore to develop a research project that focussed on the experience of women casual academics in order to "touch base with the variety of real life stories women provide about themselves" (Lugones & Spelman, 1983, p. 21).

Reflecting on my initial research process, therefore, identified that I was both emotionally drawn to the research focus, and that my political/ideological/ cognitive stance helped to shape the research methodology I would employ. Thus, research decision-making is not necessarily predominantly or solely a cognitive process, as most academic literature seems to suggest. I wonder, then, how many other qualitative researchers feel initially compelled by their/our emotional and ideological 'situation' to engage in a particular research project, and subsequently seek to verify our decisions in academic discourse as a secondary impulse, or even hide an emotional or ideological rationale behind/under/within a logical 'academic' argument?

Physical Cognition and Emotion can act as a Litmus Test to Determine the 'Fit' of a Research Process for the Researcher

Once I'd selected the research focus and methodology, I spent the following few months considering suitable research methods, engaging in a literature review and writing an ethics application. Interestingly, even though I'd initially been emotionally and ideologically compelled to engage in the research, I spent most of my time in this second phase of research cognitively engaging with others' theories and processes. In other words I spent most of this time 'in my head'. Reflecting both in and on this process I recognize that I maintained my interest in the focus of the study but was not excited or passionate about it. I found much of what I read interesting and occasionally re-read a paper as it was so 'useful' to my planned practice. But I was rarely animated or exuberant within or about the process. At times I admit it felt like 'hard work'.

In contrast, during phase three of the research, which involved meeting with women casual academics and eliciting their stories of lived experience, I noticed a strong emotional impulse and connection to the project resurface, I became very animated, enthusiastic and energized by the research again. I felt *compelled* to spend as much time as possible engaging with the women participants, ensuring that they felt comfortable, listening care-fully to their her-stories, and was physically, emotionally and empathetically absorbed by them.

In particular, cognisant that talking about personal experience is usually an emotional experience (Richards, 2011), and being open to participants' potential vulnerabilities, I spent time chatting to the women participants (usually several times) before inviting them to share their stories with me. I also let them decide to tell their stories in whichever media or medium they wished as Keats' (2009) suggests that participants may have a preference for one form of narrative expression over another. I also felt that the more comfortable the women were, the more likely they would be to share of the stories that they wished to tell. This was part of an interviewing process which resisted establishing the parameters of formal and structured interviews that can confine the responses participants can select or share (Gubrium & Holstein, 2002), I simply told the women that it was up to them what and how what talked about their experience of working as a casual academic. In this way I ceded control of the storying process to the participants and assumed the role of active listener (Jones, 2004). I simply listened to and was fully to receptive the stories the women shared. I didn't 'veer' them into any particular direction or narrative theme I instead gave my time, presence and authority to the storyteller, who I acknowledged "as the one who knows and tells" (Kramp, 2004, p. 111).

And as I sat and listened to "the ones who knew and were telling", I experienced a strong empathetic engagement with the women and their stories. I felt honoured that the women would share their time and intimate details of their lives with me. I was also humbled that they would tell me their dreams, hopes, disappointments, joys and fears. The sense of humility, and care with the women could not be easily located in a particular part of my body or head. I can only describe the experience as a "feeling of body" (Wojciehowski & Gallese, 2011), where my whole being was engaged and absorbed in and by the women and their stories, and I experienced a very strong sense of connection. Wojciehowski & Gallese (2011) similarly explain that empathy and connection are "the outcome of our natural tendency to experience interpersonal relations at the implicit level of intercorporeity" or inter-physicality (Wojciehowski & Gallese, 2011, p. 17). Thus, by listening intently to the participants and then reflecting inwardly to how I felt in/with the women and their stories I recognized a fully embodied sense of empathy. In fact the experience was all consuming and provided me with tremendous energy. I felt vibrant, 'alive', dynamic and had the sense that to sit in this stage of story gathering without rushing on was the right thing to do; the right thing for me, for the women, and for the research project.

In particular, as I sat with the research participants listening to stories of lived experience I found myself mirroring their breathing patterns, facial expressions and gestures; and later when I listened to recorded transcriptions of the interviews I noticed that I was physically still, holding my breath, afraid that a sound – even my breath – might obscure or mute the nuance of a participant's tone, pitch, pace or pause. I was physically and emotionally engrossed in the women's narratives and wanted to hear and sense them as fully as possible.

I also noticed that it was during this time, when I was most emotionally engaged in the research process, that I enjoyed the research most too. It was indeed physically, emotionally and cognitively compelling, and demanding. I cried with the women, I cried for them afterwards, many times. I also laughed with them, out loud. I shared much of their sadness and joy. I was completely immersed in collecting their stories, the detail, the texture, the unique experience and telling and was tireless in my pursuit of capturing their authentic voice and experience. It was all consuming and as I didn't resist it or try to hurry the process the experience was deeply satisfying and humanizing.

And then, once I'd collected their stories over 12 months and countless conversations, emails and phone conversations, I began to consider how I would select the narratives to re-tell. And this consideration made me pause. My relentless energy and drive halted, abruptly. This 'hiatus' seemed to coincide with (and therefore probably reflected) my emotional, cognitive and physical resistance to narrative analysis, which was the process of "handling the data" I'd originally planned to undertake. I fear/ed that the process dissecting the women's stories into themes for analysis might distort the narrative flow of their stories, limit the possibility of establishing the context of each described event or character description, and diminish the idiosyncratic nature of their individualized experience. I also shared Richards' dilemma that she would "trespass with muddy feet into the hearts of her participants" were she to deconstruct the lived experience/stories of participants into un/usable categories of data (Richards, 2011, p. 11). I responded to this emotional, physical and cognitive resistance by sitting with the data for a while, *seemingly* doing nothing. Yet all the while I was thinking (and feeling) about how I might validate and share the women's stories without dissecting and scrutinizing them as if they were discreet cells. This rest, pause, interval (call if what you will) wasn't written into my research plan. It hadn't been built into my "projected timeline" as I could not have predicted my resistance beforehand.

So, in addition to times of high energy, focus, exhilaration, and passion, the humanistic, self-reflexive researcher may find her/himself in limbo, with unplanned pit stops, or a need for reorientation. The pleasure of high intensity can be accompanied with lows of emotional and cognitive responsibility to the other/research participant. But moreover, this experience taught me that our embodied response, *our thoughts and feelings about a particular research process can actually act as a litmus test to determine if the course of action we are undertaking or planning to enact, 'fits' with us as researchers, 'fits' with who we are as people and researchers, with how we view the research participants with whom we work, and how we want to engage in research more generally.* Although the experience didn't initially 'progress' the project, it did identify that we as researchers are humans with a capacity to feel and learn and act according to our feelings and values.

Academic Scholarship Can Stimulate an Embodied Response and Research Momentum

Interestingly, whilst I was seemingly pausing I was actively considering how I might engage in a process of organizing the 'data' (the women's stories) for discussion, I encountered Maggie MacLure's 2013 paper, "The wonder of data". What was remarkable about the encounter was that rather than 'the literature' substantiating my embodied or ideological impulse, as it had done previously, MacLure's scholarship instead *stimulated* an embodied response and re-energized me, motivating me to carry out the next stage in the research process with gusto. In fact, when reading the paper my heart raced and my face flushed, I felt overcome with physical and emotional energy. MacLure suggested that it was legitimate to engage with research data emotionally as narrative data is indeed emotional. She also acknowledged the "productive capacity for wonder that resides and radiates in data", and in our interaction with it (MacLure, 2013, p. 228). That is, MacLure accepts that researchers/we can have an emotional interaction with research data that confounds the methodical, mechanical search for meanings, codes, or themes. I was relieved, and my feelings (and pause) seemed validated.

In fact, MacLure's (2103) ideas created a sense of "home-coming" for me, my shoulders dropped and once again I began to feel exhilarated in and by the research process. She offered a sound theoretical and political base for my reluctance to undertake a narrative analysis, and perhaps unwittingly, offered a practical restorying solution to me. Moreover, the ideas MacLure presented created a strong feeling of 'rightness', of 'fit', 'legitimacy' and indeed, 'pleasure'. It felt so good to have my previous uncertainties and research pause legitimized. It's OK to engage in research as a fully embodied person and to feel protective over participants' stories she suggested. It's OK to engage with research data emotionally as well as cognitively, MacLure's words seemed to sing.

Using MacLure's ideas as inspiration, I worked relentlessly, tirelessly, and with creative energy, restorying the women participant's stories into a short drama, a drama that comprised participants' stories that excited me, moved me, or stimulated thought. I included in the data re-presentation only the words, sighs and silences that resonated with me, most of which were moments of personal story and biography that were peculiar to an individual participant. They told of the loss of a child, a colleague's unexpected death and no-one in the university telling the woman's casual colleagues, the casual academic that was told she was 'off-limits' and would not be receiving any future casual teaching, and the story of domestic violence and the need for casual work to sustain a family. These were not stories repeated by more than one participant, they were instead personally experienced and defied classification. Yet these stories 'glowed' me (MacLure, 2013), they resonated and deeply affected me. The restorying process, harnessed by MacLure's scholarship, was for me the most humane, satisfying, and enjoyable research process of the project. Yes, it was emotionally and creatively challenging too, but it was *equally* rewarding and joyous to pay homage to the strong, resilient and powerful women whose voices had hitherto been unheard in academia. I'm not suggesting though that the research process *has* to be emotionally challenging in order to being pleasurable and rewarding, but in my experience academic challenge can *also* be pleasurable and gratifying.

The result of my change of heart/process in deviating from my plan to narratively analyse the gathered research data, resulted in the creation of a performed drama that was presented live (at a research conference) and recordings of the drama were presented at an international and two national conferences. Moreover, the recordings of the drama (uploaded onto YouTube) received over 1000 views. It's doubtful that an academic paper would have generated such 'reach'. Yet if I had not been so emotionally engaged and self (and bodily) reflexive in and on the research process I perhaps would not have taken the risk to reject narrative analysis. I would have probably (instead) examined the data looking common themes, oft-repeated aspects and incidence of experience, and in doing so would have presented and discussed the research outcomes in traditional academic papers and conference presentations. This process would have undoubtedly prevented me from selecting the idiosyncratic stories that 'glowed' to me (MacLure, 2013), and some of the more private of stories of women casual academics would not have been re-presented for others to experience or know. I think then that had I not been emotionally, physically and cognitively engaged in the process, many of the stories of women's experience as casual academics would remain "yet to be voiced" (Arnot & Reay, 2007). Therefore, humanistic, fully embodied research can create an opportunity for multiplicity of stories and storytellers to be presented and celebrated in academic organisations (Boje, 1995) and supports the essential human right of being able to see oneself and one's community conjured to the stage and thereby reflect on both the strengths and injustices of your world (Valentine, n.d.). The lesson I learned from this is that the researchers who are offering new insights and presenting new stories are not necessarily the ones following paths well-travelled. They may in fact be following their own path and judgment.

REFLECTIONS ON THE OVERALL RESEARCH PROCESS

On reflecting on the entire research process I see that there were times that my research was emotionally driven, and times when my rational and intellectual process dominated the process. But there were also phases of research within which my head and heart were symbiotically engaged. Moreover, when my emotional, moral and cognitive energies were simultaneously activated and I experienced an intense feeling of research flow. I was completely absorbed in the process, was excited by it, and engaged in it tirelessly for weeks – which-seemed-like-hours. Indeed, my experience of engaging with narrative research was as Patton *warned* (my emphasis) "time consuming, intimate, and intense" (Patton, 2002, p. 35), but it was also exhilarating, emerging and flow-full. I was fully immersed in the research process with a strong sense of contentment, alertness and energy (Csikszentmihályi, 1990). I was aware of a heightened experience of emotional and cognitive congruence (Hektner & Csikszentmihályi, 1996). Without full bodied engagement I doubt I would have reached such a pleasurable and satisfying experience.

A second reflection I have is that qualitative research when undertaken with full embodiment and humanity inevitably *unfolds* or *evolves*, it cannot be predetermined or systematically planned. For instance, I could not have predicted that I would feel the need to employ a data restorying process that privileged the unique narrative moments of participants until I had experienced an intense reaction against analytically ordering the stories into theoretically organized themes. As Merriam (1998) suggests "where to focus or stop action cannot be determined ahead of time" (p. 97). Thus, it seems that the humanistic researcher cannot know the path or destination of the research at the outset of a project. Instead, s/he initiates an action then responds with a fully embodied openness to context, to research participants, and to self. Furthermore, this process requires time and academic freedom. In particular, humanistic fully embodied research is dependent upon the researcher discerning how s/he feels about each stage in the research process before s/he/we can respond to what becomes physically, emotionally or cognitively apparent. In this regard fully embodied research is closely aligned to slow scholarship, an academic process where ideas are allocated time to 'marinate' and 'ripen' (Mountz et al., 2015, p. 3). Similarly, it is harmonious with feminist research which refuses to adhere to 'masculine' linearity or the placing of logic over emotion. Feminist research instead 'promiscuously' invites researchers to create 'in-the-making', unfolding, and responsive scholarship (Childers et al., 2013) that deviates from the restricted and tired timelines and formulas of traditional discourse. Fully embodied research, like feminist and slow scholarship, therefore requires researchers' presence, self-reflexivity, time, and internal and external flexibility to engage in care-full research practices. Unfolding and evolving processes are also conducive to a flow full and joyful experience for the researcher.

CONCLUDING STATEMENTS AND CLOSING THOUGHTS

Qualitative research is often described as having a humanizing effect on research participants and research audiences. Yet little has been written about the researcher's human and humanistic process of engaging in qualitative research. In this chapter, I have therefore discussed a fully embodied, reflexive account of a narrative inquiry. It is offered up as a "personal tale of what went on in the backstage of doing research" (Ellis & Bochner, 2000, p. 741). Reflecting in and on my research process helped me to identify and communicate that I was emotionally and ideologically drawn to a particular research focus and approach, and that some scholarship, as well as research data, can resonate or 'glow' (MacLure, 2013). Indeed both published literature and research data can compel the researcher to an emotional call to action, and when stimulated, engaging in research can be an intense, highly productive and creative 'flow-full' experience. Finally, when we work tirelessly, creatively, and compulsively we can find intense joy and satisfaction in the research process.

Yet, fully embodied, self-reflexive research is perhaps paradoxical to the p/restrictive traditional structures of academia where budgets, timelines and detailed research plans and outcomes are expected to be communicated before the research process begins. It occurs to me, through reflecting on this research process, that fully humanistic, fully embodied research, like slow and feminist research, inhabits a human resistance that challenges "neoliberalism's metrics and efficiencies" (Mountz et al, 2015, p. 19). It is not a resistance that requires fight, or angry determination, it is instead simply requires presence, self-knowledge and care-full engagement with each stage of the research journey. It is a resistance worth preserving as the alignment of heart and head, or affect and cognition, during the research process can bring a sense of humanism, integrity, and flow to the research process so that our work as academics can, and indeed *should*, be pleasurable and gratifying.

REFERENCES

Anderson, H., & Goolishian, H. (1992). The client is the expert: A not-knowing approach to therapy. In S. McNamee & K. J. Gergen (Eds.) *Therapy as social construction* (pp. 25–39). London, UK: Sage.

Boje, D. (1995). Stories of the storytelling organisation: A postmodern analysis of Disney as 'Tamara-Land'. *The Academy of Management Journal, 38*(4), 997–1035. doi: 10.2307/256618

Childers, S., Rhee, J., & Daza, S. (2013). Promiscuous (use of) feminist methodologies: the dirty theory and messy practice of educational research beyond gender. *International Journal of Qualitative Studies in Education, 26*(5), 507–523. doi: 10.1080/09518398.2013.786849

Coates, H., Dobson, I., Edwards, D., Friedman, T., Goedegebuure, L., & Meek, L. (2009). *The attractiveness of the Australian academic profession: A comparative analysis*. Melbourne, VIC: LH Martin Institute, University of Melbourne & Australian Council for Educational Research & Educational Policy Institute. Retrieved from http://repository.unimelb.edu.au/10187/8900

Csikszentmihalyi, M. (1990). *Flow: The psychology of optimal experience*. New York, NY: Harper and Row.

Dewing, J. (2002). From ritual to relationship: a person centred approach to consent in qualitative research with older people who have a dementia. *Dementia: The International Journal of Social Research & Practice, 1*(2), 156–171. doi: 10.1177/147130120200100204

Ellis, C., & Bochner, A. P. (2000). Autoethnography, personal narrative, reflexivity: Researcher as subject. In N. K. Denzin & Y. S. Lincoln (Eds.) *Handbook of qualitative research* (2nd ed., pp. 733-768). Thousand Oaks, CA: Sage.

Gallese, V. (2009). Mirror neurons and the neural exploitation hypothesis: From embodied simulation to social cognition. In J.A. Pineda (Ed.) *Mirror neuron systems* (pp. 163–190). New York, NY: Humana Press.

Gerrish, K., & Lacey, A. (2006). *The research process in nursing* (5th ed.). Oxford, UK: Blackwell Publishing.

Gray, R., Fitch, M., LaBrecque, M., & Greenberg, M. (2003). Reactions of health professionals to a research-based theatre production. *Journal of Cancer Education, 18*(4), 223–229.

Hektner, J., & Csikszentmihalyi, M. (1996). *A longitudinal exploration of flow and intrinsic motivation in adolescents*. Paper presented at the annual meeting of the American Educational Research Association, New York, NY. Retrieved from http://files.eric.ed.gov/fulltext/ ED395261.pdf

Hesse-Biber, S. N., Leavy, P., & Yaiser, M. L. (2004). Feminist approaches to research as a process: Reconceptualizing epistemology, methodology and method. In S. Naggy Hesse-Biber, & M. L. Yaiser (Eds.) *Feminist perspectives on social research* (pp. 3–26). New York, NY: Oxford University Press.

Huitt, W. (2009). Humanism and open education. *Educational Psychology Interactive*. Valdosta, GA: Valdosta State University. Retrieved from http://www.edpsycinteractive.org/topics/affect/humed.html

Lugones, M., & Spelman, E. V. (1983). Have we got a theory for you? Feminist theory, cultural imperialism and the demand for 'the woman's voice'. *Women's Studies International Forum, 6*(6), 573–578. doi: 10.1016/0277-5395(83)90019-5

MacLure, M. (2013). The wonder of data. *Cultural Studies ↔ Critical Methodologies, 13*(4), 228–232. doi: 10.1177/1532708613487863

May, R., Strachan, G., Broadbent K., & Peetz, D. (2011). The casual approach to university teaching; Time for a re-think? In K. Krause, M. Buckridge, C. Grimmer, & S. Purbrick-Illek (Eds.) *Research and development in higher education: Reshaping higher education* (Vol. 34, pp. 188–197). Gold Coast, QLD: Research and Development Society of Australasia.

Merriam, S. (1998). *Qualitative research and case study applications in education*. San Francisco, CA: Jossey-Bass Publishers.

Mountz, A., Bonds, A., Mansfield, B., Loyd, J., Hyndman, J., Walton-Roberts, M., Basu, R., Whitson, R., Hawkins, R., Hamilton, T., & Curran, W. (2015). For slow scholarship: A feminist politics of resistance through collective action in the neoliberal university. *ACME: An International E-Journal for Critical Geographies, 14*(4), 1235–1259. Retrieved from http://ojs.unbc.ca/index.php/acme/article/view/1058

Pagis, M. (2009). Embodied self-reflexivity. *Social Psychology Quarterly, 72*(3), 265–283. doi.org/10.1177/019027250907200308

Patton, M. W. (2002). *Qualitative evaluation and research methods* (3rd ed.). Thousand Oaks, CA: Sage.

Richards, J. C. (2011). "Every word is true": Stories of our experiences in a qualitative research course. *The Qualitative Report*, *16*(3), 782–819. Retrieved from http://www.nova.edu/ssss/QR/QR16-3/richards.pdf

Rogers, C. R., Lyon, H. C. Jr., & Tausch, R. (2013). *On becoming an effective teacher – Person-centered teaching, psychology, philosophy, and dialogues with Carl R. Rogers and Harold Lyon*. London, UK: Routledge.

Schön, D. (1983). *The reflective practitioner: How professionals think in action*. New York, NY: Basic Books.

Smith, J. A. (2008). *Qualitative psychology: A practical guide to research methods* (2nd ed.). London, UK: Sage.

Taylor, B. (2013). Introduction. In B. Taylor & K. Francis (Eds.), *Qualitative research in the health sciences: Methodologies, methods and processes*. London, UK: Routledge.

White, M., & Epston, D. (1990). *Narrative means to therapeutic ends*. New York, NY: Norton.

Wojciehowski, H. C., & Gallese V. (2011). How stories make us feel. Toward an embodied narratology. *California Italian Studies*, *(2)*1. Retrieved from http://escholarship.org/uc/item/ 3jg726c2

Gail Crimmins
School of Communication & Creative Industries
University of the Sunshine Coast, Australia

CAROL A. TAYLOR

9. FOR HERMANN: HOW DO I LOVE THEE? LET ME COUNT THE WAYS

Or, What My Dog Has Taught Me about a Post-Personal Academic Life

INTRODUCTION: THE MUSIC OF HIS NAME

The very music of the name has gone
Into my being (Keats, [1816] 1977, Endymion)

Hermann
That's two 'n's not one
Named after Melville
A salty dog
A dog of the sea, of the tides, of the waves
But mostly of the rivers, gulleys, ditches and ponds
Anywhere dirty water gathered that you could sink into like a little furry hippo
And smile back up at me.

Hermann German, Hermann munster
Popsie pupsie, little sweetie, Old Boy.
You tolerated all the names I made up for you
Giving me that coy look which said
Nothing you call me gets near to who I am.

Who are you, Hermann?
Water, earth
You make language stammer
Fire, air
Good for my soul, believe it
Hermann.

In March 2016 Hermann had a second attack of vestibular syndrome, a problem of the inner ear that, when it comes, seems like a stroke and makes the dog feel constantly seasick. The first attack a few months ago left him with a lopsided head that gradually righted itself and threw his balance out. This second one has made him stagger like a drunken man, taken his appetite away for two days, and

> made him sleep, sleep, sleep. More and more, he wants to sit next to me on the floor and lean on me, lie next to me as I ruffle his ears and run my fingers into his lovely, black and white fur, so that he can fall asleep knowing I am there. I want to let him know he is safe but all I can do is stroke him, make tasty food treats for him, and play the games we've always played but gently now, not too fast or too rough because otherwise he'll fall over. I want to cry but I don't. My tears will only upset him needlessly. My job now is to make his time with us as good as it can be because that is what he has done for me all his life.

In the acknowledgements page of my doctoral thesis after thanking various humans – academics, family and friends – I wrote the following: "Final thanks go to the furry guru and the daily fun and games which helped me live in the moment and retain perspective during the long doctoral journey". I wrote that a long time ago when Hermann, aka the furry guru, was a young dog in his prime. He's been with me since then as I have worked to develop a career in academia. He's given me all sorts of unbidden help as I wrote articles, chapters, conference abstracts and papers; as I prepared teaching sessions, marked undergraduate assignments and gave feedback on doctoral work; and as I struggled to construct research bids. His consideration, inventiveness and sheer *joie de vivre* have threaded their way into the complicities, negotiations and contestations that have marked my rhizomic passages in a changing university landscape. Against the staticky pressure, the white noise hiss, of institutional targets, performativity and competition, Hermann has been a fizzing draught, a doggy alker seltzer, a beaker full of the warm south, a spice on the tongue, a tickle on the toe, the beat inside the beat. Now an older dog, a dog whose muscles are in decline, whose breath smells of seaweed, whose body now bears little lumps, pips and bumps under his beautiful fur, whose hearing is poor and whose sight is slowly failing, Hermann is still as committed to our daily fun and games. And so, for all he has given me, I write this chapter as a paean to Hermann.

As a posthuman, post-personal paean to Hermann, this chapter is my own way of making a little push against anthropocentrism and its violent and excluding legacy. I deploy a post-species, speculative pragmatics of human-animal relation as an opportunity to rethink the constitution of the 'we' in more relational, ethical and creative terms than the rational, individualized and hierarchizing straight-jacket of Humanism has so far permitted. My purpose in doing this is to widen the orbit in thinking about who and what matters in higher education and, in particular, to begin to develop a posthuman, post-personal stance on the pursuit of intellectual joy in higher education. The chapter is structured around five diffractions which engage an animal politics of mutual inclusion. Diffraction, as developed by Barad (2007) from a basis in quantum physics, refers to patterns of interference. I deploy diffraction as a writing experiment to activate a series of "small but consequential differences" which interfere with dominant modes of thinking and doing about higher education (Taylor, 2016a). By inserting what is normally excluded in intellectual pursuits – the human-animal relation – I seek to materialize "how these exclusions matter" (Barad, 2007, pp. 29–30). As a creative imaginary for writing otherwise, for starting somewhere else (Taylor and Gannon, f.c.), diffraction helps map an affirmative ethics of relation amongst companion species (Haraway, 2008). *Contra* the traditional Humanist paean which pays homage to the exceptional man, this post-personal paean to Hermann, attends to the ordinary, the mundane, and the playfully profound entanglements that emerge in the human-animal zone of indiscernibility.

DIFFRACTION 1. A POSTHUMAN, POST-PERSONAL PAEAN. OR, BREACHING THE WALL BETWEEN HUMAN/ANIMAL

Paean, in Merriam-Webster's dictionary, is a joyous song or hymn of praise, tribute, thanksgiving or triumph; it is a work that praises or honours its subject. As a literary form, a paean tells of the exceptional man, the man of courage, heroism, the man whose glorious deeds mark him out as unique and set him apart from the rest 'us'. As such, a paean has historically been in deep service to ideals of human – and usually masculine – exceptionalism. A paean in its literary form and content is an exemplary denotation of Humanist values: it both explicitly and implicitly activates a way of thinking that divides those apparently thinking beings ('humans') from those with apparently unthinking lives and instinctual ways of being ('animals'). In Humanist frame, the former possess all the moral and intellectual virtues of 'culture', as well as rational, cognitive and reflexive modes of understanding to propel goal-directed action, while the latter exist in a state of 'nature', driven purely by instinct, and without the cognitive means to reflect upon and improve their lot. From this fundamental ontological separation of human/ animal, other binaries flow: man/ woman; brain/ body; reason/ emotion; civilized/ savage; inside/ outside; public/ private; extraordinary/ ordinary. Furthermore, the binaries on which Humanism has been based have helped establish and maintain an elaborate edifice of hierarchy, separation and dispossession which positions the 'human' not just as necessarily superior to animals, things, objects, anything that is 'nonhuman' (Snaza, 2015) but which also positions some particular humans as superior to other categories of humans. Thus, White, male, western, middle-class humans have arrogated to themselves the virtues and beneficences of 'culture' and 'civilization', enabling them for many years to cast their privilege as 'normal', 'natural' and 'right'. I have noted elsewhere that Humanism is "grounded in the separation of, and domination by, a small-ish section of 'mankind' from/of the 'rest of' nature, humanity, and nonhuman 'others' in accordance with its god-given civilizing mission" (Taylor, 2016b, p. 8). By installing the 'civilized (White) man' as the centre and yardstick of the universe, Enlightenment Humanism both brings into being and upholds the hierarchies and separations of colonialist violence, as well as the injustices borne of racism, classism, able-ism, and speciesism (Said, 1994; Braidotti, 2013). While the twentieth century has seen if not a dismantling then certainly a destabilizing, of many of the binaries that Humanism gave rise to and attempted to hold so firmly in place, it seemed until recently that the fundamental distinction between human/ animal still held fast. Not so any longer.

While animals have been the derogated species par excellence against which 'man' measures himself – animality is a *sine qua non* for that which is base, dirty, disgusting, low, lacks reason, licentious, bestial, instinctive, natural – the scientific and philosophical bases of such thinking is now being questioned. On the biological front, it seems that there has been and is much more cross-breeding going on in nature across microbe, plant, and animal communities, producing much messier and tangled genetic webs, than we (humans) thought. 'We' have known for a long time but keep conveniently forgetting that 'our' (human) genetic heritage places us as kin to the great apes: 'our' genome is 1.2% different from chimpanzees and bonobos, about 1.6% from African apes, but that chimpanzees, bonobos, *and* humans all show a same amount of difference from gorillas (Smithsonian, 2016); 'we' have 90% of homologous genes with cats, and 82% with dogs (eupedia.com, 2009); while the genetic difference between individual humans today is about 0.1% (Smithsonian, 2016). "The DNA evidence leaves us with one of the greatest surprises in biology: the wall between human, on the one hand, and … animal, on the other, has been breached" (Smithsonian, 2016). Findings such as these are leading some evolutionary biologists to argue that our whole fundamental view of biology needs to change – because the issue is not simply that we are related to the great apes, we *are* one (Massumi, 2014).

Biological evidence such as this is acting in concert with contemporary philosophical moves to variously question, undermine, and do away with presumptions of a dichotomous human/ animal paradigm. In this, Brian Massumi's thinking is key. Massumi (2014, p. 2) argues that we need to envisage a "different politics, one that is not a human politics of the animal, but an integrally animal politics". Crucially, the aim of such an animal politics is to free us from "traditional paradigms of the nasty state of nature" with its presuppositions about instinct as blindly-induced and automatic behaviour. The purpose of Massumi's philosophical animal politics project is clear: to situate the human on the animal continuum. This project does not involve erasing what is different about the human – or the animal. Rather, it is about trying to create a politics which moves beyond the arrogant image we have of ourselves as standing apart and above other animals; it is about questioning "our inveterate vanity regarding our assumed species identity, based on the specious grounds of our sole proprietorship of language, thought and creativity" (Massumi, 2014, p. 3).

DIFFRACTION 2. REFUSING THE LOGIC OF THE EXCLUDED MIDDLE. OR, DEVELOPING THE LIFE-ENHANCING LOGIC OF MUTUAL INCLUSION

Massumi's development of an animal politics is based on a philosophical thought experiment which deconstructs the principle of the excluded middle. In traditional philosophical logic, the excluded middle:

> Means that a statement is either true or false. Think of it as claiming that there is no middle ground between being true and being false. Every statement has to be one or the other. That's why it's called the law of excluded middle, because it excludes a middle ground between truth and

falsity. So while the law of non-contradiction tells us that no statement can be both true and false, the law of excluded middle tells us that they must all be one or the other (web.stanford.edu, 2016)

In place of, and as a life-enhancing replacement for, the law of the excluded middle Massumi proposes the logic of mutual inclusion. This is a logic of sympathy, creativity and play (here Massumi draws on Bateson's work); it is a logic which depends on differing and difference on a spectrum of continuing variation (drawing on Deleuze); and it is a logic which releases a force of transindividual transformation (drawing on Simonden). Massumi's development of the philosophical bases of the logic of mutual inclusion is grounded in an analysis of animals' play-fighting: the animals agree and know that this is both play and something else, something which is allied to combat but which is not 'real' fighting, something which in its style is combatesque. This ability of animals to performatively embody a ludic gesture entails an element of metacommunication: it is an immanent form of embodied thinking-doing which shows they can stage a paradox, that they can gesture beyond the immediate to something else, that they are adept at adapting their behaviour performatively as the moves of the game unfold, and that they can modulate an embodied act as an abstraction (via a performative –esqueness that points to the something else that this current game references). The logic of mutual inclusion packs two different logics into one situation: play and combat come together, and their coming together makes three: "there is one, and the other – and the *included middle* of their mutual influence" (Massumi, 2014, p. 6). What, you may be asking at this point, has this got to do with producing pleasure in the contemporary university? For me, quite a lot, as I go on to show below.

The logic of mutual inclusion produces, sustains and nourishes a zone of indiscernibility where Hermann and I have played and continue to play, participate and creatively propagate our lives together. It is in-with-through our daily fun and games that Hermann and I become-together-with-each-other. So, it is not just that the logic of mutual inclusion suspends traditional logic; it is more that the ludic gestures which give it its force open onto vivacity, vitalism, and verve, and it is these qualities which helps sustain a mode of living as an enactive and joyful pragmatics of emergence. In the zone of indiscernibility that the ludic gesture opens up, living-doing-being-thinking are mutually entailed. What my dog has taught me is that academic life (a life which for me as for many academics seems to spill into our many 'other' lives), ought to be oriented by a desire to increase the fund of joy with which we are learning to inhabit our world together. When I've stumbled, become discouraged and disheartened (a failed bid, a rejected paper, a desperately boring meeting, a difficult teaching session, an overwhelmingly stressful workload, yet more targets piled on already unmeetable targets), my dog has taught me that bad times pass and pass slightly more quickly if you'll just come outside with me, go for a walk and have a little play. He's done his best to teach me that the future is unknowable, and that worry, guilt and anxiety are usually unproductive ways to expend energy and time. Hermann has taught me the value of patience, the importance of living in the moment, and the necessity of relaxation.

When I have failed to learn, he has repeated his lesson sometimes with urgent, sometimes with gentle, persuasion, never tiring of doing so. Sometimes I've got it, sometimes not, in which case, he's taught me that sometimes it is good to just let it (whatever the 'it' is that seems so vital at that moment) go.

DIFFRACTION 3: HERMANN GETS ON WITH IT. OR, WHAT MY DOG HAS TAUGHT ME ABOUT ROUTINE AND HABIT

> Your back legs are shaky when you walk and you can't walk very far. The distance has contracted from roaming the fields, woods, and hillsides to a slowish amble around the block. Living on a four-way corner, though, gives you four choices each time we exit the house. Every journey begins with an immediate piss on your favourite tree right outside then you stand pondering – which way? – before taking off at a slow but utterly determined trot, rolling a little from side to side as you proceed. The intensity of your sniffing has not lessened. You'll stand for ages inhaling a privet hedge, a tissue in the gutter, or a mark on the pavement, head bobbling up and down, nose in air, breathing deeply as an unseen aroma, some "soft incense [that] hangs upon the boughs" (Keats, [1816] 1977) traverses the air, flowing over your 147 million scent receptors. I stand next to you wondering what it's like to be zapped with smells up to ten thousand times stronger than my poor nose can identify. I'm sorry about all the times I've made you hurry or dragged you away from a scent you're imbibing as you continue your ever complex mapping of our neighbourhood. As you trot, I see the non-malignant but growing fatty lump on your side jogging up and down. I watch you stumble and you look up at me with embarrassment as if to say "Did you see that? What's happening to me?" When I come home from work now you take ages to come and greet me. No bounding now. I am in, coat off, shoes changed, making a cup of tea before you peer round the door, looking confused at my interruption. My old boy, you sleep most of the time now, and so deeply that when I enter the room I look carefully at your belly to make sure it is still gently rising and falling as you breathe. Deepest sleep. I imagine you dreaming your younger self back into your body, roaming, gamboling, ferreting.

Whenever I work at home – writing, doing bids, marking or teaching preparation – Hermann structures my day for me. Morning, up and out, walking round the block. Three hours work. Out again at lunchtime, this time to the park. Three more hours work. As he has his afternoon nap on the sofa in my study room, I struggle with putting one word in front of another or, on better days, take a flight with theory. Then, at 4pm, Hermann comes over, lays his head on my knee, sometime with paws too, and lets me know it is time to stop this nonsense and get outside for a longer walk before teatime. Sometimes I also work in the evening before he ushers me out for a final leisurely stroll around the block again for the deep sniffs of evening. Dogs and humans share a deep need for, perhaps love of, routine. The habits of routine ward off chaos, disorder, and fear. The habits Herman-and-I share are a set of ongoing, known practices that bind us to each other, to our environment and to the world. They act as a form of ontological and epistemological social glue that help us get up each day and work together to make the world anew in its known contours that are, at the same time, replete with emergent differentiation. This moment has never happened before and has always happened before: as Dewsbury and Bissell (2015, p. 22) say, "habit archives the past that *is* for the present that *was*". The habit routines that Hermann-and-I engage in daily might, then, be seen as a sort of lived and bodied post-personal continually emergent treaty. While the outlines of this treaty are known, its intimate mappings occur daily anew, in the to-and-fro more-than-human negotiations at the micro-level of bodily enactment. Together – at mutually agreed times – we get out and take in the air, breathe, let our bodies move together in an ambulatory rhythm. We participate daily in something (whatever, the unknown) together.

Habit and routine have had a lot of bad press. They denote the boring, dull, same; a recipe for staleness, repetition and regularity. Habits have often been seen as endemic to the governmentality of educational practices that school bodies and minds over a long period of time. Foucauldian analyses argue that habit in education transforms us into docile bodies, willingly subjectifying ourselves to regimes of truth and technologies of the self that enable power to do its work on and through us. Sociology of knowledge analyses suggest that the purpose of education is to habituate us to modes of being that support capitalist reproduction. Indeed, the emphasis in contemporary higher education is towards harnessing bodies to an increasing dependency on the habits that derive from measurement and metrics, which are undoubtedly oriented to the reproduction of a neoliberal, capitalist, patriarchal power-knowledge matrix.

And yet. These neoliberal habits do not nullify those other habits which activate daily the pleasures of human-animal relation. This is because these other habits are desiring forces (Deleuze & Guattari, 1987) drawing into their orbit the energy, force and flow of affect. Something escapes. Something always escapes. Anderson (2009, p. 77) talks about how affective experience occurs "beyond, around, and alongside the formation of subjectivity" and that it is the in-betweenness of affective atmospheres that give them their ambiguity and potency. Affects are transpersonal. They circulate, flow across and infuse bodies, rendering individuality redundant. When we're walking together where does Hermann end and I begin? More than this, it is important to note that affective habits 'occur' by virtue of the body, they are corporealized events. Habits are a bodying that indicate the "lived importance" (Massumi, 2014, p. 29) of being in this situation at this moment together, both doing what we usually do *and* innovating ('oh, I must go and look at that over there right now, come with me') when the impulse of the moment takes over. Affective habits anchor us in the given and produce a way to 'finesse' the given, to go beyond it and surpass it. Massumi suggests that the words 'bodying' and 'corporality' are better than 'embodiment' because the latter suggests a body that exists prior to and as container for the affective force that inhabits it. On the contrary, 'bodying' is the '"movement by which corporeality surpasses itself: it includes the mental pole of the event" (Massumi, 2014, p. 30). Here, the philosophies of Bergson and Whitehead lend support to the future development of a post-personal speculative pragmatics of human-animal relation: the bodying of enactive thinking-doing by all living beings contains elements of reflexive consciousness that presuppose no definitive boundaries between species.

What Hermann has taught me is that a post-personal academic life is enriched by the rhythms borne of shared human-animal routine. It takes the sense of a dog to show me the productive joy in having a schedule and sticking to it *and* innovating on it as the moment or necessity demands. Habit is not about the production of the same or of inducing stasis. It is, conversely, about practices which continually work and *rework* the same to form new intensive figurations of experience within known contours. Minute innovations – choosing to walk this way today rather than that in order to ponder this puddle and this bit of rubbish in the gutter, or to say hello to these people-and-dogs and listen for a while to this bird's song – are the occasion for the release of a present and joyful daily doing-together that is a not inconsiderable unpicking of the Humanist iniquities that normally attend the human-animal binary.

DIFFRACTION 4. HERMANN FINDS A PLASTIC BOTTLE. OR, WHAT MY DOG HAS TAUGHT ME ABOUT CREATIVITY

> A long time ago when you were young we went for a walk up on the high chalk hills overlooking the sea. Salty, sunny, summer, breeze, bright as you like, high sky with hot sun, sea deep blue, glittering glare and white wave points. After a long walk, we relaxed, sat on the green, patterned-with-daisies grass, had a picnic with sandwiches and dog biscuits, followed by water brought in plastic bottles. Do you remember? After lunch, you started fizzing, looking for fun. Now's the time for play, you decided. However, we'd forgotten the vital object: a ball. After some foolish human mime on our parts – empty hands held out and shoulders shrugging – you responded with a gesture of "ok, enough of that, let's innovate". You seized the half empty water bottle in your mouth, ran a short distance away, turned, dropped it, did a play bow which you thought told us clearly enough "look at this, this will do instead". Being only human, and slightly slow to cotton-on to this new game, you barked at us in an encouraging and peremptory way to let us know 'let's do it now, you half-wits'. And we did. We played for a long while, amazed by your ingenuity and inventiveness in starting and then prolonging the game. Sheer fun.

Hey presto. Hermann the furry magician. This is one instance of many during our long life together in which he has effectuated a creative transformation of the mundane into the magical, which does not erase the mundane but transports it – and him and me – into a new zone in which "merely to breathe was enjoyment"

(Poe, 1967, p. 179). He has en-couraged – given me heart – to do the same, so a found pine cone becomes a ball, getting first to the letter as it drops to the mat becomes a bounding race which "*everybody* [wins], and all must have prizes" (i.e. biscuits) (Carroll, 1865), and physically greeting each other every morning becomes an act of joy. Such enactive pragmatics constitute what Massumi (2014) considers to be the 'third' – the excluded middle – that occurs in/as the zone of indiscernibility.

In relation to the post-personal, human-animal politics of the in-between Hermann-me that I am developing in this chapter, the zone of indiscernibility emerges via an emplaced intensive bodying. It is emplaced, in the sense that it instantaneously creates an onto-epistemological *terrain vague* which exists both as an emergent interstitial space which heightens the senses, and as a physically situated place in the domestic and daily environments we inhabit (kitchen, living room, garden, wood, streets etc). It is intensive in that it is an alert, attuned, expressive, surplus-value, a feeling-thinking of life as an enthusiastic intensity, a sort of surplus-value, a spilling over (Massumi, 2014). And it is a bodying in that what occurs here-and-now in this place is a material practice of mattering which constitutes the 'we' in the event's emergence. The magic of the play act that emerges between Hermann-and-I works by force of abduction; it is a "thinking-feeling flush with subjectlessly subjective doing" (Massumi, 2014, p. 107). Its improvisational force is contagious, its vitality affect sweeps one up with the other.

What Hermann has taught me about a post-personal academic life is that every pedagogic situation, like every game we play together, is an unrepeatable and unique occurrence. *This* (pedagogic encounter) will occur now, once, one time only. Likewise, as Arendt (1958) notes, every human being is unique, an unrepeatable existence – as is every dog, cat, microbe, chicken etc. All of these unique elements come together in a particular space and time – say, 9am to 12am on a Tuesday morning for a seminar on a specific module – in an emergent and only temporarily stable assemblage to constitute this or that pedagogic encounter. Thinking pedagogy in this way as what Deleuze and Guattari (1987) would term a singularity has, over the years, and following Hermann's example, become less and less a cause of anxiety (oh dear, there is so little time to stuff these difficult theories into recalcitrant heads) and more and more an incitement to play (for example, by pursuing the question "what happens if ...?").

Working in the key of pedagogic play might, then, be about pursuing a theory by adding something a bit weird to it which resituates it oddly; it might be about getting up and moving out of the classroom to walk the campus to see up close how university buildings arrange power and discipline space; or it might be about bringing a treasured personal object into the classroom to talk about how its thing-power (Bennett, 2010) influenced an educative path. Such sensory-mobile-material dimensions to pedagogy are usual in early years' education but it seems that the closer one gets to a university education the less they occur, so that contemporary higher education (at least in the UK) seems an immaterial pursuit, cognitive, rational, ordered, skills-based and outcomes-focussed. What Hermann has taught me is that to have a go at inventing, creating, innovating is better than not having a go. Sometimes you take a tumble, fall flat on your back, but that's ok. The pursuit of pedagogic creativity is about creating the conditions for the force of the ludic gesture to take hold. When it does, it may just work its magic and induce a "qualitative change in the nature of the situation", so that the 'we' that is assembled at that moment are transported out of the usual. Doing higher education pedagogy differently is risky and sometimes unrewarding (a student may ask "how will doing this activity get me a better mark?") but on the occasions when a 'ludic gesture releases a force of transindividual transformation' (Massumi, 2014, p. 5) then it may be worth it. And who knows what the longer term effects may be? Barad's (2007) materialist ontology does not presume that 'things' exist as separate entities but that they are constituted relationally as phenomena by their coming to existence through an event's emergence. If that is so, then all pedagogic encounters enfold their emergent sense into the ongoing space-time-mattering that is the worlding of the world (Barad, 2007). In that sense, then, every pedagogic intra-action, like every game Hermann-and-I play, matters.

DIFFRACTION 5. HERMANN NEEDS LOOKING AFTER. OR, WHAT MY DOG HAS TAUGHT ME ABOUT CARE AND CONCERN

> Over our many years together, Hermann has been hurt a few times, and got ill at others. His worst hurt was when he charged enthusiastically out of the conservatory door, catching his claw on the plastic threshold, and ripping it out at the root. I can still smell the stink of dark blood as you rushed back in, huddled under the table and shook with the shock of the pain. Two days later you looked as pleased as punch to be sporting a bright green half-leg bandage and hopping round the block, puffing yourself up like a proud solider as people bent down to inquire "poor little thing, what happened to you?" Illness has been infrequent and often related to tasty things gobbled up off the pavement and swallowed quickly before I could get them out of your mouth. There have also been bald patches to do with insect bites, eye infections to do with foul water, plus occasional bouts of we don't know what where you've kept away from us, slept all day, not touched any food, and looked miserable as hell. Through all of this, I've tried to look after you in a hit and miss sort of way. I've coddled you with rice and chicken, paid some outrageously expensive and probably pointless vet bills, stroked you when your body told me you wanted me to, and left you alone when you let me know that was what you needed.

Barad (2007, p. 185) says that "each intra-action matters" and it is in this mattering that the ethical dimension of a post-personal enactive pragmatics comes into focus. Enacting ethics in a post-personal sense is less about putting in place an ethic of care and more about enacting an ethics of concern. This is because an ethic of care is located in a notion of care *for* the other which, in an animal rights-inflected discourse of human-animal relations, is based in presumptions that animals are more vulnerable than humans, less able to articulate their needs, and have a diminished sense of agency. These presumptions assume a dependency of animals on humans and so privilege the human as care-giver *for* the animal. Some go further and trace care's violent, exclusionary and instrumental side (Giraud and Hollin, 2016). An ethic of concern, in contrast, is rooted in a process ethics of relation which presumes no such hierarchical difference between subject (human) and object (animal). Inspired by Whitehead (1938), a post-personal ethic of concern sees "each occasion [a]s an activity of concern". Shaviro (2008, p. 1) usefully elaborates: "*concern* implies a weight upon the spirit. When something concerns me, I cannot ignore it or walk away from it. It presses upon my being, and compels me to respond. Concern, therefore, is an involuntary experience of being affected by others. It opens me, in spite of myself, to the outside". Concern, then, is fundamentally relational in its feeling and aim. As used by Whitehead (1933, p. 226), concern is imbued with an 'affective tone' which constitutes it as a supra-individual impulse fusing subject-object in-relation. Concern is a connective force, tying individuals together in deep, often pre-conscious, ways. More than that, concern has a connection with enjoyment, in that the occasion's processual emergence involves the realization that it is tied into the universe that lies beyond it (Whitehead, 1933).

What Hermann has taught me about a post-personal academic life is that considering concern as an *involuntary* experience of being affected by all sorts of human and nonhuman others, the other is not 'other' but is a vital part of a felt sense of relational responsibility that tangibly suffuses all occasions. Higher education pedagogy (and research, and academic writing), in this view, unfolds as processual relation of enjoyment in which flux and impermanence point to an open future. Not everything is decided in advance. A post-personal academic life would open up more scope not just for acting well in-relation-to human and nonhumans bodies, things, materialities of all kinds. Its activation of concern would provide an ethical push against the competitive individualism that is such a feature of contemporary higher education.

(IN)CONCLUSIONS: DEVELOPING AN ENACTIVE PRAGMATICS FOR INTELLECTUAL JOY

Is it not the height of human arrogance to suppose that animals do not have thought, emotion, desire, creativity, or subjectivity? (Massumi, 2014, p. 51)

The above five diffractions gesture towards just some of the things that my dog has taught me about a post-personal academic life. He has, of course, taught me much more than can be contained in this short chapter. He has taught me that love is not a zero-sum game but that it increases the more of it you give; that apprentices (our young, new dog) learn as much from careful mentoring by wiser, older furry ones as by human ones; that knowing when to sit-with, flop-by and lean-against someone is as important as knowing when to keep your distance; that a silent gesture of concern (a head on the knee or a lick of the hand) can help a lot when someone is upset; that wisdom resides in the eyes, and is bodied forth in action as much as voice; and that energy, effervescence and enthusiasm need to be nurtured in the slow time of rest, relaxation and sleep. And there are many more 'ands'. What he has taught me has infused my academic life in ways which are known, felt, enacted, unknown, ungraspable, unsayable. His irrepressible spirit is enfolded into so many of my academic doings.

I have used the phrase 'my dog' frequently in this chapter. That 'my' is, of course, an inaccurate and arrogant presumption of human ownership. Hermann belongs to no-one but himself. Or, rather, he belongs to life and the universe, with whom he shares his irrepressible spirit. Being-with Hermann induces a transindividual ontological understanding of reality; it requires an ethical relationality of concern that expands our (human) sense of spiritual reality (Willett, 2014); and it inspires a post-species, nonhuman epistemology. What 'my' dog has taught me is that enacting an 'animal politics' (Massumi, 2014) of higher education would mean orienting teaching and learning towards the disclosure of the category of the 'human' as an undeniably normative, political, and cultural one. It would mean creating curricular and disciplinary spaces to explore the historical installation of Humanism and its categories, hierarchies, and distinctions as a sense-making assemblage. And it would mean providing the resources for students to engage with many other modes of knowledge-making (feminist, materialist, indigenous, post-colonial, intersectional, posthuman) which contest, decentre and expand the category of the 'we' in order to think and do who 'we' are differently. As he lies on the decking, blinking in the hot sun in what may be his last summer, Hermann lets me know that sounds like a good way forward.

REFERENCES

Anderson, A. (2009). Affective atmospheres. *Emotion, Space and Society, 2*, 77–81.
Arendt, H. (1958). *The human condition*. Chicago, IL: University of Chicago Press.
Barad, K. (2007). *Meeting the universe half way: quantum physics and the entanglement of matter and meaning*. Durham: Duke University Press.
Bennett, J. (2010). *Vibrant matter: A political ecology of things*. London: Duke University Press.
Braidotti, R. (2013). *The posthuman*. Cambridge: Polity.
Carroll, L. (1865) *Alice's adventures in wonderland*. Retrieved from https://www.cs.indiana.edu/metastuff/wonder/ch3.html
Dewsbury, J. D., & Bissell, D. (2015). Habit geographies: The perilous zones in the life of the individual. *Cultural Geographies, 22*(1), 21–28.
Deleuze, G., & Guattari F. (1987). *A thousand plateaus: Capitalism and schizophrenia*. London: Continuum.
Eupedia.com (2009). http://www.eupedia.com/forum/threads/25335-Percentage-of-genetic-similarity-between-humans-and-animals (accessed 8 July 2016).
Giraud, E., & Hollin, G. (2016). *Affective labour and care-work within the animal laboratory: Dwelling on "the trouble"*. Presentation at the Gender, Work and Organisation conference, University of Keele, UK, 1st July, 2016.
Haraway, D. (2008). *When species meet*. Minneapolis: University of Minnesota Press.
Keats, J. (1977). *The complete poems*. London: Penguin.
Massumi, B. (2014). *What animals teach us about politics*. Durham: Duke University Press.
Poe, E.A. (1967). *Selected writings*. Harmondsworth: Penguin.
Said, E. (1994). *Culture and imperialism*. London: Vintage.

Shaviro, S. (2008). Self-enjoyment and concern: On Whitehead and Levinas. http://shaviro.com/Othertexts/Modes.pdf (accessed 18 April 2016).
Smithsonian. (2016). *What does it mean to be human?* http://humanorigins.si.edu/evidence/ genetics (accessed 8 July 2016).
Snaza, N. (2015). Toward a genealogy of educational humanism. In N. Snaza & J. Weaver (Eds.), *Posthumanism and educational research* (pp. 17–29). London: Routledge.
Taylor, C. A. (2016a). Close encounters of a critical kind: A diffractive musing in/between new material feminism and object-oriented ontology. *Cultural Studies<=>Critical Methodologies, 16*(2), 201–212.
Taylor, C. A. (2016b). Edu-crafting a cacophonous ecology: Posthuman research practices for education. In: C. A. Anon & C. Hughes (Eds.), *Posthuman research practices in education*. London: Palgrave Macmillan.
Taylor, C. A., & Gannon, S. (f.c.). Doing time and motion diffractively: Academic life everywhere and all the time. *Qualitative Inquiry*.
web.stanford.edu (2016). IV. The law of the excluded middle. An introduction to philosophy. Stanford University.
http://web.stanford.edu/~bobonich/glances%20ahead/IV.excluded.middle.html (accessed 10 July 2016).
Whitehead, A.N. (1933). *Adventures in ideas*. London: Cambridge University Press.
Whitehead, A. N. (1938). *Modes of thought*. New York: The Free Press.
Willett, C. (2014). *Interspecies ethics*. New York: Columbia University Press.

Carol A. Taylor
Sheffield Hallam University, UK

PAULINE COLLINS

10. WHERE HAVE ALL THE FLOWERS GONE?

The Future for Academics

Change the way you look at things and the things you look at change.
(Albert Einstein)

INTRODUCTION

Giroux (2006, p.8) likens the post 9/11 American university to a militarized knowledge factory. Isaac Cordal (Wang, 2015) an artist, captures this in his miniature installations which depict factory-like settings, but in which no items are actually produced. The industrial setting of rows of white lab-coated middle-aged men engaged in busy work conjures a sterile, pointless environment in which students and academics have become slaves of production. Skeletal overlords supervise the industry in which universities are now a business and students have turned into customers.

Studies on academic satisfaction and stress abound across Western countries (Gillespie, Walsh, Winefield et al 2001; Kinmen, 2013). These clearly indicate a need to improve alarming imbalances in work-life, stress and depression levels. However, the higher education 'agenda-setters' commitment to a neoliberal ideology moves against the direction needed for improvement. The market vision encompasses a growing number of students in need of ever greater teaching support, with an added consumer attitude that calls for increasing academic flexibility, while all the time overseen by managers in a 'big-brother is watching you' institutional context.

The political philosophy of Hayek (1952) underpins the public management model in which autonomy is highly constrained by externally defined goals, increasing social control, and reducing academic freedom. A radical critical break is required, but is difficult to birth. Neoliberalism has become the reinforced norm in the current university discourse. While the term itself is dominant in describing the current economic political approach of Western states, its ubiquitous nature requires some clarification. The following provides a useful definition of neoliberalism:

> [It is] in the first instance a theory of political economic practices that proposes that human well-being can best be advanced by liberating individual entrepreneurial freedoms and skills within an institutional framework

characterized by strong private property rights, free markets and free trade. (Baron, 2004 p. 274, citing Harvey, 2005 p. 2)

The marketing rhetoric overflows into all domains delivering a creeping sameness not unlike that seen in any military. Huntington (1957) portrayed a vision of military values that he suggests civil society would be better to align with. Such values are 'pessimistic, collectivist, historically inclined, power-oriented, nationalistic, militaristic ... in brief ... conservative ...' (p. 68). This black and white binary view enables the otherness of alienation, and exclusion of difference, developing insider and outsider dichotomies in a militarization of the civil.

Hayek's belief that there is nothing new to be discovered or imagined, and that all theory is just reconstructing existing knowledge, leaves little for academics to be doing in the critical thinking space, and presents a challenge for researchers and PhD students who are required to add new knowledge (Marginson, 2009). The drive for change produced by neoliberalism creates a futile pursuit and by its endorsement of coercion of the social order ironically leads to high levels of uniformity. Like the cat chasing its tail, the Hayekian neoliberal world relies on a circularity produced by three false beliefs. First, a naturalizing of competitive economic markets; second, the politics of state driven markets; and third, that the human drive for wealth and personal gain predicts human reaction to market signals (Hayek, 1952, 1979). There are assumptions in this that leave little room for other values, or scope for a self-reflecting and self-determining agenda.

Giroux (2006) sees the current plight of the academe as: 'an ideological war against liberal intellectuals who argued for holding government and corporate power accountable as a precondition for extending and expanding the promise of an inclusive democracy' (p. 4). In this vision academics become mere cogs in the wheel of capitalist production. The urgency for disruption and space for academics to pushback, resist and open room for pleasurable intellectual pursuit and sustaining of democratic ideals is apparent. Giroux (2006) suggests the neoliberal ideology of the Right in the US dominates. The election of President Trump gives some credence to this claim, signalling the endgame of these ideals. The drive to unity is supported by hierarchical command and control concepts found in the military (Saltman, 2007). The spectre that Eisenhower warned against, regarding the power of the industrial–military complex is re-envisioned by Giroux. Eisenhower (1961) said:

> We should take nothing for granted. Only an alert and knowledgeable citizenry can compel the proper meshing of the huge industrial and military machinery of defense with our peaceful methods and goals, so that security and liberty may prosper together.

Marginson (2009) describes the new public management model as providing benefits for a privileged few. Thornton (2009) refers to the heroes it produces as the 'technoprenuers' combining technological and scientific knowledge, with business acumen (p. 388). This new public management model is seen as suppressing university autonomy, academic criticism, free inquiry and creativity. Marginson (2009) argues this occurs through the channelling and limiting process by which academics are tamed to economic or market interests (outputs) and state control. Preferring the term 'academic self-determination', Marginson (2009) suggests what is lost in this process is space for critique and creativity (p. 87). The need for freedom, or the capacity for the radical critical break, described by Marginson as vital, does not occur.

This chapter addresses a number of issues and possibilities for university academics struggling in a managerial neoliberal world to find purpose, creativity, pleasure and excitement in their work. The issues in the 'technopreneurial' 'militarized knowledge factory' of the privatizing public university are considered (Saltman, 2007). What might be some of the disruptions needed in order to provide for creative reflection time and personal wellbeing for academics and why is this essential? This chapter introduces some suggestions based on creativity theory (Agamben, 1995), psychology (Jung, 1967), the politics of difference (Young, 1986) and resistance theory (Cixous, 1997) that enable a disruption of the militarized invaded space. First identification of the extent of the problem is outlined.

WHAT IS THE PROBLEM?

Thornton (2009) recalls the history of the university in three phases. The first was 'Modernization', when the early 1800s saw Von Humboldts – bourgeois' revolutionary education create a rational, universal, secular and enlightened – liberal university in which freedom to inquire permitted the pursuit of knowledge for its own sake (p. 377). The second phase arose during the late 20th century with the second wave of feminism which sought to transform the nature of knowledge and structures of power. Women disrupted the established social order by revealing how denigration of the 'other', being women, enabled the sustaining of male power. In turn this led to postmodernism, concerned with deconstruction of notions of truth, neutrality and universalism (p. 379). This critique delivered the 'crisis of legitimation' with the voices of race, poor and LGBTI destabilizing feminism. The third and current phase is described by Thornton as "knowledge capitalism" with the filling of the space by corporatization, the new knowledge economy, new public management, and neoliberalism. "New Knowledge", it is suggested, now equals "useful knowledge" (p. 381). No longer is the pursuit of pure knowledge for knowledge's sake seen as useful. Rather, like the pure aesthetic experience of a rare flower it is seen as an expensive indulgence, and not for the common people.

A hierarchical militaristic command and control value system, stands in opposition to democratic civilian notions that embrace the politics of difference in a fragmentary world. The 'technoprenurial' creation of the neoliberal institution seeks to wash away feminist gains made by the second stage transformation of universities. Thornton (2009) argues the technoprenurial favours the male, "they work alone, taking risks and promote the self, unconcerned about collegiality and collective good" (p. 388).

Factors putting pressure on creativity, pleasure and freedom that feed into the current crisis are numerous. The end of the Cold War, the Arab Spring and the increasing push to so called democratization, result in fragmented borders that challenge the traditional state mechanisms for raising revenue (Becher & Trowler, 2001). Universities become entangled in the vortex attempting to pursue private funding in an environment of declining and destabilized government. Driven by continuous improvement and change cycles, they seek to compete in a globalized market of a commodified higher-educational industry (Taylor, 2015 p. 12).

Under this influence, public universities have morphed from participating in a democratized civil society, to the market. Nation states pursue knowledge production through education which is exploited as a source of wealth. Teaching is concerned with imparting skills to produce the future clones necessary for continued production and wealth generation for the few. The information they soak up is used as data to be applied, not as wisdom to advance and improve humankind. Rather the university graduate is now put through a vocational training mill to be work-ready for the conveyor belt of the capitalist state. In this world flowers do not bloom, but rather neat little rows of sameness are produced represented by students as both product, ready to reach the market, and consumers. They exist on the conveyor belt of sameness as equal quality-control tested and credentialed products. The neoliberal world sees new thought as dangerously disruptive, and unity and conformity as essential for this market.

The push for 'quality' graduates brings with it a regime of testing instruments and systemized language of accountability and number crunching. Compliance and audit are the dominant rituals preferencing management and bureaucratic norms over professional, moral and ethical requirements (Elliott, 2001). The 'quality' assurance, however, is only as good as the testing instrument and its ability to genuinely assess the 'quality' of the outcomes. Poorly designed evaluation systems where perceptions mean the highest ratings of teaching are based on the "ease of the course" lead to bad information and bad outcomes (Bansel, Davies, Gannon, & Linnell, 2008). Thus audit is subject to considerable manipulation and questionable construction. The rise of standardized testing and curricula prioritize rote memorization and regurgitation over critical thinking, a messy and more time consuming process.

Quality assurance testing is sold as a requirement to justify government expenditure of tax payers' funds and to work as a carrot-type incentive that inspires academics to ensure they produce 'quality' graduates. Trust is no longer placed in the academic to be professional in their assessment and grading of the student (Rosser, Johnsrud, & Heck, 2003). Despite all the literature on good pedagogical practices, time and cost pressures reduce assessment to standardized and regimental practices involving online multiple choice testing, a written paper and an exam. Student/clients have expectations of this regimented norm and are likely to complain if there is deviation. Creative teaching is discouraged in this sterile garden. The large number of students also reduces the academics own ability to apply creativity, innovation and critical thinking in their research space, as they have to teach more courses in continuously overlapping semesters (Heath & Burdon, 2013).

Despite these concerns the neoliberal transformation of the university has been rapidly adopted by faculty, students and academics. How this has been accepted is a question that has been given little attention. No longer being treated as a professional independent worker, trusted to get the job done with a necessary degree of autonomy, academics experience the loss of respect and correspondingly loose trust in their universities (Groundwater-Smith & Sachs, 2002). The nature of the neoliberal program, placing onus on the individual, leaves many in their isolation feeling unable to respond to the political-economic system that sees a dog-eat-dog survival of the fittest mentality prevail. Collegium in academic deliberations, the *sanctum sanatorum* of academic decision making, is removed.

Academic careers are disrupted through casualization, making the career choice an uncertain and low level aspiration (Castellóa et al., 2015). The academic given an insecure casualized employment ensures not only that they lack continuity in professional development as a tertiary educator, but they remain constrained due to their hierarchy of needs, leaving them unlikely to challenge the neoliberal world. Tenure clearly is important in empowering the critical approach and the dissenting voice (Flaherty, 2016). It is possible, however, that aging academics, those who would resist, have given up and retired, or taken up consultancies.

Blum and Ullman (2012) describe the neoliberal individual as "an entrepreneur of the self" (p.370) and as such they are responsible for all that befalls them. As noted, the technoprenurial and neoliberal experience sees a few rising to the demands and being sated as the hero that academics should all aspire to be, but know they can never quite achieve. In this high pressure competitive yet constraining environment, the individual is left accounting for their ethical, physical and mental wellbeing, which excuses the organization for its own inbuilt institutional lack of support when wrong outcomes occur. An environment of competition over collegiality is an undesirable knowledge environment. The intensification in work demands, bureaucratic audit and managerialism, fosters bullying and other unethical behaviours such as cheating and plagiarism that grow like weeds and have to be constantly screened for (Hutchinson & Eveline, 2010). Workplace bullying can extend to whole groups and: "… can be stimulated by workgroups or organisations that normalize abusive, or even competitive, behaviour" (Al-Karim & Parbudyal, 2012, p. 585 cited in Baron 2015). Australia ranks sixth out of thirty-one OECD countries for "bullying in the workplace" (Dollard, Bailey, & Webber, 2014). Perhaps it is time to consider Buckminster Fuller's (2008) suggestion, "when the situation does not suit, one should play in another garden" (p. 205).

WHAT CAN BE DONE?

What can be done in light of the issues raised in this chapter, and other chapters of this publication, as the many voices set out the concerns of working in a neoliberal world? Practical ideas and recommendations, new theory or theory amalgamation, creative, and political solutions are required. This section invites thought about what tools one can use as possible strategies to resist and disrupt, to enlarge the creative space, to dream new thoughts and critique existing thoughts? A culture of being continually 'on', available and responsive, leaves little opportunity to experience the pleasure in thinking cognitively and deeply as university researchers should. Watson (2010) claims:

> ... our attention and our relationships are getting atomized ... We are in danger of developing a society that is globally connected and collaborative, but one that is also impatient, isolated, and detached from reality. A society that has plenty of answers but very few good questions. A society composed of individuals who are unable to think by themselves in the real world. (p. 3)

Baron (2009 pp. 47–52) proposes some practical suggestions that universities could use to help academics thrive. These include promoting collegiality, practising time management strategies – including factoring in free 'thinking' time, having realistic expectations, utilizing mentoring, having a supportive and alert management, maximizing professional autonomy and development of the individual academic. While such tools are important it is at the individual's deeper philosophical and psychological level that real achievement of goals are obtained.

Philosophers provide us with some of the keys to breaking through the many concerns outlined. Nietzsche (1997) refers to disruption as that which enables alternative forms of humanity and new paradigms for life. Nietzsche's "disruptive wisdom" is called for in a neoliberal world in which critique and self-reflection are essential, but lacking, components (Hicks & Rosenberg, 2005). Nietzsche looked to psychology, over history, as a way to release humans from their loss of power and control to enable the body to fulfil its will to power (Hauke, 2000; Hicks & Rosenberg, 2005). Castoriadis (1987; Giroux, 2006) describes creativity and critique as the capacity to act upon our limits – enhancing or negating what we know, giving rise to new and unpredictable thoughts for ourselves. The removal of philosophers and philosophy from universities, along with the intellectual collegial discussion spaces such as philosophy clubs and debating societies, adds to the technoprenuerial sterility depicted by Cordal (Wang, 2015), and the Hayekian (Marginson, 2009) neoliberal notion that '[c]omplete intellectual self-understanding is impossible' (p. 95). Heidegger (1959) posed that "granted that we cannot do anything with philosophy, might not philosophy, if we concern ourselves with it do something for us" (p. 12). Encouragement of philosophical discussion, and pursuits that engage in healthy debate, will improve the future outlook for universities seeking to distinguish their institution from others by creating a fertile garden for minds to explore in.

The failure to value plurality, difference and a range of views weakens the human's lifeworld (Hauke, 2000, pp. 152-159). The power of the dissenting voice is mollified in a neoliberal world in which conformity and noncritical thinking are optimized. People who are judged as highly creative by their peers tend to conform consistently less often to the group's opinion than do people judged as less creative (Sternberg & Lubart, 1995, p. 229). Heffernan (2011) claims:

> ... what we see is significantly determined by what we know those around us see. Some people can resist this some of the time. Good decision making

positively depends on it. Which is why minority voices are so essential in any group discussion. (para. 8)

The outcome of the suppression of dissent is to be seen in political institutions where party enforced unity of voice, has resulted in sudden rupturing leadership spills, instead of gradual changes. Greater rending in the fabric of society, such as the Arab Spring (Morris, 2012), Brexit, and now the Trump Presidency are in response to disjunctions between the claims of democracy and the experience of reality resulting from the long suppression of dissent. The WikiLeaks (2010) and Panama Papers (2016) seek the transparency that democracy claims to rely on, yet fails to provide, as capitalism and neoliberal pursuits support the few, 'commanders', in sustaining their power. Academics are looked to, for provision of the critical voice that assesses and proposes new ideas suggesting the way forward, aiding society through these political and social periods of upheaval.

Jung took up the creativity cause in his search for individuation enabling the 'I' to integrate complex conflicts both internal and external (Hauke, 2000, p. 71; Storr, 1973). Jung's idea of individuation deals with the struggle of the inner unconscious, encompassing "the infantile, personal and collective" at the same time as dealing with the outer world of society (Hauke, 2000, p. 169). Jung's advances in psychological thinking provided the beginning of a concept of reflexive individuation, a process involving attention to the fragmented self. This however, is only the beginning as neuroscience becomes the newest way of seeing how the human brain functions. For instance, the demands of technology such as email, smart phones and the like, create attention deficits that place the human brain in its most primitive and reactive state: the limbic brain. This is the antithesis to the demands of learning that require the brain has quiet space to engage the cortex in deep thinking (Newport, 2016; Sheehan & Pearse, 2015).

Jung's devotion to the inner life responded to the enlightenment and its drive to power over nature through an internal self-referential loop satisfying utilitarian abstract notions based on rationality and logic. In modern neuroscientific analysis this could be described as bringing the whole brain (including the primitive, emotional and cognitive) together in an acknowledgment that each serves a purpose in the working of the whole. There is little recognition in the academe, of the impact of fear and stress in causing the human brain to act out of primitive survival, diminishing the ability to operate from the cortex, or thinking brain. To be truly free to think from the cortex, engaging the whole brain is essential (Newport, 2016). In the neoliberal controlling environment demanding constant change, the academic's stress levels diminish their ability to engage in clear thinking, or integrated brain activity. Jung, operating without the benefit of the MRI scan, talked of the self-regulating psyche in which something within us holds a greater awareness than just our conscious self. Jung argued

... in today's world people are inclined to pursue scientific work for the sake of success ... They evaluate their field of study in terms of its future income ... Strictly speaking, [this means] no science is the least bit useful ... until it abandons its exalted status as a goal in itself and sinks to the level of an industry. (Jung, 1898, cited in Hauke, 2000, pp. 36–37)

Creativity theory is deeper than the addition of the slogan that 'creative' implies when added to marketing and business applications. It goes to the fundamentals of who we are as humans. Here, Carl Rogers' view of creativity is preferred to that of Guilford's. The latter, speaking in 1959, could just as easily have been speaking now of creativity as 'slogan' adopted by the neoliberal drive to produce and foster capitalism. Guilford (1959) appealed to the American way of life and military values of power and might stating, "… we are in a mortal struggle for the survival of our way of life in the world. The military aspect of this struggle, with its race to develop new weapons and new strategies, has called for the stepped-up rate of invention" (cited in Vernon 1970, p. 167). It is telling that over six decades later these clarion calls for innovation remain current. Whereas Rodgers, even earlier, in 1940, had identified the need for personal growth and development of the individual in a democratic manner stating,

> In education we tend to turn out conformists, stereotypes, individuals whose education is "completed", rather than freely creative and original thinkers … in the sciences, there is an ample supply of technicians, but the number who can creatively formulate fruitful hypotheses and theories is small indeed. (Vernon, 1970, pp. 137–128; Pope, 2005)

The desire to pursue a creative vision is what produces pleasurable drivers in an individual that can push the boundaries of knowledge. Baron (2009) discusses the need for a creative life to bring about a 'thriving' person while a compliant life requires 'adaptation and fitting in' leading to a feeling of futility and that nothing really matters (p. 30). One of the toughest factors for creative people is their environment:

> Some environments nurture creativity and others squelch it. … Creativity is in part the product of an interaction between a person and his or her context. A setting that stimulates creative ideas, encourages them when presented, and rewards a broad range of ideas and behaviours will surely foster original and nonconformist thinking. (Sternberg & Lubart, 1995, pp. 9–10)

Hence universities urging academics to be creative and innovative within a neoliberal constraining organization will not succeed. A self-regulating creative person is motivated most strongly from their internal motivators, with the external environment often negatively affecting this motivation: "… in a nutshell … extrinsic, motivation is to creativity what strychnine is to orange juice" (Sternberg & Lubart, 1995, p. 238). However, Amabile (1988) has suggested that it is a little more nuanced. Extrinsic, in the absence of intrinsic motivation, can undermine creativity, extrinsic combined with intrinsic motivation may, however, improve creativity. The indication is that intrinsic motivators are important in the initial and idea formulating stages. Extrinsic motivation can become more relevant during the labour stage in bringing a creative idea to fruition (Amabile, 1988, cited in Sternberg & Lubart, 1995, p. 243).

Many academics are drawn to the scholastic life because they are creative thinkers and the university was perceived as a space that would enable them to have time to incubate and pursue their inner creative drive. However, stress levels rise and academics become disheartened when external drivers whip them to do more for students, and produce more research, overloading their ability to become the person they are. Creativity requires mindfulness in producing ideas that do not always have to show immediate application. This pursuit is essential to the development of humankind. To become the 2015 Nobel Prize winner in chemistry, Professor Paul Modrich noted that his tenured professorial position and the freedom that gave him "helped him to pursue 'curiosity-based research' with no guarantee of returns" (Flaherty, 2016).

Resistance requires effort to maintain and strengthen freedom and to avoid being trapped in the binary dimension (Rowland, 2002, p. 127). Heath and Burdon (2013) argue for a power that frees academic agency in opposition to neoliberalism. Bauman (2001) argues that democracy needs a questioning culture to:

> ... keep the forever unexhausted and unfulfilled human potential open, fighting back all attempts to foreclose and pre-empt the further unravelling of human possibilities, prodding human society to go on questioning itself and preventing that questioning from ever stalling or being declared finished. (p. 4, cited in Giroux, 2005, p. 216)

The postmodern contests the ideal of fixed narratives that knowledge is a stable of conscious rational belief and humans consist of binary gendered opposites such as male/female (Rowland, 2002). The drive to conformity relies on hegemonic exclusion over inclusivity, whereas a politics of difference addresses dislike of physical differences, different ideas, thinking and approaches (Paull, Omari, & Standen, 2015). In discussing the politics of difference, Young (1986, 2011) identifies the possibility of an 'openness to unassimilated otherness' (1986, p.301). Young's likening of the "unoppressive city" as a model that encompasses a social relations among strangers, a place of excitement and possibilities, that 'welcome anonymity and some measure of freedom' (1986, p. 317) could easily be adopted as a model for a healthy university. Such a model evokes the thriving jungle promising much more than a neat row of cultivated sterile blossoms.

It is for each individual to find who inspires their own path of individuation. Jung through the idea of the unknowable unconscious loosens the nature of scientific empiricism. He provides inspiration for the seeker of creative pleasure by the use of alchemical references as metaphor for this mystical process. If not Jung then others such as Deleuze and Guattari's ([1972] 1982) schizoanalysis may suit, as they depart from notions of dualism and binary splitting, such as the conscious and unconscious, linking this to a politicization of the psyche. Instead they speak of a continuous becoming and offer the rhizome, like a tuber that can sprout from any part of its surface, spreading in an underground manner as a creative power that invites perceptions of labyrinthine subterranean creative energies (Deleuze & Guattari, [1980] 1988). Perhaps Jung's (1967) description of Joyce's *Ulysses* encapsulates this idea of the continuous whole as human becoming's: "It not only begins and ends in nothingness, it consists of nothing but nothingness. It is all infernally nugatory. As a piece of technical virtuosity it is a brilliant and hellish monster-birth" (p. 110). Cixous (1996) contests the use of culturally structured notions of gender objecting to the binary of male and female as hierarchical and limiting. Instead she draws on the idea of "other" as an unknowable creative source.

Cixous' contribution to creativity brings a call to think inventively and differently from the patriarchal hierarchy of a binary world view (Cixous & Clément, 1996). After all, women have suffered through lack of autonomy and the restrictions of unifying conformity across historical periods. Cixous (1997) invokes women to resist the unifying objectivity imposed on women, and to celebrate. The isolated madness of women suppressed in their inability to express their individuated self can find release. As Alexander (2004) argues Cixous suggests '… by expressing the self and transgressing fixed lines … woman rebels against passivity forced on her literally, economically, emotionally, and physically' (p. 5). Cixous (1997) entreats woman to:

> … continue to look inside the self … to give the world artistry, as a mother of the creative world, whether literally or metaphorically; woman serves as her own inspiration … no longer a commodity in a masculine economy but creative of 'life, thought, [and] transformation'. (p. 893)

Feminist writers therefore provide another possibility to inspire pushback against neoliberal tendencies through resistance theory. Howson, Coate and Croix (2015) support Thornton's (2012) assertion of the re-masculinization of universities. Hostility to women invading perceived male domains still occurs (Baron, 2015). Empirical studies of gendered bullying and discrimination in masculine dominated cultures shows "aggressive, dominant behaviours" are rewarded (Omari, 2010). Recognition that women should not carry the burden of non-prestigious tasks, but rather they should be shared across gender and employment, along with more rewarding of collective success, would help support the majority, statistically, of mid-career women (Howson et al., 2015). Ensuring support for women and positive recognition for good work in any of the university domains provides another form of resistance. Relational mentoring programs are a meaningful tool for encouraging this human dimension of support and nurture.

The underlying values of the collective, or *Weltanschauung* (world-view), change in response to the knowledge of the period (Jung, 2015). A change in direction for researchers and educators is required given the pressure of dying (natural) environments. The move towards considering quality of life, means people are disenchanted with Huntingtonian military values and Hayekian neoliberalism, such as honour, power, wealth, and fame (Storr, 1973, pp. 86–87). Klein's (2015) admonishment to abandon the core free market ideology, restructure the global economy, and remake our political systems suggest the current ideology is no longer an option. Instead knowledge for humanity is required as climate crisis challenges us to either embrace radically new ways of being or suffer the consequences. In other words the garden bed is ripe for a radical overhaul and new landscaping.

The inexplicable dimension of the human makes the certainty of science uncertain and challenges Hayek's claim that everything is already known. Rather than the heroic technoprenuer each individual is on their own heroic journey, seeking pleasure, be it through individuation, creativity, and/or resistance. Finding spaces within the university environment, little jungles that enable support, nurture and incubation of creativity is essential in allowing this process to bloom.

Baron (2009) suggests feelings of wellbeing are supported by having a social environment in which leadership provides a warm, empathetic and attending aspect encouraging academics to feel part of a collegial group who are free to communicate and participate in a non-threatening, non-competitive, and a non-audit focussed atmosphere. A meeting group for Post Graduate and Early Career Researchers is an example of a safe social environment providing space for reflection and flowering. This meeting space is loosely based on a community of practice approach. The concept of a "community of practice" (CoP) (Lave, 1982; Wenger, 1998) has blossomed in academia as it provides a safe and creative refuge for like-minded members sharing common interests or purposes.

The community of practice (CoP) is an example of one possibility for a space that can foster pleasure and creative freedom in a constraining university. It represents a bottom-up self-organizing enterprise of individuals grappling with unmet needs or common problems. They provide an environment in which support and fostering of creative inspiration can improve and encourage the academics exploration and grow, both in their teaching and research. CoPs beauty can be their independence from the organizational university structure enabling freedom in their informal enterprise (Becher & Parry, 2005). This provides a space to test new ideas and new approaches outside of official spaces. The CoP provides both an acknowledged and a subversive role that can provide opportunity to permit some of Nietzsche's disruptive wisdom.

A CoP can also break down the risk of dominance by elite's helping overcome the bullying syndrome. Bourdieu (1979/1984) has argued that social positions develop within fields, and become a means of enabling attribution of status that distances undesirable socio-economic identities (Taylor, 2015, p. 20). The modes of perception of elites can then be imposed on dominated groups, in what Bourdieu argues (1990), is a symbolic violence. Awareness of the practices of elitism and bullying enable academics to resist the dominant social capital and create their own participatory democratic flat structures through such mechanisms as CoPs, mentoring, or providing another garden in which to play.

CONCLUSION

Giroux (2005) suggests a moral responsibility exists for both the condition for politics and agency to recognise the importance of becoming accountable for others through their ideas, language, and actions in a struggle between hope and despair.

These are real questions for academics to contemplate, embrace and enact their resistance.

Young (1986) proposes in her outline of the politics of difference an embracing of the diversity that abounds in society. Creating a jungle of exciting possibilities. Like the modern city, in which humans interact, or not, on their own terms finding empowerment and support that suits their needs. Universities could do well to embrace the exciting mix of different possibilities.

Sadly, scholarship and research, producing public goods is disappearing as the university is co-opted by private economic interests seeking research to support the competitive market. Cordal (Wang) says "[b]enefit culture has destroyed the values of knowledge, considering useless everything that is not productive ... We have immersed in the industrialization of thinking that makes us slaves of production away from an enriching personal development through education" (p. 2). Some argue that academics are motivated to resist the pressures because they are capable critical thinkers (Anderson, 2008). However, others suggest there is little evidence of this with academics seemingly accepting the changes or else leaving academia altogether (Heath & Burdon, 2013). Both present a bleak outlook.

It becomes the duty of academics to avoid these unhappy outcomes and sustain the substantive purpose of ensuring the university provides a future for knowledge, learning, education and research that is not destroyed by a questionable audit system of control and commercial interests alone. More space for creativity and acceptance of the critical dissenting voice is called for. Academics with these abilities will inevitably seek out these spaces where they can flourish.

Opportunities for resistance, dissenting stances and openness to difference provide academics with possibilities to ensure they fulfil their lives. Academics should reflect and determine what they want. Should they be content in the corporatized university or should they resist the pressures and seek pleasure that satisfies their self-fulfilment? Practical examples, like a community of practice or mentoring programs embrace the lifeworld. Using reflexivity, mindfulness, the path of individuation, the knowledge given to us by the new field of neuroscience, together with psychology and philosophy, all help the academic stay on track in a fulfilling life. Mindfulness in maintaining the academe as 'profession' over the academe as 'business' is essential in this reclaiming of space. Reducing the militarization, regimentation and commodification of the university will enable an environment that can incubate a profusion of blossoming creativities in a co-creative space ripe for intellectual cross fertilization; a veritable jungle of colour, perfume and beauty.

REFERENCES

Al-Karim, S., & Parbudyal, S. (2012). Twenty years of workplace bullying research: A review of the antecedents and consequences of bullying in the workplace. *Aggression and Violent ehaviour, 17*(6), 581–589.

Alexander, L. (2004). Hélène Cixous and the rhetoric of feminine desire: Re-writing the Medusa. *Literary Journal, 1*(1).

Amabile, T. M. (1988). A model of creativity and innovation in organisations. *Research in Organisational Behaviour, 10*, 123–167.

Anderson, G. (2008). Mapping academic resistance in the managerial university. *Organization 15*(2), 251–270.

Bansel, P., Davies, B., Gannon, S., & Linnell, S. (2008). Technologies of audit at work on the writing subject: a discursive analysis. *Studies in Higher Education, 33*(6), 673–683. doi: 10.1080/03075070802457017

Baron, P. (2009). Thriving in the legal academy. *Legal Education Review*, 27–52.

Baron, P. (2013). A dangerous cult: response to 'the effect of the market on legal education'. *Legal Education Review, 23*(1/2), 273–289.

Baron, P. (2015). The elephant in the room? Lawyer wellbeing and the impact of unethical behaviours. *Australian Feminist Law Journal, 41*(1), 87–119. doi: 10.1080/ 13200968.2015.1035209

Becher, T., & Parry, S. (2005). The endurance of the disciplines. In I. Bliekle & M. Henkel (Eds.), *Governing knowledge* (pp. 133–144). Dordrecht: Springer.

Becher, T., & Trowler, P. (2001). *Academic tribes and territories: Intellectual enquiry and the cultures of disciplines* (2nd ed.). Buckingham: Open University Press.

Blum, D., & Ullman, C. (2012). The globalization and corporatisation of education: The limits and liminality of the market mantra. *International Journal of Qualitative Studies in Education, 25*(4), 367–373.

Bourdieu, P. (1979/1984). *Distinction: A social critique of the judgement of taste*. New Haven: Harvard University Press.

Bourdieu, P. (1990). *The logic of practice*. Stanford: Stanford University Press.

Castellóa, M., Kobayashib, S., McGinnc, M. K., Pechard, H., Vekkailae, J., & Wiskerf, G. (2015). Researcher identity in transition: Signals to identify and manage spheres of activity in a RiskCareer. *Frontline Learning Research, 3*(3), 1.

Castoriadis, C. (1987). *The imaginary institution of society* (K. Blamey, Trans.). Cambridge: Polity Press.

Cixous, H. (1997). The laugh of the Medusa. In R. R. Warhol & D. P. Herndl (Eds.), *Feminism: An anthology of literary theory and criticism* (pp. 334–349). New Brunswick, NJ: Rutgers University Press.

Cixous, H., & Clément, C. (1996). *La Jeune Née Tauris transformations (The newly born woman. Theory and history of literature)* (B. Wing, Trans.). London: I.B.Tauris.

Deleuze, G., & Guattari, F. (1983). *Anti-Oedipus: Capitalism and schizophrenia* (R. Hurley, M. Seem, & H. R. Lane, Trans.). Minneapolis, MN: University of Minnesota Press.

Deleuze, G., & Guattari, F. ([1980] 1988). *A thousand plateaus*. London: Athlone.

Dollard, M. F., Bailey, T. S., & Webber, M. (2014). The economic burden and legal framework of work stress in Australia. In M. F. Dollard & T. S. Bailey (Eds.), *The Australian workplace barometer: Psychosocial safety climate and working conditions in Australia*. Samford Valley, Queensland.: Australian Academic Press.

Flaherty, C. (2016). *Professor pay up 3.4%*. https://www.insidehighered.com/news/2016/04/11/ annual-aaup-salary-survey-says-professor-pay-34?utm_source=Inside+Higher+Ed&utm_ campaign=0be8b923a0-DNU20160411&utm_medium=email&utm_term=0_1fcbc04421-0be8b923a0-198897377

Fuller, R. B. (2008). *Utopia or oblivion: The prospects for humanity* (1st ed.). Lars Müller Publishers.

Giroux, H. A. (2005). Translating the future. *Review of Education, Pedagogy, and Cultural Studies, 27*(3), 13–218. doi: 10.1080/10714410500228876

Giroux, H. A. (2006). Academic freedom under fire: The case for critical pedagogy. *College Literature, 33*(4), 1–42.

Groundwater-Smith, S., & Sachs, J. (2002a). The activist professional and the reinstatement of trust. *Cambridge Journal of Education, 32*(3), 341–358. doi: 10.1080/0305764022000024195

Hauke, C. (2000). *Jung and the postmodern. The interpretation of realities*. London: Routledge.

Hayek, F. A. (1952). *The sensory prder: An inquiry into the foundations of theoretical psychology*. Chicago: The University of Chicago Press.

Hayek, F. A. (1979). *The political order of a free people: Volume 3 of Law, legislation and liberty*. Chicago: University of Chiocago Press.

Heath, M., & Burdon, P. D. (2013). Academic resistance to the neoliberal university. *Legal Education Review, 23*(2), 379–401.

Heffernan, M. (2011). *The power of a dissenting voice*. http://www.inc.com/margaret-heffernan/the-power-of-a-dissenting-voice.html

Heidegger, M. (1959). *An introduction to metaphysics* (R. Manheim, Trans.). New Haven: Yale University Press.

Hicks, S. V., & Rosenberg, A. (2005). Nietschke and disruptive wisdom. *Dialogue and Universalism, 15*(5/6), 7–19.

Howson, C. B. K., Coate, K., & Croix, T. d. S. (2015). *Mid-career academic women: Strategies, choices and motivation*. Leadership Foundation for Higher Education.

Hutchinson, J., & Eveline, J. (2010). Workplace bullying policy in the Australian public sector: Why has gender been ignored? *Australian Journal of Public Administration, 69*(1), 47–60.

Jung, C. G. (1967). *The spirit in man, art and literature* (R. E. C. Hull, Trans.). London: Ark Paperbacks.

Jung, C. G. (2015). *Collected works of C. G. Jung: The first complete English edition of the works of C. G. Jung*: Routledge.

Klein, N. (2015). *This changes everything: Capitalism vs. the climate*. Simon & Schuster.

Lave, J. (1982). A comparative approach to educational forms and learning processes. *Anthropology and Education Quarterly, 13*(2), 181–187.

Marginson, S. (2009). Hayekian neo-liberalism and academic freedom. *Contemporary Readings in Law and Social Justice, 1*(1), 86–116.

Morris, K. (2012). The Arab Spring: The rise of human security and the fall of dictatorship. *Internet Journal of Criminology*. Retrieved from http://www.internetjournalofcriminology.com/Morris_The_Arab_Spring_IJC_July_2012.pdf

Newport, C. (2016). *Deep work rules for focussed success in a distracted world*. Grand Central Publishing.

Nietzsche, F. (1997). *Untimely meditations* (R. J. Hollingdale, Trans.). Cambridge: Cambridge University Press.

Omari, M. (2010). *Towards dignity and respect at work: An exploration of work behaviours in a professional environment* (Doctoral dissertation, Edith Cowan University, WA). Retrieved from http://ro.ecu.edu.au/cgi/viewcontent.cgi?article=1045&context=theses.

Paull, M., Omari, M., & Standen, P. When is a bystander not a bystander? A typology of the roles of bystanders in workplace bullying. *Asia Pacific Journal of Human Resources, 50*(3), 351–366.

The Panama Papers. (2016). *The international consortium of investigative journalists*. https://panamapapers.icij.org/

Pope, R. (2005). *Creativity: Theory, history, practice*. Milton Park, Abingdon, Oxon: Routledge.

A primer on early WikiLeaks coverage. (2010). *Columbia Journalism Review*. http://www.cjr.org/campaign_desk/a_primer_on_early_wikileaks_co.php?page=2

Rosser, V., Johnsrud, L., & Heck, R. (2003). Academic deans and directors: Assessing their effectiveness from individual and institutional perspectives. *Journal of Higher Education, 74*(1), 1–25.

Rowland, S. (2002). *Jung A feminist revision*. Cambridge, UK: Polity.

Saltman, K. J. (2007). Education as enforcement: Militarization and corporatization of schools. *Educating for Equity, 14*(2), 28–30.

Sheehan, M., & Pearse, S. (2015). *One moment please*. Hay House.

Sternberg, R. J., & Lubart, T. I. (1995). *Defying the crowd: Cultivating creativity in a culture of conformity*. New York: The Free Press.

Storr, A. (1973). *Jung*. London: Fontana.

Taylor, B. C. (2015). Yours, mine and ours: Theorizing the global articulation of qualitative research methods and academic disciplines. *Romanian Journal of Communication and Public Relations, 17*(3), 11–26. doi: http://dx.doi.org/10.21018/rjcpr.2015.3.165

Thornton, M. (2009). Universities upside down: The impact of the new knowledge economy. *Candian Journal of Women and Law, 21*(2), 375–393.

Thornton, M. (2012). *Privatising the public university: The case of law*. London: Routledge.

Vernon, P. (Ed.). (1970). *Creativity*. Harmondsworth: Penguin.

Wang, L. (Producer). (2015). Isaac Cordal depicts for-profit universities as horrifying dystopian factories. *Inhabitat*. Retrieved from http://inhabitat.com/isaac-cordal-depicts-for-profit-universities-as-horrifying-dystopian-factories/

Wenger, E. (1998). Communities of practice. Learning as a social system. *Systems Thinker*. http://www.co-i-l.com/coil/knowledge-garden/cop/lss.shtml

Young, I. M. (1986). The ideal of community and the politics of difference. *Social Theory and Practice 12*(1), 1–26.

Young, I. M. (2011). *Justice and the politics of difference*. Princeton: Princeton University Press.

Pauline Collins
School of Law and Justice
University of Southern Queensland, Australia

ALISON L. BLACK, GAIL CRIMMINS, AND JANICE K. JONES

11. REDUCING THE DRAG

Creating V Formations through Slow Scholarship and Story

Every seed destroys its container, or else there would be no fruition.
(Scott-Maxwell, 1979, p. 65)

INTRODUCTION

We are three women working across two Australian universities. We know the deadening, withering nature and containment of the neoliberal university. Yet, we find ourselves inspired by the wisdom of slow scholarship and recognize that with our deliberate activity with each other we have been emulating something of the cooperative reciprocity inherent in the energy-boosting-V-formations adopted by groups of flying birds. Our chapter is a breaking free of managerial containment and a proclamation that "not everything that counts can be counted" (Collini, 2012).

In this chapter we resist the insidious, diminishing drag of managerialism, comparison and metric-based audits of productivity and outputs; we have 'outgrown' these narrow containers. We recognize the joy and pleasure of responding to our longings to connect, to "care for self and others", and to "be" differently in academia. Our resistance and pleasure has been found in opportunities to listen and to converse in meaningful ways that give time to reflection and relationship; ways that enable us to work cooperatively and speak our lives into the academy.

We use this chapter to invite the reader into our deliberate storying and re/de/storying of our lived experience and our practising a politics of care and collaboration. It feels pleasurable (and naughty and rebellious too) to be subverting what it means to be a productive, accountable and useful academic and to be offering alternatives that seed new, fruitful, meaningful and altruistic ways of working.

> **It's a fine line between pleasure and pain**
>
> *Pleasure*
>
> The ongoing conversations and thinking has been something that has sustained me through the last tough years of academia – times when my workload has been beyond me, and my sense of academic worth at rock bottom.

> In this collaboration I have found that I have contributions to make, that research can be so much more than what the academy perpetuates.
>
> Our group, our wonderfully nicknamed "Wise Women" ... WOW! For the first time EVER in my academic life I have a group of women around me who are inclusive, who get me, who affirm me, who do the work, who are amazing, who are ethical, who value ongoing collaborations, who also operate from an ethic of caring.
>
> Sharing the load has felt important too. And that load sharing looks different each time, but it never feels like "here I am again, doing it all on my own".
>
> We are prolific 'responders' and so I find our informal email conversations that 'surround our research work' as meaningful as our academic writing.
>
> (Ali reflecting April 2016)

Remembering

It is important to shed light on our academic experiences – to make public the stories of what it has felt like, and feels like, to be an academic – so that collective conversations about academic culture and the current social, political and intellectual life in the academy can take place. Often our personal stories are linked directly to political contexts and so sharing them is essential to developing new understandings about the workings of larger political discourses and structures (Berg & Seeber, 2016). Stefan Collini's book, *What Are Universities For,* reminds us of the importance of making space for reflection about the complexity and uncertainty of academic work, particularly in these contemporary times where academics are feeling pressured to lead and live 'affectively thin and relentlessly diagnostic lives' due to the 'steady poisoning and paralysing effects of managerialism' (Collini, 2012).

> **It's a fine line between pleasure and pain**
>
> ***Pain***
>
> *Tired and empty*
>
> *Life-sapped, energy depleted*
>
> ☑ All forms filled in, boxes checked, still room for improvement
>
>   *All hours in the day spent*
>
> *Dragging feet, heart crying out, trying to listen, trying to add value, trying, trying, trying, dying*
>
>   *Where is the joy, the vision, the making of a difference?*
>
> ☑ Compliance, accountability, do more, do more with less

> *Pressure, guilt, drained from doing, yet not doing enough?*
>
> *Not doing what matters ... to me*
>
> *Where is what matters?*
>
> *The mattering of meaning, community, and relationships.*
>
> ☑ ☑ ☑ Compliance checks, benchmarks, performance measures by COB
>
> *Too many deadlines, too many deadlines, too many <u>deadlines</u>.*
>
> <u>Dead</u> *inside. Draw the <u>line</u>.*
>
> *I don't want to stand back and let education and systems and accountability delete the person, delete the joy and the creativity*
>
> *I don't want the shallow to delete the deep*
>
> *I don't want the far gaze to delete the looking closely*
>
> *I want to understand your life and for you to understand mine*
>
> (Snippets of longing, from a free form poem Ali penned way back in July 2010, Black, 2015)

Our current understandings have grown out of our experiences of universities as bureaucratic corporations; of feeling managed, compared, stressed, demoralized, distracted and fragmented by the constant and frantic pace, work overload and relentless demands for increased product and productivity in jobs with no boundaries (Berg & Seeber, 2016; Gill, 2010; O'Neill, 2014; Pereira, 2015).

We are not surprised to read that stress in academia exceeds that found in the general population (Catano, Francis, Haines, Kirpalani, Shannon, Stringer & Lozanski, 2010). The consequences of this academic climate can be devastating. There are human costs, as this blog on wider lessons shows: https://musicfordeckchairs.wordpress.com/tag/professor-stefan-grimm/

We think soberly of the life and needless death of Stefan Grimm (1963–2014) a 51 year old professor, who had submitted the highest number of grant applications in his faculty, who had brought in $265,000 in grant income, who had made fundamental contributions to the understanding of cell death in connection with the development of cancers and was researching an anti-cancer gene, who had published 50 journal articles and two books, and who took his own life after being told by his head of department:

> you are struggling to fulfil the metrics of a Professorial Post ... and must now start to give serious consideration as to whether you are performing at the expected level of a Professor ....

In a final email, Stefan wrote:

> What these guys don't know is that they destroy lives. Well, they certainly destroyed mine. (http://www.dailymail.co.uk/news/article-

2861588/ Professor-dead-cash-row-Cancer-scientist-said-told-fellow-academics-chiefs-treated-like-s.html

We think deeply about the human consequences of narrow measures, constant threats, relentless pressure and instruments of comparison and shame. Like Maggie O'Neill (2014) we believe it is time to pause, reflect upon and resist the relentless performativity and measurement of academic life.

It's a fine line between pleasure and pain

Pain

Hi Janice and Gail,

Just trying to follow up things that I transfer in my diary from one week to the next. GRANTS is a big one – driven by that awful institutional imperative. I have heard that without an external grant I won't get promoted back to Level C (the level I had before I came to this university, but which they refused to consider in HR appointment processes). So, I am looking for a grant space.

X Ali

***

Ali,

I am in the same boat – an external grant will be vital for me to move up to Associate Professor – but I'm not sure I care at the moment (although I change like a chameleon!)

☺ Janice

***

Ali and Janice,

I am a yes – in fact I am a yes please.

I need a grant too. I need it so that I can at least be considered 'legitimate' in 'their' eyes and would use it to try to gain an ongoing appointment.

I get tired. No, I get weary. Weary is tired-er than tired isn't it? But I do have a large capacity for work. And I would work hard to make the grant successful.

And working with you gives me my 'hum'.

Xx Gail

(Email exchanges between Ali, Janice and Gail, one Saturday in February 2016)

Sigh.

This is the type of culture in which we are situated, we three women academics/writers/artists. Our work as academics is defined by increasing demands for accountability and effectiveness (Stachowiak-Kudła & Kudła, 2015), outputs (Lee, 2007) and measurement (Burrows, 2012). We are situated in highly gendered workplaces (Husu, 2001). We are surrounded by high levels of academic dissatisfaction (Fredman & Doughney, 2011).

How can I *survive* in these cultures of measurement, audits, comparison, segregation and stratification?

No. No, my friend. This was the type of question we *used* to ask – individually, alone, and hopelessly. We had absorbed the corporatist rhetoric of individual responsibility for so long that we had begun to ask the wrong questions. We have stopped asking ourselves this question.

Figure 1. Asking questions.
Digital artwork by Ali Black (2016)

Questions are powerful tools. They elicit answers in their likeness. There is something life-giving about formulating and asking better questions (Tippett, 2016).

We have changed the questions we ask. Now, we ask: How do *we* best *thrive* in cultures of measurement, audits, comparison, segregation and stratification? We ask: What gives us meaning? And pleasure? Our work meaning? And pleasure? Our lives and relationships meaning? And pleasure?

And we listen with a different ear, not the ear of the academic assembly line, not the ear of impending doom and helplessness. We listen to our enduring questions of what it means to be human, to our questions of who we are to each other, and we listen with genuine care and presence. We listen to our shared longings to lead a good life, a connected life, a life of meaning and relationship. As we listen we are re/orienting ourselves to "ethical scholarship for the common good" (Zuidervaart, 2011).

We three women academics/writers/artists are beginning to show our resistance to the narrow academic containers of measurement, comparison, and productivity of the contemporary university. We are working *together*, a group of like-minded women, and together we are embracing the values of 'slow' – the "slow movement" (Parkins & Craig, 2006) – "slow scholarship" (Mountz et al., 2015; O'Neill 2014) – and the focus of "the slow professor" (Berg & Seeber, 2016).

Our group of like-minded women is growing … we are more than three … Julianne, Sarah, Linda … we are ten women academics … Lisa, Yvonne, Paula, Angie … and more seek to join with us … we are continually adding to our number and together we are pushing back against invisibility, shame and metrics to welcome conversation, collaboration, mentoring, and community building.

It's a fine line between pleasure and pain

Pleasure

Gentle caring enfolded embodied
Life generating
Deliberate
Careful
Slow

I sit in the stillness of your writing
Your writing – like a quiet companion who is just there
holding my hand
waiting patiently
for my return.

(Poetic observation by Sarah, about Linda and Ali sharing writing as relationship)

We are no longer individualizing our endeavours. Self-sufficient individualism, mastery and rationalism are old props which weaken community (Mijs et al., 2016). They are props we are happy to discard. We are letting these go and opening to otherness, deservingness, ethical engagement, mutual support and trust, conversation and collaboration, politics and pleasure. We are working as a collective. We are remembering what we love – flow, care, compassion, relationships, meaning, deep thinking, reflection, creative research and teaching.

In our everyday lives, complex and busy as they are, we are with deliberate care and attention giving priority to working in meaningful, sustainable, thoughtful and pleasurable ways. We are re/learning that giving time to self-care is not indulgent, that caring for another supports our own success, and that giving time to conversation, connectivity and collaboration in our local working environments has a ripple effect (Barsade, 2002).

> **It's a fine line between pleasure and pain**
>
> ***Pleasure***
>
> An opportunity to write, to tell, to share, to relive, to experience the whole of it by reliving parts of it. The journey starts always at that moment when everyone is content and involved in their own moments. I move and sit and look at the screen, the keyboard, pause for a moment and then it begins, it flows, sometimes caught like water in a dam, lapping, and then trickling through and then flowing freely, spilling over the top. Likeminded souls residing in the same eras, moved by the same social frames, coming together via awkward technologies, sharing their journeys, their lives, their most memorable, heart-wrenching, soul-giving seconds, hours, and days. In these sittings, someone else's story moves our being, confirms the challenges that must be faced by us as humans. This is life, our lives committed to words, images, metaphors, and emotions. Our emotions freely spill onto the page, and as we reflect and support one another and seek the deeper meanings, the resonance—and we find we are one, united. Together we soar high above the pages, the heartache, the challenges, the memories—we are brave in these moments when we share the what and the how and the why and the why not, and the so what, and the where to... We are women united by sorrow, loss, love and dreams. We are women who now dance bare in the twilight and breathe.
>
> (Julianne reflecting January 2016)

We want more than survival. We want life affirming, joyous, meaningful, collaborative and celebratory work. We want work that supports balance and our own and others' wellbeing.

Asking the right questions has directed us toward agency, purpose, pleasure, fulfilment and self-care/caring relationships.

We know! Crazy huh?!

Fly Like a Bird! Invoking the V formation

Many birds fly in a V. Yet they are not born with the skill of flying in a V, they learn the art of V-formation flying from *each other*. It could be they are watching the bird in front and responding accordingly; they might be using their wing feathers to sense the air flow around them; or they might be finding spots that feel good and be using this 'feel good' feedback to guide them – "this feels good when I flap like this, and when I flap like this it is easier" (Portugal et al., 2014). These are interesting observations that we too can employ: What is happening to the 'bird' in front of us? Is there good air flowing around me or do I need to do the *opposite* of what the bird in front is doing – so I don't get caught in its downwash? What feels good for me, what makes my work feel easier, pleasurable, freeing?

We like the last question a lot. *What feels good for me?* Recognizing the importance of affective functions and moods, Mihaly Csikszentmihaly asserts the more a person experiences 'flow' – an optimal state of inner experience – the happier he or she will be (2008. P. 6). We are now recognising, and looking for, those conditions that support our flow – our highly focussed, present-moment, imaginative, joyful work.

By engaging in our writing and research as a collective we are tapping into pleasure, togetherness, connectedness, interest and joy. These positive emotions are undoing the damage of our highly managed work environments, and we are finding ourselves more resilient and creative, and our collective outputs intellectually expansive and prolific.

It's a fine line between pleasure and pain

Pleasure

Black, A., Crimmins, G., & Jones, J. K. (2017). Reducing the drag: Creating V formations through slow scholarship and story. In S. Riddle, M. K. Harmes, & P. A. Danaher (Eds.), *Producing pleasure within the contemporary university*. Sense Publishers (this volume).

Loch, S., Black, A., Crimmins, G., Jones, J., & Impiccini, J. (in press). Writing stories and lives: Documenting women connecting, communing and coming together. Book series Transformative Pedagogies in the Visual Domain, Common Ground Publishing. Eighth title *Embodied and walking pedagogies engaging the visual domain: Research co-creation and practice.* Kim Snepvangers & Sue Davis (Eds.).

Loch, S., & Black, A (2016). We cannot do this work without being who we are: Researching and experiencing academic selves. In B. Harreveld, M. Danaher, B. Knight, C. Lawson, & G. Busch (Eds.), *Constructing methodology for qualitative research: Researching education and social practices.* Palgrave MacMillan: UK and US.

Crimmins, G., Jones, J., Loch, S., Black, A., Albion, L., Impiccini, J., & Berryman, A. (written, looking for a home). Telling lives of women: (Re)presenting personal memoirs collectively.

Black, A., Impiccini, J., Crimmins, G., & Jones, J. (2016). Finding connectedness, finding belonging, finding our voice: Contemplating creative and connected futures through storytelling and narrative. Paper presented at the *RUN Regional Futures Conference*, Rockhampton, 21–24 June, 2016.

> Black, A., & Henderson, L. (2016). Stories of mourning: Reclaiming personal/professional identities through writing. Paper presented at the *Australian Women's and Gender Studies Biennial International Conference*, Brisbane, June 29–July 2, 2016.
>
> Crimmins, G., Black, A., Jones, J., Loch, S., Albion, L., Impiccini, J., & Berryman, A. (2016). Risky discourses: Promiscuously storying women's lives. Paper presented at the *Australian Women's and Gender Studies Biennial International Conference,* Brisbane, June 29–July 2, 2016.
>
> Crimmins, G., Jones, J., Loch, S., Black, A., Albion, L., Impiccini, J., & Berryman, A. (2016) Telling lives: Women, stories and healing. Paper presented at The inaugural Narrative, Health and Wellbeing Research Conference. *Enlightened: Narratives and narrative strategies to awaken applied and creative humanism,* 8 February, Noosa.
>
> (Collective outputs from our group of 'Wise Women', with more in preparation)

By working together we have optimized our individual and collective experience; we have created a collective advantage.

Science shows there is actually no aerodynamic advantage to be had in leading a V formation – and so it would be reasonable to expect birds to want to minimize the amount of time they spend up front. What researchers have found is that birds are often working in pairs and matching the time they spend in each other's wake by taking frequent shifts in the lead position (Voelkla, Portugald, Unsölde, Usherwoodd, Wilson, & Fritz, 2015). The birds are taking turns, sharing the load, and benefiting from this shared arrangement. By working together, a flock of birds is greater than the sum of its parts. By working together they create a collective advantage; by invoking the V formation they are optimising the collective experience.

> **It's a fine line between pleasure and pain**
>
> *Pleasure*
>
> Ali had set up a space where *all* the women in the group, *all* of whom had stolen five minutes here and there from busy lives to write about their lives, were to share their work, and expose an inner layer of self. More so, Ali shared her 'chapter' and exposed her soft and tender underbelly. She trusted us. So through *a joint vulnerability* I ceased to be 'me' and we (the group, wise and warrior women) became 'we' and 'us'. We were all asked to share something of ourselves. We were all invited to read and see each other's lives with a shared sense of fragility and transparency. And so I shared, and the other wise warrior women shared their stories in a process that births a sensitivity and trust for not only the work we produce but for the women we are.

> And it was this process of *everyone* contributing, *everyone exposing* their writing and selves that allowed me to share my developing story.
>
> And without there being a particular moment of transformation or one event which shredded my cocoon, somehow over time and conversation and sharing and laughing/crying at and with our stories/lives my 'I' disappeared. Even in the most personal of ventures of writing of and about oneself, the 'I's have gone. Now fearless and fortified by solidarity and vulnerable-strong women we are ready to share more publicly our work, just part of which happens to be written by me.
>
> (Gail reflecting January 2016)

What can we learn from the V formation? For the academic, 'flying'/working together in this kind of formation allows room for togetherness, it allows room for others, and otherness. Flying in this kind of formation is an ethical choice. It isn't the common choice. If we take our metaphoric cue from birds, and their long-flight migratory hauls, we can see that collaboration, cooperation and relationship is enabling. We can see the value of working together, of joining knowledge – together we are stronger than we would be flying isolated and alone. Curiously, our 'publication outputs' demonstrate this truth. As a collective we have an 'enhanced spirit of enquiry, and more intelligence, deductive speed, and inventiveness than we possess as individuals' (Brennan, 2004, p. 62). (Note, Teresa Brennan, at the time of editing her manuscript, which we are citing, left her house to complete an errand and was struck by a car and killed – a stark reminder that life is precious and short and that if we have to work it should be meaningful and hopeful, joyful and pleasurable.)

The V formation runs counter to the individualistic, competitive formation that current metrics and measures seem to/aim to generate. Adam Grant (2014, p. 4) identifies that 'every time we interact with another person at work, we have a choice to make: Do we try to claim as much value as we can, or contribute value without worrying about what we receive in return?'. Grant's (2014) research persuasively emphasises that success is increasingly dependent on how we interact with others, that 'givers' dominate the top of the success ladder, and that giving positions us for success – and creates more ripple effects to enhance the success of people around us.

> **It's a fine line between pleasure and pain**
>
> *Pleasure*
>
> Being part of this group has been like the unfolding of a net. It started in a small way – and Ali your leadership and input has been essential to the life of what we do. Your energy has encouraged us to create a network – but let's ignore the implications of contemporary and neutral virtual links. This group is different in intensity and focus: it is not about sharing cute stories on Face

> Book, or commenting briefly on a political issue. Instead we wrestle with that light – those ideas, weaving them back and forth across our virtual loom. Our Wise Women group has never met as a body yet we have created a rich and powerful process for writing. From sharing those tentative first steps in writing our lives, to the sharing of video conversations about those works – the giving of critical but wise feedback and encouragement has given life to trust and much shared humour and wisdom. Like light, ideas shoot along the networks – rapid fire emails, drafts of narratives wrestled over for hours, or flung out from an hour's creative passion, photographs, words of support – come together to create a mesh of light as sharp as the nerves of a living being. That mesh is a weaving of light – the stories of women whose complex lives include academic and emotional labour, care for others, challenges to care for ourselves.
>
> This is the first time I have felt that my unique voice is heard and valued. I have been able to offer wisdom and encouragement to women who like me are struggling to balance lives full of turmoil, joy and the routines of caring. This time has allowed me a space to understand and to begin to voice the enormity of grief at the loss of my life-partner. But – beyond the therapeutic value of the word, there is that steely focus: we are writers with purpose, and with a critical ear and eye. Our intellectual life flows along those neural pathways, and I am so glad of that richness.
>
> (Janice reflecting January 2016)

Figure 2. Delighting in V formations.
Digital Artwork by Ali Black (2016).

Working in V formation, each member of the group remain close, receiving nourishment and rest, and help with supporting her own weight. Strength is gained and regained over time. Affiliation and belonging sustain and positive feelings expand to influence group dynamics, attitudes and emotions. This changes the emotional culture from one of suppression and dispiritedness to one of satisfaction, caring, motivation, joy and belonging (Barsade & O'Neill, 2016).

The members gain lift and energy, and are uplifted by the 'good air'. Working in this way is subversive, efficient, supportive and altruistic.

We are joyfully experimenting with V formations and V signs. We are resisting the academy's gaze and judgement and changing our way of doing things. We are boosting our efficiency, stamina and range. We are reducing 'the drag' and 'sharing our flight fatigue' and this is enhancing our energy, productivity and creativity. We are experiencing a collective wellbeing and vigour from working deliberately and thoughtfully in ways that feel gloriously rebellious and taboo. These are signs of contempt and defiance, these are gestures of victory and peace. These are working for us!

Every Seed Destroys Its Container, or Else There Would Be No Fruition (Scott-Maxwell, 1979, p. 65)

In the drying and dying of everything comes a new way, a new form. Over a year ago, seven women academics/writers/artists, of which we are three, started to share stories, memoirs, images and extended poems in order to express our lives, share our joys and challenges, and to connect with other women academics/writers/artists. Over this year, through initiating and sustaining conversations, we have formed a trusted group of colleagues and we are acquiring responsive, personal and aesthetic ways to address and reconcile our personal/professional lives. We are unearthing our individual and collective voice, and creating and expanding safe spaces for scholarly, professional and personal disclosure and meaning-making.

Through this time to write, and share, and become friends, we three + more academics/writers/artists are finding our courage to resist those cultures that diminish who we are as people, cultures that rarely recognize the fullness of our contribution, or the fullness of our lives including families and personal lives and raising children/caring for elderly parents. We resist conditions that build cultures of "care-less workers" (Lynch, 2010), because we do care.

We do care – for ourselves, our students, our work, our families.

And as Pereira (2015) suggests, in order for us to enact our care it is absolutely crucial to resist this tendency of individualization which pervades performativity in the academy.

When we enact our care, this care that values human nature and human expression, this care that values community and connectedness, others feel – and we feel – heard.

We have been heard.

It's a fine line between pleasure and pain

Pleasure

Heard.
Being wise woman
I'm a beginning wise woman
I'm no one special
But I used the invitation to write the story that was
stuck
through all my other writing
stuck
in overcoming my situation
stuck
and in my falling-asleep, to stop berating, stop waiting, stop picturing
what was sad, but just would not be

I used the writing to take some power
to tell my story to women who really cared
and even cried,
who asked questions
because they cried.
Tears in their eyes.

and I stopped my waiting, living in the nether-land
and told my story
just as it came.
There was no judgment
There was no shame.
Just my life
at that time

but now, with the story slipped to one side,
away from the front
I have some space
as the word that
gorged on me
is killed.

Dead.

Failure.

Failure? fail her …? for her?

> ... I have by these women,
>
> been heard.
>
> (Sarah, offering her experience of our group of 'wise women' January 2016. Sarah's response epitomizes our collective experience of feeling/being 'heard'.)

Seeding New, Fruitful, Meaningful and Altruistic Ways of Working

We imagine, conceptualize, share and write collaboratively. Simple really. And without consciously or deliberately doing so we are reducing the drag that accompanies academic cultures, the drag of writing on our own, and the drag of feeling in competition with other academics. Such burdens only support the neo-liberalist system, they are weighty and we now realize, are unnecessary.

Our coming together in vulnerability and trust has supported our learning to write, to converse, to relate collaboratively in a V formation. Single file vying for the front position is exhausting. We don't do that. We take turns. In our V Formation one of us (often organically) provides the primary support for the flock, supporting the motion and lift and direction. And the others watch the motion, observing the unfolding, enjoying the opportunity to fly on the tips, imagine destinations and catch the updraft. Soon we are lifting together, producing together, supporting, motivating, and energising each other. By flying as a team in this formation, each of us feels the assistance of another as we fly. We rotate (also organically) and someone new moves to the front. Fatigue is avoided, strength and vigour is renewed. We learn and grow as a team, always observing, responding, and staying close. Caring. Keeping sight of each other.

Instead of working to unsustainable directives and time-frames we give time to sharing, regularly sharing – and deeply listening to – stories of life, of worth, of resistance. We write creatively, without the pressure to add citation to each claim made, without the formalities of 'masculine' discourses based on myths of objective research, without the time pressure to meet 'by close of business' deadlines.

We are creating spaces for joy and daring and togetherness. We are listening with deep attentiveness to one another's stories. By doing so we are achieving something that none of us, or our broader group of female academics could have imagined.

We are creating worlds of delight, where uncomfortable, contradictory, in-between, challenging and boisterously disrespectful ideas are given new life and space. Our joy in listening, and of allowing and encouraging ourselves and each other to speak of and attend to aspects of our lives that we believed could not be told, is creating a rich space for thinking otherwise. Breathing life back into the crushed spirit of iconoclasm we are finding great contentment in attending to the slow rhythms, the balance and the flow of our lives as women who are academics. Yes, we still are wrestling with the challenges of caring for others and ourselves, of being heard in academia, and of negotiating our way beyond the boundaries, the habitus and the 'way things are done here' in the university. But with our storying, our friendship and bravery, we are questioning 'what counts' and rising above fear.

> **It's a fine line between pleasure and pain**
>
> ***Pleasure***
>
> Rising above fear
> *Ah,* Relief immediately follows.
> Our shoulders drop
> Our guards drop
> Our fear subsides
>
> And we slowly take off our 'academic' attire, and share and listen to the women inside the women academics. And what amazing stories and voices we hear. We hear of the love and heartache of a woman grieving for her partner lost to alcoholism. We hear of the beauty in the chaos of living with a child with Downs Syndrome; of a women overcoming the hidden shame of ivf (intentionally lower case). We hear of the strength of a mother, supported by a father, who created equality of opportunity within a working class community in the 1960s and 70s. We hear of a journey through depression and are reminded of the gift of story and connection. We are energized by this 'good air' that surrounds us, our group of courageous, living, loving, and caring women. We listen and our bodies sing with relief, joy and acceptance of ourselves and each other.
>
> (Gail reflecting May 2016)

We know, with great certainty that we are enough. Our work can make us feel that we do not 'measure up'. But we have been reminded we are more than our citation index, or student evaluation scores or grant income tally.

The sense of verification and acceptance in our group's sharing and caring experience is powerful. Through our sharing, listening and connecting with each other we are establishing value in each other and ourselves; we recognize a different value to the metrics and measures that are being held to us as carrots and sticks. And something fundamental is shifting. We are beginning to understand that the metrics and standards being imposed and reified are simply constructions, they are versions of someone's truth – not necessarily *the* truth or a truth we accept. So we reject those measures, and we establish for ourselves a new set of values, an alternative guide for our academic and non-academic practice. In doing so we interrupt and 'rupture the bounds of what is permissible and possible' in academia, in writing, and create for ourselves a manifesto of caring and care-full collaboration.

*Figure 3. A manifesto for 'Reducing the drag'.
Digital image by Ali Black (2016)*

"Curiouser and Curiouser!"

After working with each other, we now wonder if we have ever before been properly heard. Such is the careful listening. The thoughtful responding. The authentic caring. Of this group of women.

We have found sacred ground – a sense of place, identity, authenticity, belonging, safety, beauty.

We are relishing our forms of communication and connection – arts-based methods, poems, storying, and writing as research. And with these tools we are creating our own definitions of productivity.

It has been so curious to see that in our sharing of selves, our shedding of academic cloaks, our breaking away, we have become more focussed, more productive, and more passionate. In academic terms, we three+ women academics/writers/artists are engaging collaboratively in developing conference presentations, academic journal articles, book chapters, grant applications, edited book collections, and so many pleasurable projects and processes.

It has been curious to find that with our escaping from the 'pressure to publish', to perform, to evidence our academic selves, we are creating spaces to share memory and meaning, to unveil the veiled women underneath our pain-(t)ed academic faces. Quite organically, these spaces are generating and opening new opportunities. We find ourselves wallowing in warm, comfortable and passionate spaces of collective scholarship. We are reconciling inner and academic lives. And this sweet resistance to managerialism feels incredibly pleasurable.

We are,

s
l
o
w
l
y

with our practising slow scholarship and a politic of care and caring, subverting what it means to be productive and what it means to be an academic. It is not a subversion that requires anger or fight – well, maybe just a V sign or two!

Subverting pressure to pleasure naturally follows the rejection of the metrics and measures of the corporate, and the embracing of a slow and ethical scholarship for the common good.

We are engaging in a strategic and highly pleasurable V formation shaped REFUSAL of the quantifying stupefying delimiters of academic production. We are finding work lives that are reflective, rich, life-enhancing, deep, collective and invigorating. The drag of work can still mess with our flight, and we still experience days of discouragement, disillusionment, exhaustion and disappointment. But, the care of our group offers spaciousness, deservingness, appreciation, and acknowledgement. We are no longer alone in this experience. And knowing this togetherness is uplifting. And so we rest a while, enjoying the good air coming from in front of us; and we float in the certain knowledge that we are indeed enough.

ACKNOWLEDGMENTS

The authors would like to thank our collective of women writers for their ongoing enthusiasm and care and to acknowledge Sarah, Linda and Julianne in particular for their contribution and permissions to include their personal observation and reflections in our chapter.

REFERENCES

Barsade, S. (2002). The ripple effect: Emotional contagion and its influence on group behavior, *Administrative Science Quarterly*, 47, 644–675.

Barsade, S., & O'Neill, A. (2016). Manage your emotional culture. *Harvard Business Review*, January–February. Retrieved from https://hbr.org/2016/01/manage-your-emotional-culture

Berg, M., & Seeber, B. (2016). *The slow professor: Challenging the culture of speed in the academy*. Canada: University of Toronto Press, Scholarly Publishing Division.

Black, A. L. (2015). Authoring a life: Writing ourselves in/out of our work in education. In M. Baguley, Y. Findlay, & M. Kerby (Eds.), *Meanings and motivation in education research* (pp. 50–71). London, UK: Routledge.

Brennan, T. (2004). *The transmission of affect*. Ithaca: Cornell University Press.

Burrows, R. (2012). Living with the H-Index? Metric assemblages in the contemporary academy. *The Sociological Review, 60*, 2, 355–372.

Catano, V.M., Francis, L., Haines, T., Kirpalani, H., Shannon, H., Stringer, B., & Lozanski, L. (2010). Occupational stress in Canadian universities: A national survey. *International Journal of Stress Management, 17*, 232–258.

Collini, S. (2012). *What are universities for?* London: Penguin.

Csikszentmihalyi, M. (1990). *Flow: The psychology of optimal experience*. New York: Harper & Row.

Fredman, N., & Doughney, J. (2011). Academic dissatisfaction, managerial change and neo-liberalism, *Higher Education, 64*(1), 41–58. doi: 10.1007/s10734-011-9479-y

Gill, R. (2010). Breaking the silence: The hidden injuries of the Neoliberal University. In R. Ryan-Flood & R. Gill (Eds.), *Secrecy and silence in the research process: Feminist reflections* (pp. 228–244). Abingdon: Routledge.

Grant, A. (2014). *Give and take: Why helping others drives our success. A revolutionary approach to success*. London: Orion Publishing Co.

Husu, L. (2001). *Sexism, support and survival in Academia: Academic women and hidden discrimination in Finland*. Finland: University of Helsinki.

Lee, F. S. (2007). The research assessment exercise, the state and the dominance of mainstream economics in British universities. *Cambridge Journal of Economics, 31*, 309–325.

Lynch, K. (2010). Carelessness: A hidden doxa of higher education. *Arts and Humanities in Higher Education, 9*(1), 54–67.

Mijs, J. J. B., Bakhtiari, E., & Lamont, M. (2016). Neoliberalism and symbolic boundaries in Europe: Global diffusion, local context, regional variation. *Socius: Sociological Research for a Dynamic World, 2* (January–December).

Mountz, A., Bonds, A., Mansfield, B., Loyd, J., Hyndman, J., Walton-Roberts, M., Basu, R., Whitson, R., Hawkins, R., Hamilton, T., & Curran, W. (2015). For slow scholarship: A feminist politics of resistance through collective action in the neoliberal university. *ACME: An International E-Journal for Critical Geographies, 14*(4), 1235–1259. Retrieved from http://ojs.unbc.ca/index.php/acme/article/view/1058

O'Neill, M. (2014). The slow university: Work, time and well-being. *Forum Qualitative Sozialforschung/Forum: Qualitative Social Research, 15*, 3. Retrieved from http://www.qualitative-research.net/index.php/fqs/article/view/2226/3696 (accessed 9 June 2016).

Parkins, W., & Craig, G. (2006). *Slow living*. Oxford: Berg.

Pereira, M. M. (2015). Struggling within and beyond the Performative University: Articulating activism and work in an "academia without walls". *Women's Studies International Forum*, http://dx.doi.org/10.1016/j.wsif.2015.06.008

Portugal, S. J., Hubel, T. Y., Fritz, J., Heese, S., Trobe, D., Voelk, B., Hailes, S., Wilson, A. M., & Usherwood, J. R. (2014). Upwash exploitation and downwash avoidance by flap phasing in ibis formation flight, *Nature, 501*, 399–404. http://dx.doi.org/10.1038/nature12939

Scott-Maxwell, F. (1979). *The measure of my days*. New York: Penguin.

Stachowiak-Kudła, M., & Kudła, J. (2015). Financial regulations and the diversification of funding sources in higher education institutions: Selected European experiences. *Studies in Higher Education*. doi: 10.1080/03075079.2015.1119109

Tippet, K. (2016). *Becoming wise: An inquiry into the mystery and art of living*. London: Penguin.

Voelkla, B., Portugald, S. J., Unsölde, M., Usherwoodd, J. R., Wilson, A. M., & Fritz, J. (2015). Matching times of leading and following suggest cooperation through direct reciprocity during V-formation flight in ibis. *Proceedings of the National Academy of Sciences of the United States of America, 112*(7), 2115–2120.

Zuidervaart, L. (2011). *Living at the crossroads: Ethical scholarship and the common good.* http://faculty.icscanada.edu/lzuidervaart/files/cprse-inaugural-address (accessed 9 June 2016).

Alison L. Black
School of Education
University of the Sunshine Coast, Australia

Gail Crimmins
School of Communication and Creative Industries
University of the Sunshine Coast, Australia

Janice K. Jones
School of Linguistics, Adult and Specialist Education
University of Southern Queensland, Australia

ANDREW HICKEY AND ROBYN HENDERSON

12. TESTIMONIO AND THE *IDIOS KOSMOS* OF THE CONTEMPORARY ACADEMIC

Charting the Possibilities for Pleasure in Personal Accounts from Inside the Academy

INTRODUCTION

Jouissance is here not taken as in the sense of pain, but rather in the sense of an ejection of pleasure, where pain is overcome through the commitment to an act rather than the action itself. (Hourigan, 2015, p. 118)

This past decade has seen an increasing focus on the effects of academic bullying, workplace harassment, incivility and other disruptive workplace behaviours within the university (Fogg, 2008). Yet despite this growing awareness and charting of the costs of these behaviours – both to the individual and organization – it is evident that flawed and ineffective responses to incivility and the maintenance of organizational structures that encourage negative interpersonal behaviours remain entrenched in the academy (Chatterjee & Maira, 2014; Giroux 2014). Within a dynamic of increasingly limited funding, public questioning of the role of higher education and epistemic changes to the shape and function of the university-as-institution, stark and unyielding shifts in the way academic work is practised have resulted in university workplaces that are increasingly interpersonally competitive and, consequently, prone to disruptive behaviours.

Indeed, the "highly performative … competitive and corporatised" nature of the academy has been identified as having undesirable workplace effects on relationships and ways of working (Morley & Crossouard, 2016, p. 150). Preston (2016) provides a particularly alarming prediction that increasingly competitive academic environments will lead to decayed interpersonal relationships and the breakdown of meaningful collegiality within the university. Writing from the British context of tiered "Russell Group" and "new" universities, Preston notes: "I have heard of arrangements whereby new university teams have had to agree to disproportionate efforts in writing a joint bid with an elite university just so they could be included" (p. 15). He predicted that:

> … lack of collegiality will accelerate as research funding becomes tighter. This will happen not only between institutions but also within them. People are being nastier to each other, not directly (that would not be protocol) but in a very English polite fashion. That makes it even more brutal. (p. 15)

Preston's (2016) argument is important because it highlights the differential nature of the experience of higher education. His identification of the separation between the prestige (and agenda-setting clout) of the Russell Group universities and the rest also carries in terms of the prestige individual researchers yield upon meeting markers of approved performance; the receipt of major funding and publication in high ranking journals are predominant amongst these. What has developed is a climate of division and separation, where an academic's value is marked by the ability to mercenarily carve a place. This is ironic, given that academics are currently pushed heavily to (at least superficially) collaborate (albeit, perhaps, in an effort to prop-up university metrics).

The problem is a multi-dimensional one. The literature reports on the effects of this reformation of academic labour in terms of the breakdown of collegiality (Burns, Wend, & Todnem By, 2014; Damrosch, 1995; Preston, 2016), the discursive framing of "the ivory tower bully" (Nelson & Lambert, 2001, p. 83), the 'intimacy' of the workplace and the encroachment of work into personal and private aspects of life (Gregg & Seigworth, 2013), the relational dimensions of ineffective collaborations and the effects of exploitation (Bozeman, Youtie, Slade, & Gaughan, 2012), the nature of relationships of power and the uses of hierarchy as a bullying tool (Fox & Stallworth, 2009), and other similar areas of focus. Although the multi-perspective and multi-dimensional nature of incivility and disruptive behaviour that this body of research reports on indicates something of the prevalence and scale of the issue in contemporary academic settings, our focus in this chapter is on the personal and everyday effects of these changes in the university context. It also happens that these personalized accounts tend to be incomplete.

It is with this lacuna that this chapter will seek to provide a sense of how the landscape of higher education functions as one increasingly marked by fraught, and often problematic, interpersonal incivility. It is, we suggest, at the level of the personal that the effects of such incivility are felt, and we will set out a brief account of the nature of this dynamic. However, we will also argue, in light of these stark contextual features of the contemporary university, that collegiality and the confrontation of mercenary academic behaviours provide a space for pleasure, or as we characterise this here, *jouissance*. We do not seek to over-theorise the notion of *jouissance*, other than to suggest that there is a place for joyful enactment of academic work within the contemporary university and that through meaningful collegiality pleasure in academic work might be activated.

Typically, analyses of the dysfunction of academic labours at the interpersonal or 'collegial' level draw as their focus a whole-of-organization view of bullying and incivility (Burns et al., 2014) or, alternatively, the effects that these behaviours have on morale, productivity and workplace capacity (Keashley & Neuman, 2010; Schwartz, 2014). More broadly, the influence that these behaviours have on the organizational climate in the whole-of-organization is also highlighted (Raineri, Frear, & Edmonds, 2011; Twale & DeLuca, 2008). Although crucial in offering a sense of the manifold perspectives from which these issues might be considered, and aside from some prominent explorations of the intrapersonal dimensions of bullying and incivility (Hil, 2012; Nocella, Best, & McLaren, 2010), to date only a smattering of recent discussions broach the personal and affective aspects of these antisocial behaviours (e.g., Beckman, Cannella, & Wantland, 2013; Frazier, 2011; Honan, Henderson, & Loch, 2015; Motin, 2009; Nelson & Lambert, 2001). A cohesive sense of how the negative aspects of academic life locate the problem at the level of the personal has yet to find traction, as has any developed sense of the nature of the pleasure that might derive from meaningful collegiality as a counter to the more problematic aspects of the contemporary university.

We suggest that more attention should be given to the inter- and intra-personal dynamics of work in the contemporary university. In taking this approach we seek to focus on the ways that the academic workplace is constructed socio-cognitively by the individual academic in proximity with other academics-as-individuals, each carrying a variety of dispositional and epistemological points of reference for enacting work in the academy. More particularly, how certain behaviours come to be framed and given meaning interpersonally within the context of the university setting provides an opportunity to consider the influence exerted by the institution itself; that is, in terms of the very real effects the structural organization of the university has on the people who work within it. It is through the exploration of the personal and the retelling of the experience of being an academic that we gain a sense of how meaning is constructed and—perhaps more importantly—how it is framed to configure certain practices and ways-of-being as normalized. This is a recording of the personal narrative of the university, a charting of the experiences that are a result of the configurations of the space of the university and the behaviours it supports. But importantly, we seek to go beyond this diagnosis of the problems of interpersonality within present-day university settings to also map an articulation of where *jouissance* in academic labours might be found.

We will suggest then – as something of a counter to the inherent despair that the incivility of the contemporary university experience provokes (e.g., Honan et al., 2015) – that the expression of *jouissance* – a state of pleasure or joy – remains a possibility. We argue that, in the collegial encountering of incivility, scope for conceptualizing what might indeed remain as productive and worthwhile in the university can be uncovered. While we are keen to highlight that there are very real issues with the ways that universities function and are funded, we are also keen to point out that which stands as positive.

Jouissance, experienced through collegial dialogue and reflection, we contend, provides a means for considering the pleasures of academic life, and accordingly, we will move to suggest that it is within those 'little' moments – with colleagues and when engaged in work that is personally meaningful – that true joy can be experienced. While it appears that the changes that have befallen universities in recent times are primed to precisely confound any possibility for *jouissance* in the life of an academic, we will in the remainder of this chapter argue a case that identifies the possibilities for joyful collegiality and "the production of moments of pleasure" (Honan et al., 2015, p. 60).

THE CONTEXTS OF THIS INQUIRY

Within this chapter we present a twofold argument. Firstly, it will be suggested that the profound changes in global economic systems witnessed over this past decade are noticeable in reframed expectations over what it is that universities deliver as (primarily) public institutions, and that the subsumption and commodification of education within a privatized, neo-liberalist logic prime the university as a site for the sorts of negative behaviours that the literature reports (Chatterjee & Maira, 2014; Giroux 2014). Secondly, we suggest that new ways of capturing and accounting for the experience of these changes must be developed, if a cohesive sense of what these changes mean for academic life at the personal level is to gain any traction. But, equally, we argue that it is with collegiality and the joy of working interpersonally that spaces might be created to enable active responses to these negative aspects of academic labour.

Several assumptions drive this line of analysis. It is suggested that the restructuring of the university sector in many parts of the globe (particularly within Australia, New Zealand, the United States, Canada and the United Kingdom) over the last few decades has resulted in the creation of workplaces that not only accommodate, but implicitly reward, incivility and anti-collegial practices as intuitive behaviours linked to competitiveness and corporate acumen (Berryman-Fink, 1998). This shift also carries a reformation of how incivility is itself configured according to quite specific iterations that are unique to the university (Nelson & Lambert, 2001).

In these terms we will suggest that a method for uncovering the personal, everyday and often mundane or 'ordinary' experiences of the university—the normalized locations of practice—must be deployed in order to chart fully the experience of academic life. We suggest that *testimonio*—as a method of inquiry, critique and action—provides an opportunity to explore the experience of the contemporary university and, as such, offers a point from which the intrapersonal dimensions of incivility and similar other problematic behaviours might be engaged.

Testimonio as a research method has been both celebrated for the insights it provides into the personal and critiqued heavily for much the same reasons: on issues of validity and rigour (Albert & Couture, 2014; Beverley, 1991; Blackmer Reyes & Curry Rodruiguez, 2012; Yúdice, 1991). High-profile applications of *testimonio*, such as Menchú's (1984) *I, Rigoberta Menchú* and its subsequent critiques (see particularly Stoll, 1999), highlight the tensions *testimonio* carries when considered within existing paradigms of research. How might the personal be gathered to provide a testimony of what *was*? How can personal narrative be used to provide insight into the experience of the moment?

In this chapter, however, a *testimonio* approach will be used as a method for recalling the authors' own experiences as illustrative moments of the less-than-positive aspects of academic life, as well as a technique that itself provides an expression of collegiality. We were not interested in the retelling of the past as a truth to be uncovered, but we used this form of narrative reflection, in conjunction with the act of writing through our experiences, as a means for exploration. In recalling how we came to experience the university, we sought not to tell the past as it was, but to reflect on the effects this left with us. Equally, it was from this critical accounting of the personal experiences of the university shared through dialogue that a commonality was forged. We did not always agree and often held differing views about moments of shared witness; but that was where the value of accounting for individual experience lay.

In recording these experiences and sharing these moments in considered reflection, accounts of both the university and the formation of a strong collegiality materialized. It was here that *jouissance* emerged and these expressions of our collegiality found meaning as joyous camaraderie and shared experience. These outcomes took us beyond the "writing, recording, crying, reading, viewing, and crying some more" that the university sector has induced in others, towards experiences that "open us to the productive possibilities of a strong commitment to pleasure" (Honan et al., 2015, pp. 60, 44).

At times our dialogues were irreverent. Sometimes, these were cathartic expressions that drew on exasperated critiques of what was witnessed. On other occasions, these dialogues caused deep empathy with colleagues or amazement over decisions made for the university. In this regard, our dialogues were *dangerous*. These dialogues opened a chance to speak freely—with *parrhesia*—to unburden frustration and anxieties through shared negotiation. *Testimonio* offered a chance to speak openly with candour and irreverence. In short, *testimonio* was deployed as a method of utility for excavating personal experiences of the university and to commence dialogue.

It is to this end that the title of this chapter – and, more explicitly, its reference to the *idios kosmos* – finds application. *Testimonio* provides scope to chart the *idios kosmos* of personal experiences of the university, via accounts that record the affective, personal and *inner* reactions to contemporary academic labours. While we are cautious in taking the idea of the *idios kosmos*, what has been called the "unique private world" of the individual (Dick, 1975, p. 32), too literally and prescriptively, we suggest that as a metaphor it opens for view the internal sense-making and emotional realizations personal experiences provoke. In drawing some form of definition to the term, we borrow from Philip K. Dick (1975) who suggests that each person has "two unique worlds, the idios kosmos, which is a unique private world, and the koinos kosmos, which literally means shared world (just as idios means private); indeed, "no person can tell which part of his total worldview is idios kosmos and which is koinos kosmos, except by the achievement of a strong empathetic rapport with other people" (pp. 31–32).

Two aspects of this account are significant. Firstly, Dick (1975) highlights the inner 'private world' of personal sense-making drawn from experience and the shared accounting that this process of reflecting on and negotiating with the world prescribes. In our collaboration, this existential process of drawing into consciousness personal productions of meaning was created via *testimonio*, written through personal narrative as testimony (Park-Fuller, 2000). The process of bringing to consciousness the minutiae of experience and making sense of these experiences through writing – the production of narrative – provided the means for uncovering the *idios kosmos* of the authors.

Secondly, Dick's (1975) assertion of the "strong empathetic rapport" (p. 32) was embraced via narrative. Through the act of writing and sharing with others the sense of the experiences encountered, a shared world (or *koinos kosmos*) of what these experiences meant was generated. Through the sharing and further dialogic co-construction of these narratives, a sense of what it meant to work within the contemporary university was exposed. This realization of how the experiences of the Self might also be shared by others through dialogue and narrative provided moments of empathetic rapport. This was central to the approach to *testimonio* detailed here and the opportunities that this offered for irreverent *jouissance*.

In this regard, accounts from the *idios kosmos* point toward a view of the experience of the present-day university currently missing in the literature. By framing *testimonio* as a useful methodological approach mobilized by a focus on the sense-making processes individuals engage in as part of the realization of the *idios kosmos*, a powerful view of the effects (and *affects*) of the modern-day university emerges. Our interest was in charting what the experience of the contemporary university is *like*, and how this comes to be understood and reacted against according to how meanings of it are produced and rationalized through the Self and in empathetic rapport with Others (who are also experiencing these instances).

METHODS OF INQUIRY

We are two long-term academics with backgrounds in the disciplines of Cultural Studies and Education and interests in research that records the experiential, the phenomenological and affective aspects of being-in-the-world. These concerns are hopefully already apparent, but in placing emphasis on this approach to research we hope to demonstrate the usefulness of *testimonio* for *jouissance*.

Our specific approach drew on the capture of, and reflection on, what we came to refer to as *narrative artefacts* of our experiences of the university. These artefacts presented as *moments* – encounters, experiences, events – that were retold and narrativized as instances of experience. We recorded short narrative accounts in the form that Bleakley (2000) identifies. Upon working into narrative our personal experiences and reflections of these moments – all subjectively and idiosyncratically crafted from the point of view of the Self (our purpose here was not to attempt the recording of some form of an objective or immutable *Truth*) – we shared the narratives and opened what we had recorded for further discussion and reflection.

These reflective narratives had a multiple effect. At the superficial level, this retelling of our experiences brought to consciousness accounts of events and moments that otherwise would have been lost in the busyness and turbulence of an *ordinary* work day. We shared between us illustrative but ultimately *everyday* examples of the ways that we felt the university was formulated as a site of incivility. These narrative artefacts did not necessarily detail explicitly (physically or symbolically) *extraordinary* moments, nor did they attempt to represent universal, generalizable accounts of the experience of the contemporary university shared by anyone else other than ourselves. But these narratives did draw important attention to the more benign and everyday instances of academic life that *we* had each encountered.

The narratives that formed offered something of a *bildungsroman* of our experiences as academics. The stock of material that was captured via our *testimonio* narratives offered more than just accounts of the moments we noticed and reflected upon. As with any personal narrative, we too were written into these accounts, with the narratives standing as indicative of *where we were* in relation to the university and what we were noticing. The accounts grew and merged as our reflections developed. These narratives came to represent what Linda Park-Fuller (2000) identifies as "autobiographical staged personal narratives in which the autobiographical material performed is not collected from others and embodied by the performer, but is, rather, the performer's own story" (p. 21). These were our stories as much as they were accounts of discrete moments.

It soon emerged that as we drew attention to the sorts of everyday expressions of incivility and similar anti-social behaviours that further instances surfaced. We were beginning to recognize and were becoming sensitive to other instances. It also occurred that many of these moments were experienced by each of us—in most cases with some nuance that reflected our relative positions, but nonetheless as moments that were mutually recognized as significant. We had found an approach that provided us the space to reflect on these seemingly benign expressions of life in the contemporary university. As these dialogues developed, we crafted an increasingly sophisticated approach for not only recognizing moments that otherwise would have been accepted as 'ordinary' (and hence forgotten), but also for problematizing that which was taken-for-granted in the interactions we were having. Ordinary moments turned out to be not so ordinary when considered against the growing stock of reportings we had developed.

We do not wish to suggest that what was at play here was some form of *false-consciousness* or something from which we had developed the critical keys to unlock an awareness of the full 'horror' of academic life. Indeed, what this approach to noticing the otherwise everyday and ordinary enabled was an awareness of the ways certain practices and actions came to be normalized. While we did notice and reflect on the multiple ways that positive interpersonal behaviours find activation in the contemporary university (such as the way very positive interpersonal relationships formed and prospered in response to some of the more problematic aspects of the university), our focus was primarily to chart the ways that those less-than-positive aspects of academic life materialized and became rationalized as *normal.*

We take the approach that Ira Shor (1987) advocates according to his critical pedagogical approach of *extraordinarily re-experiencing the ordinary.* The ordinary provided the terrain upon which the workings of the university could be examined, and from which the responses and reactions to the everyday engaged by each of us as academics could be explored and considered. The narrative artefacts we reflected on, recorded and shared between us offered an insight into the terrain of the university – one that is simultaneously intra-subjectively symbolic and reflective of the complex interpersonal relationships that shape current academic life.

It was with this, however, that a major implication in this approach to using *testimonio* recordings of experience developed. In short, our narratives and the dialogues we shared were *fun*. While our subject matter dealt with often worrying observations of incivility, in sharing these accounts and charting our relative experience of the university we inhabited, a collegiality developed between us. While we had worked together previously, and shared friendship beyond our formal collegial connection, this process of writing offered a further insight into how we each encountered the university and undertook our practice. It was with this that the joy of shared experience emerged. Our narrativized reflections provided a chance for laughter, candid appraisal, irreverent critique and most of all, shared collegiality – an experience of emerging *jouissance*.

In detailing this approach, we seek to contribute to accounts of the university already present in the literature that draw variously on ethnographic (Fox & Stallworth, 2009), case study (Bozeman et al., 2012) and even statistical (Twale & DeLuca, 2008) methodologies and data sources to highlight that the contemporary university is in something of a crisis. As a site increasingly prone to incivility, we suggest that it is through the personal narratives that *testimonio* provides that an image of the personal terrain of the university might be cast into view, and from which some sense of the shared experience of the work lives and practices of academics might be understood.

MOMENTS FROM THE ORDINARY

As one expression of the approach detailed here, the following discussion is taken from one particular entry of the *Testimonio Log* we compiled. This entry was not selected for use in this chapter for any reason other than that it represents the sorts of discussions we had, and that it provides insight into how it is we came to think about and construct meaning from moments and experiences that were otherwise innocuous and *ordinary*. Although in the moment we felt something was not right with the experiences we came to recall later, it was not until we came to share our experiences in dialogue and commit these to writing that they took on their full meaning.

Email provided a useful method for recording our dialogues. This method of writing and transferring ideas was immediate, captured, easily appended and continuous. While we did on occasion share concerns that we were indeed figuratively using the master's tools to dismantle the master's house (to poorly paraphrase Audre Lorde's famous maxim, see Lorde, 1984), and that email like most other aspects of the contemporary university was monitored, it remained that email provided a mechanism to effectively capture and share our reflections.

Over the course of several months through 2014 and 2015, we set out our dialogue and our *testimonio*. The following entry, as one example from this log, was recorded in July–August 2014.

Hi Robyn,

I had an interesting experience this afternoon in my [School's staff research forum] ... In short, we had an address from [a senior member of staff], and as part of the presentation (in which a vision for the Faculty and how this aligns with current funding climates, the University's strategic initiatives and so on was offered), discussion turned to the recent [University climate survey results].

This discussion was fascinating! It followed some perhaps 'usual' lines of inquiry (particularly around how reported issues of academic 'disgruntlement' have been pacified and massaged), but turned specifically to the growing divide between Academic staff and Professional staff of the University.

It was noted by one of my colleagues, who happens to hold a formal Administrative role as a School Coordinator, that she had recently witnessed during a significant University-level committee meeting an Academic staff member being spoken to 'like she was a recalcitrant preschooler'. She went on to highlight her concerns with anyone being spoken to – young or old, high rank or low rank – in this way, and conjured the imagery of having witnessed this colleague being 'barked at' by the Professional staff member for asking questions of a new teaching and learning policy that had been devised by a group of managers in the University; one it turns out that had received no input or advice from Academic staffers (the people who will now be obliged to follow this policy). Apparently the meeting then descended into something of a farce, whereby Academics generally were castigated and demonized by the majority Professional staff present at this meeting.

Andrew

Hi Andrew

I read your email with interest. The example you discuss seems to describe the everyday workplace practices that I am noticing as well. As an example, a recent email was sent by a member of the senior management ... That email was pleasant enough. It was addressed to 'Dear Colleagues' and invited academic staff to participate in a divisional initiative. A month later, a follow-up email was sent by a professional staff member. This time the message was simple:

REMINDER Deadline for submissions is 5pm, Monday 28 June

Although the words seem innocuous, it was the presentation of the message that shocked me. It appeared in red lettering in a font twice the size of the font of the original email and the message was in bold. What was the over-riding message here? One reading, of course, is that the professional staff member was sending a timely and supportive reminder to academics so that they wouldn't miss the deadline. However, on the other hand, intertextuality comes into play. Capital letters are recognized widely in netiquette rules as yelling or being angry, and bold, larger font suggests the same. Traditionally in schools, the red pen was used as the pen of judgement – the red pen of judgement. So another reading is that the reminder is an imperative, a directive – meet the deadline! There have been other emails too that have used similar emphasis techniques – yelling in a sense – and have seemed more explicit in their message – public displays of professional staff directing academic staff. In one example, the techniques described earlier (large size, red, bold font), along with three asterisks at the beginning and another three at the end seemed to 'bark' an order to academics:

All course examiners are required to check the draft ... timetable and forward any changes to ... by ...

The remainder of the email contained a conglomeration of bold, underlining and italic font for emphasis, with a set of rules. For example:

Any requests for specific times/days will be disregarded unless there are extenuating circumstances and will require the approval of the Head of School; **Requests to change the timetable after enrolments open will not be considered unless there are unforeseen circumstances.**

Interestingly, "please" had been added to a number of these 'rules', but there is something contradictory about adding please to an imperative: for example:

Please <u>do not</u> assume or expect it to remain the same; Please notify ... Please inform ...

Perhaps I'm overly sensitive, but these did not seem like friendly instructions to me. Am I being oversensitive?

Robyn

We do not wish to suggest that our dialogue, as reported here, stood for anything more than the reactions we each had to this specific moment. Our point was not to vilify colleagues – professional colleagues especially – nor identify for scrutiny any specific section within the university for any particular reason. What we sought to do was to share our frustrations, and how these were provoked in these moments, and to share commonality of experience. This had several effects.

Firstly, it offered a chance to unburden these frustrations and to excise the angst of the situation. It also offered a chance to take stock of our own situatedness within the university and to consider how things were and how we were perceived. In relaying these accounts of how others engaged with us (albeit often negatively), we took time to take stock of our place in the university and how it was that the university positioned our work and place as academics. But perhaps most significantly, this recording of narrative also offered the chance for collegiality – to trade notes and to share experiences. We realized that the experiences we each had were not unique and there was, within this, a comfort of knowing that there was something bigger at play than just the encounters we had each had. It was with this that *jouissance* emerged; there was relief in knowing that we were not alone in these experiences and that the joy of finding collegiality in shared experience was always present.

FINAL NOTES

A critique of the approach detailed in this chapter might suggest some "so what?" questions: Why does this matter, and how does the sharing of experience via *testimonio* result in anything other than indulgent self-realization, let alone meaningful change?

We do not wish to claim that, through *testimonio* and shared narrative, structural change of the university will result. To argue accordingly would be to extend the effects of dialogue and shared narrative too far. But when considered in terms of the isolation many academics feel, and the alienation from the work environments of the university that life in the academy provokes, a comfort is borne from knowing that the experiences of the Self are not singular or idiosyncratic and that other colleagues too might be experiencing similar things.

It has become something of a taboo to acknowledge doubt or anything other than total confidence in one's abilities in academia. In a world of stark competition for positions, funding and resources, to declare vulnerability is generally seen as a sign of weakness. This is a great shame, and when considered in terms of the problems of toxic academic environments (including growing mental health issues as Wilcox, 2014, highlights), finding opportunities for collegiality and shared experience is important. This is not a therapy, but something more profoundly human. The dialogues that we each shared moved us to realize that we were not alone in our experiences and that problematic changes to the landscape of the university were experienced in ordinary, everyday ways. Although structural responses to these changes still require enactment, as a first step at least, collegiality was found. It was also the case too that *jouissance* borne from this collegiality was generated.

For Hourigan (2015), *jouissance* stands as "the pleasure taken from suffering and most often this suffering is the result of some symbolic limit ... that prohibits or entices certain actions on the part of the subject" (p. 125). Our articulation here differs slightly from Hourigan's in that our pain was not inflicted purposefully, but it was witnessed in events occurring around us. The manifestation of incivility in the practices of the university provoked this inquiry and the recording of the personal experiences that provided impetus for our *testimonio*. From this, the joy of collegiality emerged, with *jouissance* materializing when the "pain is overcome through the commitment to the act" (Hourigan, 2015, p. 118) of writing through and engaging in dialogue of our experience.

REFERENCES

Albert, M-N., & Couture, M-M. (2014). Explore new avenues: Experiential testimonio research. *Management Decision, 52*(4), 794–812.

Beckmann, C. A., Cannella, B. L., & Wantland, D. (2013). Faculty perceptions of bullying in schools of nursing. *Journal of Professional Nursing, 29*(5), 297–294.

Berryman-Fink, C. (1998). Can we agree to disagree? Faculty-faculty conflict. In S. A. Holton (Ed.), *Mending the cracks in the ivory tower: Strategies for conflict management in higher education* (pp. 141–163). Bolton, MA: Anker Publishing.

Beverley, J. (1991). "Through all things modern": Second thoughts on testimonio. *Boundary, 18*(2), 1–21.

Blackmer Reyes, K., & Curry Rodriguez, J. E. (2012). Testimonio: Origins, terms and resources. *Equity and Excellence in Education, 45*(3). Available at http://works.bepress.com/julia_curry/1/

Bleakley, A. (2000). Writing with invisible ink: Narrative, confessionalism and reflective practice. *Reflective Practice, 1*(1), 11–24.

Bozeman, B., Youtie, J., Slade, C. P., & Gaughan, M. (2012). The "dark side" of academic research collaborations: Case studies in exploitation, bullying and unethical behavior. In *Annual Meeting of the Society for Social Studies of Science (4S)*, October, pp. 17–20.

Burns, B., Wend, P., & Todnem By, R. (2014). The changing face of English universities: Reinventing collegiality for the twenty-first century. *Studies in Higher Education, 39*(6), 905–926.

Chatterjee, P., & Maira, S. (2014). *The imperial university: Academic repression and scholarly dissent*. Minneapolis, MN: University of Minnesota Press.

Damrosch, D. (1995). *We scholars: Changing the culture of the university*. New York, NY: Harvard University Press.

Dick, P. (1975). *Electric shepherd*. Melbourne, Vic.: Norstrilia Press.

Fogg, P. (2008). Academic bullies. *Chronicle of Higher Education, 55*(3), B10–B13.

Fox, S. & Stallworth, L. E. (2009). Building a framework for two internal organizational approaches to resolving and preventing workplace bullying: Alternative dispute resolution and training. *Consulting Psychology Journal: Practice and Research, 61*(3), 220–241.

Frazier, K. N. (2011). Academic bullying: A barrier to tenure and promotion for African-American faculty. *Florida Journal of Educational Administration and Policy, 5*(1), 1–13.

Giroux, H. A. (2014). *Neoliberalism's war on higher education*. New York, NY: Haymarket.

Gregg, M., & Seigworth, G. J. (2010). *The affect theory reader*. Durham, NC: Duke University Press.

Hil, R. (2012). *Whacademia: An insider's account of the troubled university*. Sydney, NSW: NewSouth.

Honan, E., Henderson, L., & Loch, S. (2015). Producing moments of pleasure within the confines of an academic quantified self. *Creative Approaches to Research, 8*(3), 44–62.

Hourigan, D. (2015). *Law and enjoyment: Power, pleasure and psychoanalysis*. New York, NY: Routledge.

Keashley, L. & Neuman, J. H. (2010). Faculty experiences with bullying in higher education: Causes, consequences and management. *Administrative Theory and Practice, 32*(1), 48–70.

Lorde, A. (1984). *Sister outsider: Essays and speeches*. Trumansburg, NY: The Crossing Press.

Morley, L., & Crossouard, B. (2016). Gender in the neoliberalised global academy: The affective economy of women and leadership in South Asia. *British Journal of Sociology of Education, 37*(1), 149–168.

Motin, S. (2009). Bullying or mobbing: Is it happening in your academic library? *Library Faculty Publications*, Paper 28. Available from http://repository.stcloudstate.edu/lrs_facpubs/28/

Menchú, R. (1984). *I, Rigoberta Menchú: An Indian woman in Guatemala*. London: Verso.

Nelson, E. D., & Lambert, R. D. (2001). Sticks, stones and semantics: The ivory tower bully's vocabulary of motives. *Qualitative Sociology, 24*(1), 83–106.

Nocella, A. J., Best, S., & McLaren, P. (Eds.). (2010). *Academic repression: Reflections from the academic industrial complex*. New York, NY: AK Press.

Park-Fuller, L. M. (2000). Performing absence: The staged personal narrative as testimony. *Text and Performance Quarterly, 20*(1), 20–42.

Preston, J. (2016). No future? Education research at new universities. *Research Intelligence, 129*, 14–15.

Raineri, E. M., Frear, D. F., & Edmonds, J. J. (2011). An examination of the academic reach of faculty and administrator bullying. *International Journal of Business and Social Science, 2*(12), 22–35.

Schwartz, M. (2014). *How the education of healthcare professionals became corrupted*. New York, NY: Brill.

Shor, I. (1987). *Critical teaching and everyday life*. Chicago, IL: University of Chicago Press.

Stoll, D. (1999). *Rigoberta Menchú and the story of all poor Guatemalans*. Boulder, CO: Westview Press.

Twale, D. J., & DeLuca, B. M. *Faculty incivility: The rise of the academic bully culture and what to do about it*. San Francisco, CA: Jossey-Bass.

Wilcox, C. (2014). Lighting dark: Fixing academia's mental health problem. *New Scientist, 2990*, 112–116.

Yúdice, G. (1991). Testimonio and postmodernism. *Latin American Perspectives, 18*(3), 15–31.

Andrew Hickey
School of Arts and Communication
University of Southern Queensland, Australia

Robyn Henderson
School of Teacher Education and Early Childhood
University of Southern Queensland, Australia

ERICH C. FEIN, RAHUL GANGULY, THOMAS BANHAZI, AND
PATRICK ALAN DANAHER

13. SELF-DETERMINATION THEORY AND ACADEMIC LIFE

Strategies for Reclaiming Pleasure and Professionalism Distilled from Universities in Australia and Europe

INTRODUCTION

Contemporary scholarship is replete with accounts and analyses of the challenges and complexities of current academic life. Much of this scholarship sounds alarm bells – even clarion calls – with regard to the sustainability and value of academics' work. For example, Olson (2013) lamented that "Academe is often plagued by inexcusably rude and uncollegial behaviour" (p. 1) and that "This culture of incivility is becoming ubiquitous" (p. 1).

Against the backdrop of this growing concern about the integrity and professionalism of those who work in and for universities, it is timely to consider possible counternarratives to these dominant discourses attending contemporary academic work. Again there is a considerable and growing body of research devoted to these counternarratives. For instance, Gannon, Kligyte, McLean, Perrier, Swan, Vanni and van Rijswink (2015), a largely Australian group of feminist researchers, drew on "feminist scholarship about race and diversity" to propose "that the methodology of collective biography might engender more sustainable and ethical ways of being in academic workplaces because it provides the resources to begin to create a new collective imaginary of academia" (p. 189). Arguing against the "responsibilisation discourse, promoted as 'distributed leadership', [which] is a technology of indirect management" in universities currently, Amsler and Shore (2017) advocated critically informed textual analysis as a technique for rendering explicit and transparent these kinds of strategies of control of academic work from a New Zealand perspective.

These selected snapshots of multiple accounts and competing discourses related to the work and identities of contemporary academics help to situate this chapter, which constitutes the inaugural collaboration among all four authors. We exhibit a wide range of disciplinary backgrounds (organizational behaviour, special education, agriculture, and education), research paradigms and theoretical perspectives; moreover, we have worked as academics and researchers in a number of countries and continents, including Australia, Europe, Malaysia and the United States. Significantly, what brought us together in this chapter were initially disparate and incidental conversations about the seemingly inexorable onrush of the forces of managerialism and marketization in the current higher education sector. Working at the same campus of the same Australian university afforded us the opportunity to use the writing of this chapter as a means of reflecting deeply on how we understand those forces individually and collectively and the strategies – with varying degrees of effectiveness – that we have put in place to reclaim some elements of pleasure and professionalism in our work. The chapter is accordingly intended to contribute to the broader project of the book in which it is located in relation to both the specific conceptual framework, centred on SDT, that we mobilize below and the distinctive experiences and our analyses of those experiences that we present later in the chapter as a demonstration of the application of this conceptual framework.

The chapter has been divided into the following three sections:
- A combined literature review and conceptual framework that posits the three fundamental psychological needs identified by SDT – competence, autonomy and relatedness – as encapsulating wider concerns of contemporary academics;
- A discussion of vignettes as a viable and valuable research method to advance the analysis in this chapter;
- A presentation of the vignettes and their accompanying analysis.

LITERATURE REVIEW AND CONCEPTUAL FRAMEWORK

The Nature of Human Needs

Given the posited vicissitudes of current academic life both in Australia and internationally outlined above, it is clearly important to examine the psychology of human needs in order to analyse how and why contemporary academics understand and engage with the material conditions framing their work and identities in university organizational environments. From this perspective, needs-based theories of motivation are an important part of understanding people – how they make decisions and function in everyday life and across the lifespan. In recent years, the framework of SDT has been supported by large amounts of empirical research (Greguras & Diefendorff, 2009; Lee, Sheldon, & Turban, 2003), which has been a key factor driving the resurgence of needs-based theories in applied psychology and management (Prentice, Halusic, & Sheldon, 2014). Within these needs-based theories, there is an assumption that people require one or more "nutrients" – something from the environment that a person must access and use as part of fulfilling basic life processes. The term "nutrient" often connotes physiological elements like food and water, but within motivational contexts it can also refer to psychosocial stimuli that drive the fulfilment of basic psychological needs. Accordingly, within the social context of needs theories, people must derive more than physical nutrition from their environments. People must also draw social and psychological nutrients – such as positive human relationships – from environments if they are to function effectively and to live with an integrated sense of health and wellbeing.

Needs theorists claim that there is a dialectic, or an ongoing interaction and balance, between the quality and level of nutrients afforded by environments and the fullness or emptiness of internal states within a person (Ryan & Deci, 2002). Here there are two important assumptions: firstly, that a person must have a basic level of fulfilment with respect to some nutrients in order to have healthy function; and secondly, that there must be an ongoing balance between need states within people and the level of nutrients afforded by the environment. It is important to note the implication that adequate levels of psychosocial nutrients must be present in an environment if that environment is to be good for people.

Self-Determination Theory (SDT)

SDT starts from these assumptions but goes further in positing that there are three specific types of social and psychological nutrients required by people for healthy functioning. Within this framework, SDT assumes that people have inborn or innate tendencies and corresponding basic needs for growth and integration, where growth is evident via effective learning and adaptation to environments, and where integration points towards states of interconnection with aspects of the self and others (Ryan & Deci, 2002). SDT assumes that these tendencies for personal growth, intrapersonal integration (inner organization and integration of aspects of the self) and interpersonal integration (integration with other people) are innate and programmed into people by their basic design. Therefore SDT claims that these tendencies are not acquired or learned motives, but rather that people must live out these innate tendencies as part of their human essence. As essential foundations, such basic tendencies are universal across all places and times, although exactly how such tendencies are fulfilled and manifested can vary by culture.

According to the structure within needs theories, people will seek to fulfil deficits in their needs by activating their corresponding action patterns, and we note in this context that SDT claims that humans have three fundamental psychological needs, each with corresponding action patterns or tendencies. The first fundamental psychological need, *competence*, can be considered a need to enhance and practise skilled action – in essence, practising skills that result in the successful attainment of goals. Here corresponding action patterns or tendencies would include actions that enhance the felt sense of confidence and effectiveness in choice and behaviour, actions that allow the feeling and judging of oneself as effective in social environments, and the act of seeking challenges optimal to one's skills and abilities (Deci & Ryan, 2002).

The second fundamental psychological need, *autonomy*, is essentially about perceiving the self as the origin and source of one's own behaviours. It can be seen when people generate goals and behaviours on their own or when people honestly endorse the goals and behaviours of others (Ryan & Deci, 2002). It is important to note that the need for autonomy does not equal the need for independence. Autonomy does not mean that people do not permit or rely on external influences – it would be difficult to have effective human functioning in the absence of all social influence. The need for autonomy does, however, suggest that one can autonomously enact values and behaviours that others have requested, provided that they are genuinely endorsed by the actor (Kasser, 2002). Thus, autonomous individuals would show action patterns rich in generating novel behaviours and endorsing and believing in the utility of the goals and the corresponding behaviours requested by others.

The third fundamental psychological need, *relatedness*, can be considered as the effective integration of oneself with others. The need for relatedness implies that people must have some amount of interpersonal connection with others. Here corresponding action patterns or tendencies would include actions that enhance felt connections such as caring for others and being cared for by others. It includes a sense of belonging with others and with a larger community, as well as a secure sense of communion and unity (Skinner & Edge, 2002).

SDT and Work Contexts

Because of the dialectical aspects of needs theories, there is a constant negotiation and balance between internal, personal levels of the three fundamental psychological needs and the quality that environments afford in satisfying each of these three needs. SDT assumes that there is a personal, ongoing search for social contexts that nurture humans based on these three fundamental psychological needs, and that the affordances of rich contexts will allow people to pursue healthy patterns of activities. Thus, it is possible to consider high quality work contexts to be characterized as work environments that enable and promote psychological states that enhance competence, autonomy and relatedness.

With respect to competence, a work environment should generally enable individuals both to maintain levels of skilled action and to develop new patterns of action. Such activities must be attuned to outcomes that are valued by the social contexts that people navigate. However, at the same time the goals and actions should be relatively autonomous, in that individuals are enabled to pursue skills and goals of their own choosing or endorsement – so that they either generate their own goals or honestly endorse the goals of others. In such environments, individuals should be allowed, encouraged and empowered to learn or practise skills and actions that are personally important and meaningful to personal as well as organizational fulfilment.

With respect to autonomy, a work environment should generally allow individuals either to develop goals and behaviours on their own or to accept genuinely the goals and behaviours that are required by the work context. Such genuine acceptance requires a belief in the usefulness and merit of the goals and actions required. We note here that considerable SDT research has offered distinctions between different patterns of behaviour that are relatively higher or lower in elements of autonomy (Deci & Ryan, 2002; Ryan & Deci, 2002). On the autonomous side of choice and action, the terms *integrated regulation* and *identified regulation* imply that the behaviours required by the workplace have been accepted as valuable and are incorporated into the goal and action patterns of individuals. The notion of *introjected regulation* implies choice and action that are in between autonomous and controlled behaviours, where the actions demanded by the work environment are internalized into a person's work-specific goals and action patterns, but they are not truly accepted. *External regulation* describes action patterns that are extrinsic to, and the least autonomous for, the actor. In these cases, people do things only to obtain rewards or avoid punishment and one's reasons for behaviour are to satisfy external demands or social contingencies (Deci & Ryan, 2002; Ryan & Deci, 2002).

With respect to relatedness, healthy work environments allow the time and space for interpersonal connection with others. Such connections would be based on goals and patterns of practice that enhance felt connections. Examples of such work activities can include mentoring, leadership and the development of informal relationships with peers, as well as the phenomenon of allowing oneself to be cared for by others. It includes a sense of belonging with others and a sense of belonging to a larger community of practice. In such work contexts, people do not generally feel under threat, and there would usually be a secure sense of communion and unity of action and purpose. Table 1 lays out the types of goals and action patterns afforded in work environments that are healthy with respect to the three fundamental psychological needs deployed in this chapter. Based on SDT, employee wellbeing would be related to the relative strength of these contexts, although we recognize that, within the neoliberal enterprise, it would be unusual to have all types of goals and actions supported by any individual organization.

Changes in the Academic Working Environment

Table 1 enables us to situate the specific psychological needs of academics in a broader perspective. For instance, numerous authors have noted academics' perceptions of the changing nature of academic work (Enders & de Weert, 2009). Some of the major trends across these changes include new types of students with different expectations, less public support of higher education, the rise of neoliberal hybrid institutions mixing profit motives with traditional state support and an according rise of audit cultures in institutions (Enders & de Weert, 2009). The latter trend has been interpreted as a new form of public management that threatens the power, legitimacy, autonomy and status of members of the academic profession and their identities (Enders, de Boer, & Leišytė, 2009). Our question, then, is how these trends translate into changing the nature of the academic employment context.

One way to address this question is to look at other specific, relevant global changes in the life space of academics that have been noted by numerous authors (Fairweather, 2009; Finkelstein & Iglesias, 2015) as having a direct and continuing impact on academics' lives and work and on their opportunities for enacting their professionalism and producing pleasure in doing so. We turn in the next section of the chapter to propose vignettes as a viable and valuable research method for investigating our selected experiences of academic work and for considering our proposed strategies for maximising the enjoyment and value of those experiences.

Table 1. SDT-based healthy work environments

	Characteristic goals	**Action patterns supported**
Competence	To promote skill maintenance relative to one's work context. To promote skill mastery relative to one's work context. To promote skill acquisition relative to one's work context. To explore the potential utility of possible new skills. To evaluate the means for acquiring new skills. To increase personal self-regard through the mastery of skills.	The maintenance of already valued activities. The chance to develop new skills and patterns of action. Practising patterns that result in increased confidence in personal action. Practising patterns that allow one to judge oneself as effective in social environments.
Autonomy	To develop personally-set goals. To achieve the honest endorsement of organizationally-set goals. To experience low or no felt threat from organizationally-set goals.	The chance to plan, organize and live out one's work day in one's own way. The chance to say "no" to goals that one does not endorse or support. The chance to say "no" to goals that compete with or take time from more important goals.
Relatedness	To increase positive social interactions during job performance. To increase community connections within the workplace. To promote a de-emphasis on organizational politics and impression management. To promote external connectedness and felt benevolence for the natural world and others.	Spending time with co-workers and colleagues without immediate performance pressures. Spending time mentoring new arrivals and early career employees. Spending time specifically to build team cohesion.

RESEARCH METHOD

Vignettes are an increasingly effective and popular research method in qualitative research accounts (Tracy, 2013). Furthermore, vignettes have been deployed in a range of scholarly disciplines, including business (Bryman & Bell, 2015), criminology (Maxfield & Babbie, 2016) and nursing (LoBiondo-Wood & Haber, 2014).

According to Arthur, Mitchell, Lewis and McNaughton Nicholls (2014), "Vignettes are short descriptions of a particular circumstance, person, or event, which might be described verbally by the researcher or shown in a written or video version" (p. 166). While Bryman and Bell (2015) associated vignettes with "presenting respondents with one or more scenarios and then asking them how they would respond when confronted with the circumstances of that scenario" (p. 270), we have elected to construct our vignettes (outlined in the next section) based on our perceptions of how our colleagues and we would respond to questions about the three key concepts in SDT outlined above: competence, autonomy and relatedness. Our deployment of the vignette research method is therefore close to the characterization by Tracy (2013):

> A vignette is "a focused description of a series of events taken to be representative, typical, or emblematic" (Miles & Huberman, 1994, p. 81). Vignettes are similar to exemplars in that they exemplify a key argument or claim. They are different in that the researcher (re)constructs the example by purposefully collecting and piecing together data (rather than by *finding* the exemplar intact within the data). (*emphasis in original*)

With regard to this chapter, the distilled character of the vignettes presented below has enabled us similarly to discuss sensitive issues in ways that are still rigorous and grounded in material realities while minimising the ethical dilemma of analysing contentious situations without infringing anonymity and confidentiality. We have also found the generation of the vignettes to be simultaneously pleasurable and therapeutic.

DATA ANALYSIS

Having outlined the chapter's conceptual framework, clustered around the three concepts of competence, autonomy and relatedness in relation to SDT, having located these concepts in selected literature about contemporary academic work and identities, and having proposed the use of vignettes as potentially powerful encapsulations of broader psychosocial issues, we turn now to deploy three such vignettes in order to illustrate threats to the academic environment in relation to the three critical psychological states within SDT. We present these vignettes in the order in which the states were presented in Table 1: namely, competence first, followed by autonomy and then by relatedness. In doing so, we contend that these narrative constructions constitute a striking synthesis of wider issues pertaining to reclaiming pleasure and professionalism in contemporary academic life, gleaned through the insights afforded by SDT and its concepts of competence, autonomy and relatedness.

The Vignettes

Competence We begin with the competence vignette, in which we have characterized competence as a state where individuals both maintain levels of skilled action and develop and internalize new patterns of action that reflect outcomes valued by their social contexts. From that perspective, it is no secret that academic life presents a demand to "publish or perish". For instance, the current university research environment in Australia is dominated by Excellence in Research for Australia (ERA), Australia's national research evaluation framework (http://www.arc.gov.au/excellence-research-australia). Research evaluation frameworks in other countries include the Research Assessment Exercise [RAE] and subsequently the Research Excellence Framework [REF] in the United Kingdom and the Performance Based Research Fund [PBRF] in New Zealand.) The scheme places a high value on the quality of publcations, which in turn drives researchers to higher levels of methodological rigour and demands that they keep pace with up-to-the-minute changes in methodological advances. By itself, this is a good thing. However, academics are also experiencing the bind of work intensification, where there is too much work given, based on what can reasonably be expected in a given time frame (Conway & Sturges, 2014). Our previous research about work intensification (Fein, Skinner, & Machin, in press) illustrated that work intensification promotes burnout and other depletion-based outcomes. The threat to competence exists based on the climate of work intensification experienced by most academics, which means that the demands of everyday academic life (e.g., high teaching loads, pressure to publish) crowd out the mental and temporal resources required to learn and master new knowledge and skills (Meyers, 2012).

One example is the situation experienced during one author's tenure at a large, metropolitan university in Australia with an enrolment of more than 35,000 students. This situation started at the beginning of an academic year, when a university research centre paid for all research active staff to attend training in state-of-the-art methodology. This required some five days in residence. Here we had a significant investment of time as well as money. Unfortunately, after the week of training, each staff member who attended the training was forced immediately back onto the treadmill of teaching and administration that accompanies the beginning of an academic term. With the exception of one individual who entered a period of sabbatical research leave and who was wisely able to practise applying the software to data on hand, the staff members were unable actually to sit down and use the software until the end of the term (if they confined this practice to normal working hours). This significant delay seriously harmed the process of skill transfer, and frustrated the staff members' genuine desire to master the new skills immediately after instruction.

In the Australian university system, it is common to attend effective training at one point in time, but paradoxically to be denied the work hours needed to transfer the training to everyday practice. The embedding and application of skills and knowledge learned in a discrete training context are vital to experiencing the benefits promised by the training (Zumrah, Boyle, & Fein, 2013). Furthermore, the process of transfer is very close to the idea of experiencing competence as a critical psychological state, as experiencing competence would be a logical by product of the effective transfer of training.

Autonomy As we noted above, autonomy does not necessarily equate with independence; it is possible for individual actors to accept others' goals and behaviours, provided that they endorse those goals and behaviours. Nevertheless, autonomy implies actors having a reasonable capability to generate their own goals and behaviours and/or to have a high degree of influence on the goals and behaviours generated in collaborative enterprises in which they participate. This is against the broader backdrop of changing government policies towards "[t]he concept of 'regulatory autonomy' [that] captures the use of organizational autonomy of universities as a tool of a new regime of governmental autonomy" (Enders, de Boer, & Weyer, 2013, p. 5).

Accordingly, it is salutary to consider the situations of academics who increasingly teach in courses with more than one staff member teaching in them. Potentially such courses can generate significant benefits for students and academics alike, with enhanced insights being derived from multiple perspectives (Kolluru, Roesch, & Akhtar de la Fuente, 2012). Yet often the reasons for such courses are economic, related to cost efficiencies and economies of scale, as much as they are educational (Bowen, Chingos, Lack, & Nygren, 2014). From another perspective, sometimes angst and stress result when academics with contrasting viewpoints about the character of a course and how it should be taught and assessed are required to work together. Occasionally these conflicts derive from personality clashes; potentially more often they reflect genuinely different positions with regard to university teaching and learning.

One site of university teaching where such conflicts are sometimes highly visible and where there can be deleterious effects on students' learning is the supervision of research students. Again the potential benefits of such students being able to draw on multiple perspectives about their research are considerable, significantly enhancing the breadth, depth and richness of their studies by mobilising deeply intellectual and finely nuanced discussions of theory, methodology and analysis. Yet supervisors do not always agree with one another, and sometimes that disagreement manifests as conflict that the student feels a requirement to mediate (Lahenius & Ikävalko, 2014).

These diverse examples derive from the same source: academics' sense of a reduced professional autonomy and their perceived lack of control over outcomes – the learning success of their students– in which they are invested significantly. Considerable stress can be generated – for academics as well as for their students – if they are unable to develop strategies for enhancing their felt autonomy, thereby reducing their perceptions of pleasure and professionalism connected with their working identities.

Relatedness Relatedness can be characterized as a state where individuals effectively integrate themselves with others. Such a state of being gives individuals feelings of connectedness, acceptance and support.

Academics are generally under high pressure to bring in external funding (Laudel, 2006), as part of broader changes to universities (Hicks, 2012). Apart from high quality publications, external funding gives the researcher and the university considerable prestige. In addition, external funding enables academics to engage in high quality research and to build industry linkages. All of these are essential survival tools for academics and also increase those academics' ability to produce high quality publications. While good quality publications can be produced without being involved in externally funded projects, quite often very high quality publications are based on results that were produced during large, externally funded projects.

In principle, relatedness should enable academics to develop better (more rounded and inclusive) ideas collaboratively. However, in reality the severe competition among different research groups results in a "bikie gang" like culture among academics. While there is an element of loyalty and co-dependence within certain groups, there is also severe and almost ruthless competition among different research groups, often within the same region (see also Etzkowitz, 2003).

This secretive, tribal attitude to research (see also Arias, 2012; Trowler, Saunders, & Bamber, 2012) can be so obvious that, for example, in Europe, when larger research consortia bid for a research project, members are often required to sign a written agreement (before the research project is developed) pledging their exclusive support for a particular research consortium and promising that they will not interact or disclose any information to other (potentially competing) research consortia. While such an attitude is completely understandable on a practical level, surely this will not improve relatedness among academics. At a certain "tribal level", it will perhaps result in a form of co-dependence, but it is unlikely to result in true relatedness.

This situation is very similar even in relation to conference attendance. Academics must be seen and heard at conferences, so that they can assert their presence in research circles (Parker & Weik, 2014). Two of the key motivations for conference attendance used to be to meet colleagues in person, and also to catch up on personal issues affecting research work, issues that cannot necessarily be published in research articles.

Nowadays, academics all try to get the "drift" of who will do what next year and are keen to form (sometimes uneasy) alliances with a handful of likeminded researchers to tackle the next big funding opportunity. Competition for research funding increased significantly in the past decade, and receiving financial support as an individual researcher (certainly in the sciences) is practically impossible these days. Thus forming alliances has become a crucial task for academics. However, while academics are trying to form alliances, they also need to guard their new ideas so as to maximize the chance of their "chosen tribe" to succeed. Academics must team up with high profile researchers and must somehow remain valuable players in the "hunting game" for research funding. Often this feels like a tightrope performance. The right balance between with whom to share and what to share must be found and quite often these relationships are mercenary in character rather than providing a sense of true relatedness with other academics.

Alliances within the research community can also change rapidly. Academics are quite often forced to switch among different groups because of the high level of competition within specific research fields. Perceived allies and friends can turn against one another rapidly in the hope of obtaining a better position in relation to the next big funding deal. The days when researchers came together to discuss freely their new, innovative ideas are something of the past. Networking and associated "scientific tribalism" have become a dangerous new game that adds further stress to the already demanding academic life (see also Howell & Annansingh, 2013).

Analysing the Vignettes

These three vignettes encapsulate many of the broader issues framing the book of which this chapter is a part. Work intensification, cost cutting, collegial competition, increased accountability without the accompanying resources to fulfil that accountability – these and other concerns traverse teaching, supervision, research and the other domains of academics' work in contemporary universities. From this perspective, the vignettes have attained their purpose of illustrating dissonances in that work that are otherwise implicit, invisible and tacit.

The vignettes have also confirmed the utility of mobilizing competence, autonomy and relatedness as three central concepts in SDT as a means of analysing the reported experiences of the authors of this chapter that are distilled in the vignettes. Each concept helped to generate productive insights into the current higher education landscape and workplace that potentially resonate more widely with academics and researchers in different countries and in diverse academic disciplines.

From one perspective, the vignettes make for depressing and discouraging reading. Yet the fact that they were underpinned by the rigorous theoretical framework of SDT also contains the seeds of a potentially more enabling understanding of higher education today and in particular of the prospects for reclaiming pleasure and professionalism in contemporary universities. Firstly, at a conceptual level, SDT affords distinctive apprehension of the notions of pleasure and professionalism specifically as the interplay among competence, autonomy and relatedness. The scholarship is clear that, when these fundamental human needs are fulfilled, the result is a greater capacity for enhancing the success and wellbeing of others – in this case, of university students and research participants.

Secondly and relatedly, these three concepts of SDT also help to launch particular and practical strategies designed to engage wholeheartedly with the work intensification canvassed above and to maximize pleasure and professionalism for academics and researchers. In this regard, the "Action patterns supported" column in Table 1 lists examples of tactics that are worthy of consideration for each concept. More broadly, while not minimising the challenges confronting contemporary universities, each author of this chapter has attained considerable success, working within as well as outside their current university workplace, in systematically helping to boost their own, their students' and their colleagues' competence, autonomy and relatedness. These strategies are not effective on every occasion, and they tend to be medium- and longer-term in character, but nevertheless they do tend to repay ongoing commitment and repeated efforts to apply them.

CONCLUSION

SDT scholarship has proposed the centrality of competence, autonomy and relatedness as basic human needs whose continued fulfilment is crucial to psychosocial health and wellbeing. This proposition has been confirmed by the three vignettes in this chapter, which have illustrated the problems for academics and researchers when one or more of these needs is not addressed in personal and professional terms. At the same time, the vignettes and Table 1 contain the seeds of more positive and productive outcomes when these needs are met.

On the other hand, the enhancement of psychosocial health and wellbeing through the fulfilment of competence, autonomy and relatedness at the individual level must be matched by corresponding fulfilment of these fundamental needs at group, institutional and sector levels if the pleasure and professionalism of academics and researchers in contemporary universities are to be maximized and sustained. As we noted above, favourable environmental and organizational principles are required to be in place to align with and support the efforts of individuals and groups. The shared interests of all stakeholders – students, academics, researchers, university leaders, governments, employers, communities and other beneficiaries of well-functioning and high quality university – demand nothing less.

ACKNOWLEDGMENTS

The authors are grateful for the editors' encouragement and support, including Dr Marcus Harmes's careful reading of the text.

REFERENCES

Amsler, M., & Shore, C. (2017). Responsibilisation and leadership in the neoliberal university: A New Zealand perspective. *Discourse: Studies in the Cultural Politics of Education, 38*(1), 123–137. doi: 10.1080/01596306.2015.1104857

Arias, C. C. (2012, March). Rituals and ceremonies of quality of higher education: New academic tribes and challenges in social recognition. *Mediterranean Journal of Social Sciences, 3*(6), 171–177. Retrieved from http://s3.amazonaws.com/academia.edu.documents/17629457/580599.mediterranean_journal_of_social_sciences_vol_3_no_6_march_2012.pdf?AWSAccessKeyI d=AKIAJ56TQJRTWSMTNPEA&Expires=1471149110&Signature=7mYL1D3xNfY4rot2Qpz1u0 cGnl4%3D&response-content-disposition=inline%3B%20filename%3DTowards_ the_Professionalization_of_Stude.pdf#page=171

Arthur, S., Mitchell, M., Lewis, J., & McNaughton Nicholls, C. (2014). Designing fieldwork. In J. Ritchie, J. Lewis, C. McNaughton Nicholls, & R. Ormiston (Eds.), *Qualitative research practice: A guide for social science students and researchers* (2nd ed., pp. 147–176). London, UK: Sage Publications.

Bowen, W. G., Chingos, M. M., Lack, K. A., & Nygren, T. A. (2014, Winter). Interactive learning online at public universities: Evidence from a six-campus randomized trial. *Journal of Policy Analysis and Management, 33*(1), 94–111. doi: 10.1002/pam.21728

Bryman, A., & Bell, E. (2015). *Business research methods* (4th ed.). Oxford, UK: Oxford University Press.

Conway, N., & Sturges, J. (2014). Investigating unpaid overtime working among the part-time workforce. *British Journal of Management, 25*(4), 755–771. doi: 10.1111/1467-8551.12011

Deci, E. L., & Ryan, R. M. (2002). Self-determination research: Reflections and future directions. In E. L. Deci & R. M. Ryan (Eds.), *Handbook of self-determination research* (pp. 431–441). Rochester, NY: The University of Rochester Press.

Enders, J., de Boer, H., & Leišytė, L. (2009). New public management and the academic profession: The rationalisation of academic work revisited. In J. Enders & E. de Weert (Eds.), *The changing face of academic life: Analytical and comparative perspectives* (pp. 36–57). Basingstoke, UK: Palgrave Macmillan.

Enders, J., de Boer, H., & Weyer, E. (2013, January). Regulatory autonomy and performance: The reform of higher education re-visited. *Higher Education, 65*(1), 5–23. doi: 10.1007/s10734-012-9578-4

Enders, J., & de Weert, E. (Eds.). (2009). *The changing face of academic life: Analytical and comparative perspectives*. Basingstoke, UK: Palgrave Macmillan.

Etzkowitz, H. (2003, January). Research groups as "quasi-firms": The invention of the entrepreneurial university. *Research Policy, 32*(1), 109–121. doi: 10.1016/S0048-7333(02)00009-4

Fairweather, J. (2009). Work allocation and rewards in shaping academic work. In J. Enders & E. de Weert (Eds.), *The changing face of academic life: Analytical and comparative perspectives* (pp. 171–192). Basingstoke, UK: Palgrave Macmillan.

Fein, E. C., Skinner, N., & Machin, T. (in press). Work intensification, work–life interference, stress and well-being in Australian workers. *International Studies of Management and Organization*.

Finkelstein, M. J., & Iglesias, K. W. (2015). The changing American academic profession. In P. Altbach, G. Androushchak, Y. Kuzminov, M. Yudkevich, & L. Reisberg (Eds.), *The global future of higher education and the academic professional* (pp. 160–198). Basingstoke, UK: Palgrave Macmillan.

Gannon, S., Kligyte, G., McLean, J., Perrier, M., Swan, E., Vanni, I., & van Rijswink, H. (2015, Winter). Uneven relationalities, collective biography, and sisterly affect in neoliberal universities. *Feminist Formations, 27*(3), 189–216. doi: 10.1353/ff.2016.0007

Greguras, G. J., & Diefendorff, J. M. (2009, March). Different fits satisfy different needs: Linking person–environment fit to employee commitment and performance using self-determination theory. *Journal of Applied Psychology, 94*(2), 465–477. doi: 10.1037/a0014068

Hicks, D. (2012, March). Performance-based university research funding systems. *Research Policy, 41*(2), 251-261. doi: 10.1016/j.respol.2011.09.007

Howell, K. E., & Annansingh, F. (2013, February). Knowledge generation and sharing in UK universities: A tale of two cultures? *International Journal of Information Management, 33*(1), 32–39. doi: 10.1016/j.ijinfomgt.2012.05.003

Kasser, T. (2002). Sketches for a self-determination theory of values. In E. L. Deci & R. M. Ryan (Eds.), *Handbook of self-determination research* (pp. 123–140). Rochester, NY: The University of Rochester Press.

Kolluru, S., Roesch, D. M., & Akhtar de la Fuente, A. (2012). A multi-instructor, team-based, active-/learning exercise to integrate basic and clinical sciences content. *American Journal of Pharmaceutical Education, 76*(2), article 33. doi: 10.5688/ajpe76233

Lahenius, K., & Ikävalko, H. (2014). Joint supervision practices in doctoral education – A student experience. *Journal of Further and Higher Education, 38*(3), 427-446. doi: 10.1080/0309877X.2012.706805

Laudel, G. (2006, October). The "quality myth": Promoting and hindering conditions for acquiring research funds. *Higher Education, 52*(3), 375–403. doi: 10.1007/s10734-004-6414-5

Lee, F. K., Sheldon, K. M., & Turban, D. B. (2003, April). Personality and the goal-striving process: The influence of achievement goal patterns, goal level, and mental focus on performance and enjoyment. *Journal of Applied Psychology, 88*(2), 256–265. doi: 10.1037/0021-9010.88.2.256

LoBiondo-Wood, G., & Haber, J. (2014). *Nursing research: Methods and critical appraisal for evidence-based practice* (8th ed.). St Louis, MO: Elsevier.

Maxfield, M. G., & Babbie, E. R. (2016). *Basics of research methods for criminal justice and criminology* (4th ed.). Boston, MA: Cengage Learning.

Meyers, D. (2012). *Australian universities: A portrait of decline.* Sydney: AUPOD. Accessed from http://australianuniversities.id.au/Australian_Universities-A_Portrait_of_Decline.pdf

Olson, G. A. (2013). *A creature of our own making: Reflections on contemporary academic life.* Albany, NY: State University of New York Press.

Parker, M., & Weik, E. (2014, April). Free spirits? The academic on the aeroplane. *Management Learning, 45*(2), 167–181. doi: 10.1177/1350507612466210

Prentice, M., Halusic, M., & Sheldon, K. M. (2014). Integrating theories of psychological needs-as-requirements and psychological needs-as-motives: A two process model. *Social and Personality Psychology Compass, 8*(2), 73–85. doi:10.1111/spc3.12088

Ryan, R. M., & Deci, E. L. (2002). An overview of self-determination theory: An organismic-dialectical perspective. In E. L. Deci & R. M. Ryan (Eds.), *Handbook of self-determination research* (pp. 3–33). Rochester, NY: The University of Rochester Press.

Skinner, E. A., & Edge, K. (2002). Self-determination, coping, and development: Patterns of action and engagement. In E. L. Deci & R. M. Ryan (Eds.), *Handbook of self-determination research* (pp. 297–337). Rochester, NY: The University of Rochester Press.

Tracy, S. J. (2013). *Qualitative research methods: Collecting evidence, crafting analysis, communicating impact.* Chichester, UK: Wiley-Blackwell.

Trowler, P., Saunders, M., & Bamber, V. (Eds.). (2012). *Tribes and territories in the 21st century: Rethinking the significance of disciplines in higher education.* London, UK: Routledge.

Zumrah, A. R., Boyle, S., & Fein, E. C. (2013, December). The consequences of transfer of training for service quality and job satisfaction: An empirical study in the Malaysian public sector. *International Journal of Training and Development, 17*(4), 270–294. doi: 10.1111/ ijtd.12017

Eric C. Fein
University of Southern Queensland, Australia

Rahul Ganguly
University of Southern Queensland, Australia

Thomas Banhazi
University of Southern Queensland, Australia

Patrick Alan Danaher
University of Southern Queensland and
Central Queensland University, Australia

KATHRYN GILBEY AND TRACEY BUNDA

14. THE PLEASURE AND PAIN OF ABORIGINAL BEING IN THE UNIVERSITY

INTRODUCTION

Aboriginal education is a relatively recent phenomenon within higher education and its inclusion has given rise to complexity that is at once subjugating and liberating. We offer stories of critical moments in teaching within the university to represent the complexity as a continuum of experience ranging from pleasure to pain. Viewed through a critical theoretical lens the stories told demonstrate how the intersectionality of race and power remains relevant to the position of the Aboriginal academic in teaching Aboriginal studies to primarily white undergraduate students or in the teaching of Aboriginal students at the preparatory level. In particular this chapter examines the race based hazards associated with teaching about Aboriginal histories and societies to the uninitiated and resistant white learner whilst the teaching about white learning codes of the university within Aboriginal ways of knowing presents a differing pedagogical challenge. We draw upon our doctoral studies and current teaching to inform how the Aboriginal academic is called upon to deflect institutional and ideological whiteness and yet needs to remain centred in this space to be effective for teaching the next generations of Aboriginal learners. Riding the pleasure-pain continuum poses challenges not only for the Aboriginal academic but also for the Australian university which has responsibility to increase its Aboriginal workforce. The chapter unpacks this problematic to reduce the harmful effects of the race/ power tangling on the body, mind and spirit of the Aboriginal academic whilst exposing and decentering whiteness in the university.

As is important within our cultural practices as Aboriginal women we introduce ourselves as Alyawarre for Gilbey and Ngugi/Wakka Wakka for Bunda. We also identify ourselves as experienced academics in the field of Aboriginal higher education though we are classed in the academy as early career researchers. Together, and at the time of writing, we constitute the permanent Aboriginal academic staff of an Indigenous academic site in a regional university. We draw on our doctoral studies to locate this chapter within a critical theoretical lens, in part informed by the study of whiteness to elucidate the intersectionality of race and power at ideological, institutional and individual levels (Dyson, 2003). Additionally we draw upon our collective experiences in teaching both Aboriginal studies/education at the undergraduate level and teaching Aboriginal and Torres Strait Islander students at the Pathways Program level. We unpack the socio-political complexities that work to position the teaching Aboriginal academic on a continuum riding through experiences of pleasure and pain. This chapter is organized in two parts with the first speaking into critical moments of teaching pleasure for the Aboriginal academic and the second part speaking into teaching pain. We conclude with strategic advice to the Australian university that struggles to build appropriate numbers of Aboriginal and Torres Strait Islander academic staff and at appropriate levels concomitant to agendas signaling the need for a National Indigenous Higher Education Workforce Strategy (IHEAC, 2011). It is our thesis that the lived day-to-day experience of the teaching Aboriginal academic cannot be negated in this consideration if the academy is to be a site of educational invitation for our communities and a site of safety for work through exposing, naming and decentering its whiteness.

CONTEXTUALISING MOMENTS OF PLEASURE

The Aboriginal and Torres Strait Islander educational site where we are employed has, within the past two years, undergone a review. In terms of course and program offerings the site offered a Pathways Program specifically for Aboriginal and Torres Strait Islander students, a core course in initial teacher education and a minor studies in Aboriginal and Torres Strait Islander Studies. The Pathways Program was offered with various levels of success, measured in terms of graduating and articulating Indigenous students into degree level studies. The particular educational circumstances of our student body meant that past structural impediments to formal education had to be eliminated.

The criteria for entrance in to the Pathways Program was often restrictive to some of older students and to our students who didn't have the luxury of full schooling. The creation of three pre-entry subjects provided opportunities that otherwise would have been denied. In post review mode, Gilbey set about transforming the program to deliver a preparatory studies that was both epistemologically and pedagogically grounded in a blackness that drew from Indigenous knowledges with an additional need to decode the skills required by our students to negotiate a higher education.

Author 1 (Kathryn Gilbey) Speaks: The Power of the Telling

The pleasure of our positions within the university sector comes from knowing that we are doing 'some good', making change, chipping away at the behemoth that is the University and western academia. Through implementing a methodology where telling and sharing our own stories, with our own people is centred we slowly begin to identify that which matters through a shared practice of knowing and being (Martin, 2008).

The pleasure experience comes from dialogue about a pathways program delivered at a regional university and uniquely written by Aboriginal and Torres Strait Islander people for Aboriginal and Torres Strait Islander people. IHEPP is the Indigenous Higher Education Pathways Program and has existed as a safe place for First Nations students to find their way into the sometimes unwelcoming environment of western academia. Translating into the whitestream (Andersen,

2009) is not without its hazards. For example, in the short time in which we have come to manage IHEPP, questions regarding the 'educational standard' of IHEPP and its validation for entry into degree level studies have been raised by white staff employed to assist in the administration of all university courses. It should be noted that being an experienced Aboriginal academic who is well versed in the hierarchical rules of the university and can therefore speak back to the institution stands in stark contrast to Aboriginal students who are in less powerful locations to navigate such terrains yet will need to do so with various degrees.

Refreshing IHEPP necessitated a transformation of approach and methodology. So now, rather than being a carbon copy of the whitestream pathways program with a few tokenistic images of Aboriginal people scattered throughout course content which was thus imagined as an authentic statement of inclusion, the program moved to deepen the First Nations content. The program also lacked any analysis of power, racism and structural inequality as evidence of the disciplinary practices of whitestream systems in justice, education and family and children services and the consequences of how such practices are deeply felt by our communities – as extraordinary, unjust and are situated in our bodies as slights, as violence and as genocide. It is critical that our students are provided with the tools to interrogate these everyday interactions with the whitestream. There is a fundamental discrepancy between the white and black lived experience in this country and when our educational and learning environments deny or refuse to acknowledge this then there is a fundamental denial of self and family and community felt by First Nations people so that a choice has to be made, to engage or not to engage. Strategic thinking needs to occur and critical questions need to be asked: is this detrimental to my sense of self? Do I deny my family and my history by engaging in this arena? If yes then why would I? IHEPP aspires to be an education program specifically designed to bring pleasure, acknowledgement and to engage our ways of being, knowing and doing and to deliver skills to unpack western education in a way that doesn't denigrate your sense of self. It is this re-positioning of Indigenous knowledges that is important and central to the movement of Indigenous academics into Indigenous education, that is the education of our peoples. Professor Marie Battiste (2000) a Mi'kmaq educator from the Potlo'tek First Nations in Canada, determines:

> Through this act of intellectual self- determination, Indigenous academics are developing new analyses and methodologies to decolonize themselves, their communities and their institutions. (p. 4)

Internationally Indigenous academics have been arguing that whilst cultural differences do exist in the classroom, those classrooms that recognise and include students' knowledge have greater educational outcomes (Bartolome, 2008, p. 137). There is also an argument for a democratic pedagogy that includes an analysis of power structures to understand why certain students' knowledges have previously been ignored. Bartolome's location of the political dimensions of culture is useful for understanding difference as a response to subordination. She argues further in regard to cultural inclusion or an essentialist difference model being the only answer:

> I use this definition of culture because, without identifying the political dimensions of culture and subsequent unequal status attributed to members of different ethnic groups, the reader may conclude that teaching methods simply need to be ethnically congruent to be effective ... all differences are treated as ethnic cultural differences and not as responses of subordinated students to teachers from dominant groups, and vice versa. (2008, p. 137)

So recognition of cultural difference is one step. Another step is the re-positioning of Indigenous ontology to the fore of classroom practice, to change the binaries so that Indigenous ways of being and knowing are privileged within the curriculum and within the classroom and have a critical power-based analysis within every course. Acknowledging the lived realities of the students, the ongoing effects of colonialism and the damaging effects of racism from the outset and embedding this knowledge within all classroom and service delivery is an imperative. Sue Stanton in her paper "Talking both ways – acting one way: looking to find the right balance" says:

> Any number of publications on 'Indigenous education' point out and explain the way for western educators to reflect on practice, on ethics and epistemology, educational practice, sometimes transformative thinking. What most western educators need to read and think about is more on teaching as activism, more volumes on colonialism and capitalism (and its effects on Aboriginal peoples), variations on assisting Aboriginal peoples with strategies on how to combat domination and oppression, especially in education and the workplace, added to that some colonial histories, and especially Marie Battiste's work on post-colonial remedies. (2013, p. 7)

For these steps to be implemented, for example is not only about one group being 'different' to another. It is about a complex history of denial and subjugation that doesn't sit only at the site of the student's body in the classroom (deficit model) but is being played out at a bigger broader national and cultural level that, in turn, returns the students' critical gaze onto the institution of education itself.

The following dialogue reflexively considers the implementation of the refreshed IHEPP program. This is how it happened.

OUR KNOWLEDGES – OUR HISTORIES

Australian History by its nature, name and definition is not inclusive of Aboriginal and Torres Strait Islanders' stories or lived realities. Australian history is based around settlement and not invasion. It does not represent through public holidays, war memorials, curricula and the collective psyche the ongoing struggle continuum that is Aboriginal peoples' realities since invasion. There have been constant and ongoing sites of resistance, freedom fighters, warriors, wars, activism and resistance to colonization. This is rarely represented in the history books taught in schools and universities. When on the odd occasion it is, it has been hotly contested by non-Indigenous historians and politicians (https://theconversation.com/australias-history-wars-reignite-57065). To counter these tendencies we spend time looking at Aboriginal resistance history (Attwood & Markus, 1999). We begin with the first written acts of resistance in the late 1830s on Flinders Island in Bass Strait. We then move through time to the ongoing struggle for land rights, citizenship and recognition up to today. This detailed looking at resistance history was often confronting and eye-opening for students. Students local to the areas included in the written historical accounts knew the histories through their own peoples' oral traditions but as a whole, as a cross-sectional snapshot of Aboriginal and Torres Strait Islander peoples' resistance, very few knew of the complete, recurring and undying struggle continuum. We started to see how much of our history had been left out of the dominant versions of history. We did this as a large group where we all participated in the process of reading about sites of resistance and sharing that back as a group.

We looked at and celebrated images and stories of our ancestor warriors; we ogled Gary Foley's Koori history Website, revelling in the telling of our histories. I gave impassioned lectures on the despicable nature of terra nullius and its dehumanizing consequences felt today.

It was also important that we had the space to tell our stories and histories in a First Nations only space as in this way the journey of telling and retelling history could happen without fear; we raged, we cried, we celebrated, we laughed and we shared.

The History Wars and who controlled the representation and arguments around Australian history was analysed. The differing versions of the Mistake Creek massacre of Peggy Patrick and Keith Windshuttle formed the basis of a robust discussion. Whole lectures on how to deal with white ignorance were given. Of course they weren't called this rather they were cloaked in a discussion around contestations of knowledge – what to do when confronted with information that you fundamentally know to be untrue. In this way we developed a resilience by acknowledging and forewarning students about a possible contested space; we arm the students with the capacity without losing their temper, or internalizing the racism, take that knowledge, theorise it and give it back.

In addition to textual analysis and academic skills we provide the building blocks to communicate our own versions of history, a re-telling from an Aboriginal and Torres Strait Islander perspective. In this way the students define what is important to them, they get to tell their story. Dion (2009) speaks of these moments in terms of "compelling invitations":

> ... within Aboriginal traditions the power of the story resides partly in the telling, our approach is to (re) tell the stories in such a way that listeners hear a "compelling invitation" that claims their attention and initiates unsettling questions that require working through ... the hope for accomplishing an alternative way of knowing lies partly in our ability to share with our readers what the stories mean to us. (p. 1)

Sharing our histories and stories in a way that was accessible, that can be heard, is an aim of the program. If the moments in history that we find important, moments that shape who we are, are the very moments that white Australia wants to forget, then telling histories from an Indigenous perspective provided forums from which more authentic discussions can begin. Again Dion (2009) supports this point from her Canadian perspective:

> If justice for Aboriginal people lies in remembering, but forgetting serves the needs of the Canadian nation, where are the possibilities for accomplishing justice found. (p. 1)

The central story being told was one of Aboriginal and Torres Strait Islander achievement, history, strength and survival. The classrooms and the offices had been hijacked and, whether it was one speech or story in particular that grabbed the audience's attention, the focus briefly was not on curriculum content or discipline specific knowledges that maintain the accustomed binary power relationships within Western Academia, but instead was all about First Nations peoples' strength, knowledge, stories and capacity.

We moved from being mere subjects of power and became agents of power. We managed to move our position on the power continuum from being passive recipients of the consequences derived from others' positions of power through their benevolent goodwill to becoming speakers of our truths. Just being an Aboriginal or Torres Strait Islander person in this country is political, our very survival is political, so when we stand up and speak our truths it changes both the speaker and the recipient.

The transition from being individuals who have historically been beholden to the power of white others to individuals holding power with space to speak was a transformative educational moment. The holding of space and agency is important on many levels. Not only is it about sharing something that has never been shared outside of the family, or something that you are passionate about, it is a personal achievement. So the act of speaking one's truths has dual meaning. It is important for the public sphere, adding to the knowledge of the room, the town, the country, but it is also important on a personal level. The public/private sphere is transformed into a collective space imbued with all the strength and power of stories never before told, or needing to be re-told with the hopes and expectations and community mindedness of the whole classroom. In this moment, the subjugation of the past is removed, the feelings of inadequacy gone, as we for a moment feel empowered. Speaking the truth of our lives, telling a story of a grandfather banned from the islands and the effects on him; three generations of one family in care because of the Stolen Generations; a story of survival from a massacre in NSW; stories of triumph against adversity, stories of survival, recollections of idyllic childhoods on the river, at the beach or in the desert; manifestos on hunting and bush food and native title claims for each student is a moment of embodying the power of an ancient culture and sharing that with an audience.

The speeches are an act, and therefore a site, of empowerment for the participants and a gift to the audience to witness a different perspective.

These performances of power were an act of breaking down some of the barriers that typically exclude First Nations people from succeeding within western higher education frameworks.

White Ancestors of Knowledge: Aristotle, Plato and Power

Relying heavily on material borrowed from Batchelor Institute's (Northern Territory) common units and material written by Dr Robyn McCormack we introduced students to the classical Greek philosophers Aristotle and Plato, the ancestors of western education. We outlined the two very different western educational traditions that arose from the thinking of these two men.

As a result loud classroom discussions about Socrates' choice of hemlock over banishment were reinterpreted into the importance of country and the pain of dispossession. If these were the ancestors of western education and the choices that surrounded them then we accorded them the respect that they deserved. By knowing the conflict between Aristotle and his teacher Plato; by knowing that they differed in their approach, meant that we could deconstruct the current western model and, in so doing, removed the omniscient power of western education to that of simply a winning model. This insight opened the door to alternatives.

By looking at the history of western education we see the influence on its structure of political ideologies over this same history. It was in this way that we used the colonizer's educative tools for integration and assimilation to our own benefit, for our self-determination.

Knowledge is power and as we discussed knowledge production; as we discussed the wisdom of our Elders; as we learnt about differing styles of education; we did so from our own uniquely varied but First Nations people's position. We felt ourselves growing more powerful through a knowledge of the white other (western education). By removing the invisible codings of the current western education system we could discuss from our own First Nation's perspective the value of our own education systems as well as the pros and cons of the various western systems.

This synthesis of knowledge came from two sources; one a non-Indigenous academic's (Dr McCormack) detailed knowledge of Greek educators and modern philosophers, the other the First Nations students' detailed knowledge of their own educational practices and educational journeys. We explored the disconnect between that knowledge being taught by family and community and what was being taught in schools. By applying this knowledge to our real world, a whole new level of understanding about the role and purpose of knowledge sharing through generations was revealed.

We called these workshops transformative and experiential. You are ultimately transformed as a result partly because of the powerful experience of listening to a room full of stories. The residential schools are transformative because of the celebration of speaking and enacting the power of our Ancestors through the students telling their stories; talking their histories into existence.

Butler speaks of this transition from subjugation to agency:

> It seemed that if you were subjugated, there were also forms of agency that were available to you, and you were not just a victim, or you were not only oppressed, but oppression could become the condition of your agency. (Butler, 2010)

It was this act of speaking up and out to an audience that is one of the key strengths of and the greatest threats to Aboriginal knowledges in the academy. The presentations were all informative and entertaining and strong, and held to Aboriginal and Torres Strait Islanders' views, worldviews, stories, and realities. This oftentimes had a profound effect on the speaker and the audience. Every speech challenged ignorance. That was the very point of this exercise, to communicate our histories to an audience and by telling our truths that are counter to dominant Australian narratives we chip away at the ignorance that exists in the whitestream.

These speeches ran contrary to other narratives that surround First Nations people. The gaze had shifted. Aboriginal and Torres Strait Islander strength and competency were being displayed and this sat at odds with the hegemonic narrative. This program runs contrary to white privilege and its pathologizing (Moreton-Robinson, 2009) narratives. The celebratory analysis and presentation that happens directly contradicts mainstream narratives of drunk, desperate, needy, hopeless Aboriginal and Torres Strait Islander people. Instead we show our strengths and that, my friend, is a game changer within the academy.

CONTEXTUALIZING MOMENTS OF PAIN

Drawing on her own experiences within the university and with the Indigenous voices of her doctoral studies Bunda gives attention to critical moments of teaching in humanities and education. These classes are primarily populated by white students who enter into their studies with poor background knowledge of Aboriginal and Torres Strait Islander histories, cultures and societies. The learning about Indigenous Studies and in the case of initial teacher education students, the learning about Indigenous education is, from Aboriginal perspectives, foundational to the quality of engagement and therefore relationships between black and white peoples in this country.

Author 2 (Tracey Bunda) Speaks: A Different Telling

Hart and Whatman remind students, teachers and researchers located within the field of Indigenous Studies that:

> much of the literature on Aboriginal and Torres Strait Islander peoples can be ideologically traced back to the emergence of 'knowledge' about native

peoples in the context of European imperialism and expansionism from the fifteenth century. (1998, p. 1)

The colonial knowing of us as *objects* of study travelled from the diaries of white 'explorers', the records of government officials, the observations of squatters and colonial news print, coalesced into 'scientific' notes in the field and travelled further to laboratories, lecture theatres and research at universities. In this way the university retained a complementary arrangement with the colonial project. The colonial project initially engaged in the dispossession of Aboriginal peoples from our lands. Together with the university the colonial project became a dispossessing of ourselves from ourselves.

At this time there were very few opportunities for Aboriginal peoples to represent ourselves and our knowledges in the university, David Unaipon, Ngarrindjeri warrior, inventor and writer, being one of the exceptions. The university engaged in acts of knowledge dispossession.

The knowledge being produced by whitefella academics was afforded status and protection. This knowledge educated, fascinated and repelled, and held a dominating authority that permeated broader communities, including Aboriginal Communities. The ramifications of this white knowledge producing and owning legacy effectively subjugated and devalued Aboriginal knowing. This dominance, invested in the white production of knowledge, auspices white race membership as having sole authority over Aboriginal knowledge, and continues the investment in this knowledge as the propriety rights of the dominant. From the outset, there was enacted a disciplinary practice of knowing the Aboriginal other. These disciplinary knowledge domains came to eat us (Smith & Hooks, 1999).

Linda Tuhiwai Smith (1998), a Maori academic and intellectual trailblazer, says that it is only through an understanding of the institutional context that we can change our lived realities, that change can be effected. Wendy Brady (1992), speaking at an Aboriginal Studies Association conference, cites Smith:

> We cannot begin to describe the dilemma which faces us in our practice without first recognizing that we exist in institutions which are founded on the collective denial of our existence ... and which not only actively continue to assimilate us, but more importantly perhaps actively compete with us and the world views we represent. (p. 314)

The teaching and learning rights of the dominant and protection of this *status quo* remains a pertinent feature of this discussion; of understanding what is happening at the teaching and learning interface (Nakata, 2007). The investment in the proprietary value of knowledge (what it is, how and where it is located, and who holds control over it) speaks into questions of authority and legitimacy that can linger within the academy when an Indigenous academic teaches.

Framed by Aboriginal practices of relationality that enabled de-identification though did not deny central markers of Aboriginality participants within my doctoral studies were referenced in relation to my own location thus Deadly Tidda South and Central of My Country (DTSWCMC) speaks to the questions of authority and legitimacy:

> I was co-ordinating one of the biggest subjects in our Centre, a core subject. As soon as you have a core subject you seem to get an element of resistance anyway but in this particular situation we had some non-Indigenous students appeal the subject under equal opportunity. How ironic! They believed it was discriminatory that they had to do a subject that focussed on Indigenous education. Thank goodness the Faculty of Education didn't accept their appeal and obviously the Equal Opportunity Unit said it was not appropriate.

Ironic indeed! Equal opportunity legislation that aimed to protect the interests of the Indigenous other has on occasion become a legalistic technology for the dominant to lay claim to reasserting white ownership of public institutional learning spaces. It seems to be imagined by the dominant that 'they' constitute a 'minority' surrounded and besieged by the others (Aboriginal, disabled, transsexual and so on) who collectively form a new dominant group with access to unfettered power to dislocate the former dominant to the margins, away from power and to a position of subordination. Aggrieved non-Aboriginal peoples reframe the equal opportunity regulations for their own purposes and lay claim to a 'reverse racism', as this group of students had done.

This strategy exposed the claimants as lacking the necessary critical tools to unpack power and white race privilege and here lies a second irony in this teaching moment. In contesting the Aboriginal education subject as unworthy of their learning for a teacher education degree, the students would have in fact benefited from being taught about the concepts of race and power. This knowledge would have provided a learning corrective to the white students' misinformed positions on equity and justice and thus saved themselves considerable grief. My colleague continues:

> The students were then required to do this subject but then that meant you had to face the students and deal with them every week in lectures and tutorials. That was really confronting because not only did I have to co-ordinate the subject but I had to protect the staff in my team.

> I think 15–20 students were engaged in this appeal. It was really complicated because not only did you have to really believe in the knowledge you were teaching, you had to believe that what you were doing was pedagogically and methodologically sound … you were up to date with the theoretical underpinnings of the discipline. Otherwise, this is where potentially you could be scrutinised and got at.

> The processes had to be absolutely perfect in terms of protecting yourself and your staff. It also meant we had to team teach for some classes because the situation got so difficult that you needed another person to observe what was actually going on just in case something went wrong. We were attacked really.

It felt like a war. It's not a war but you develop the same tactics. You protect the staff and the other students too, they had a right to feel protected as well, and culturally safe. We haven't had that since, although there is always a small minority who don't believe what we teach is relevant to them as teachers.

The metaphor of war used by DTSWCMC to describe this particular moment of teaching white students is at once revealing and shocking. I read the resistance of the white students as both a contestation over who owns the teaching space and who owns the knowledge that is being taught in that space. There is a white student violent desire to ensure the subaltern cannot speak/teach (Spivak, 1988). DTSWCMC, as an Aboriginal academic and subject co-ordinator of the Aboriginal Education subject experiences the power differential as if she is a battlefield marshal in charge of defending the subject and having to protect staff as the producers and disseminators of this knowledge, and protecting students willing to receive the knowledge from the onset of the semester.

Resistant white students will argue that Aboriginal Education/Studies has little relevance for them as learners and future teachers. In the case of teacher education students, this argument is rationalized by the white student learner who imagines that, on becoming a classroom practitioner, they will not be responsible for educating Aboriginal children *per se* because all children should be seen 'equally' as 'individuals'. It can be argued that the Deadly Tidda was preparing the white student for the actual event of teaching in culturally, linguistically different and racialised spaces as there are no guarantees that the primary/secondary classroom comes only in the colour white.

The justice efforts of liberatory teaching practices in racialized spaces, particularly where white student violence seeks to impinge on black knowledge authority, belie the exhaustive effort on the part of Aboriginal academics to bring peace when Indigenous Education/Studies have been inserted for re-shaping this space. Disruptions to common understandings of the Aboriginal other do challenge the learning readiness of white students to engage with new knowledge, particularly those Aboriginal knowledges that ask white students to interrogate their own positions with regard to race identity standpoints and within continuing colonial relationships.

The Aboriginal staff of the Aboriginal Centre engaged in the teaching about race (in this case, teaching for undergraduate teacher education students) operated with a pedagogical imperative for team teaching with Aboriginal and like-minded non-Aboriginal colleagues. In the first instance, this strategy enables a sharing of the teaching weight and intellectual labour for the semester. These are the moments of strategically deciding what armour to wear. In addition, the coming together of a coalition of teaching colleagues allows for a dialogical deconstruction of the racialized teaching and learning space and a sharing of pedagogical practices for dealing with the burdens of resistant and sometimes violent students. These are the moments of checking and repairing the wear and tear of our protective shields. The shared space also offers identity affirmation for the Aboriginal teaching staff, a confirmation of knowledge being taught and a distance and reprieve from the battling that can sometimes occur in the tutorials. These are the teaching moments of standing on point, in our armour, with our shields, together. This shared space is necessary, cathartic and regenerative for a continued Aboriginal academic participation within the university.

My own critical moment of teaching mirrors that of my colleague and Deadly Tidda. I taught in a subject designed by an Indigenous warrior woman colleague who was taking leave from her position for a year. The subject was positioned as a compulsory study for journalism students, although students from other disciplines were also enrolled. My tutorial consisted of a group of approximately 20 students who were predominately young, that is, under 30 years of age, and were predominately white.

At the completion of the subject the enrolled students were asked (with voluntarily participation) to evaluate the course and the teaching practice of the individual tutors. Student evaluation is completed as an on-line task and is constructed so as to protect the identity of the individual student. The evaluation form draws from a university constructed set list of questions for students to complete online. Anonymous responses are then returned to the subject co-ordinator and tutor respectively. This process is standard for the teaching staff in this university.

Seven students of my tutorial group of twenty participated in the evaluation task and responded to the set questions. One written response in particular stood out. In response to the question: How can the lecturer improve their teaching? A student had written: "by dying".

I shared this student's evaluation of my teaching with my white warrior woman colleague and co-ordinator of this subject, who at once showed that she felt deeply ashamed, hurt, angry and protective of me. In a career of teaching at the university level for over two decades, predominately to white students, I had never been told that the technique for improving my teaching was to die or anything else approaching such mean-spirited violence.

It is a comment that can be made, an agency that can be performed, because it is protected in its anonymity. It is an act of violence performed onto the 'black race' that I, as an Indigenous academic speaking and teaching with a critical theoretical voice, come to represent. Folded into the seams of these two words lies the complexities of the discursive formation of the black teacher/white student relationship in teaching and learning. The challenge of critical theoretical knowledge about the concepts of race and race-ing in colony Australia is confronting for the uninitiated learner. This challenge of unfamiliar and self-interrupting knowledge becomes even more so when the teaching of race is provided by one who is raced as black. It is not a common experience of the white learner in a colony Australia university to have a black (Indigenous) teacher. The realities of this situation also speaks to that residual colonialist ideology embodied in the white student that privileges the holding and production of knowledge about the other as the intellectual property of white knowers. The breaking down of the protection once offered by invisibility occurs in the moments when the Indigenous other occupies a position as a knower of how the understanding of 'race' is conceptualized; knowing how this knowledge impacts on black race membership and how this critical unpacking of 'race' conceptions extends beyond its 'normal' categorization to include the necessity of seeing oneself as white. Exposing the privileges of white race membership, in this case, can incite a hatred for a knowing black. I was being seen as having gone too far.

The goodwill that is extended to the university through sharing our stories and knowledges quickly dissipates when met with resistance; a reluctance to know; an unwillingness to understand. This protective response to whiteness is a particular type of ignorance. Lipsitz (2002) writes that white privilege and ignorance of that privilege accords advantages for white people. And that ignorance operates at the level of not knowing and therefore not able to do anything about it. His primary argument is that "part of the problem is not because of our race but because of our possessive investment in it" (p. 79). It is not about ignorance but the possessive investment in it, the deliberate maintenance of it. That ignorance is taught and structured throughout our society, that ignorance is the fundamental backbone that allows the truth about Australia's invasion and colonization to remain unacknowledged. Applebaum (2008) believes it to be a reciprocal arrangement, the system remains uninterrogated as the people that it benefits remain in power with a certain arrogance and moral imperative that sees them complicit in its construction and maintenance. The question is asked, who has the most to gain from remaining ignorant, for ignoring the systemic injustice and their complicity in it?

Within the contract of ignorance, the state of 'not-knowing', is "a social achievement with strategic value" (Steyn, 2012, p. 8). Here ignorance is not only about the lack of knowledge acquisition by individual whites but also, and more so, about the social accomplishment achievable within whiteness.

A FINAL WORD

We, in telling of critical moments, expose complexities associated with the pleasure/pain continuum for the teaching Aboriginal academic. There is generative power in teaching to produce pedagogical and political joy. It is but one of the many reasons that we have chosen this profession. To facilitate and share the learning journey with our own is agentic, a living transformation in action. Framed by our ways of being, knowing and doing, teaching and learning becomes a safe space for the First Nations learner and the First Nations teacher. It feels like home. At the other end of the continuum where teaching pain is located, the presence of the Indigenous teacher as the bearer of Indigenous and critical knowledge for the uninitiated and resistant white learner culminates in hazardous spaces where danger manifests.

Contestations of ownership of the teaching space, who is teaching and what is being taught, will remain whilst the university fails to acknowledge, chooses to be ignorant of, the prickly, racialized spaces where the Indigenous academic intellectually labors to transform the academy as less white and less bound to new forms of a colonizing ethos. National agendas to build and sustain an Indigenous academic workforce must embrace de-colonizing practices otherwise university claims of Indigenization of the teaching and learning space will remain unrealized.

REFERENCES

Applebaum, B. (2008). White privilege/white complicity: connecting "Benefiting from" to "Contributing to" Philosophy of Education. *Philosophy of Education, 13*, 292–300.
Attwood, B., & Markus, A. (1999), *The struggle for Aboriginal Rights: A documentary history*. Allen and Unwin.
Andersen, C. (2009) Indigenous studies from difference to density. *Cultural Studies Review, 15*(2), 80–100.
Bartolome, L. I. (2008). Beyond the methods fetish: Toward humanizing pedagogy. In M. Villegas, S. B. Neugebauer, & K. R. Venegas (Eds.), *Indigenous knowledge and education: Sites of struggle, strength and survivance*. Cambridge: Harvard Educational Press.
Battiste, M. (2000). Reclaiming Indigenous voice and vision Vancouver. In J. Y. Henderson (Ed.), *Protecting Indigenous knowledge and heritage: A global challenge*. Saskatoon: Purich Press.
Battiste, M. (2002). *Indigenous knowledge and pedagogy in First Nations education. A literature review with recommendations*. National Working Group on Education and the Minister of Indian Affairs Indian and Northern Affairs Canada, Ottawa ON.
Brady, W. (1992). *Indigenous control of Aboriginal and Torres Strait Islander research*. Paper presented to Aboriginal Studies Association conference.
Butler, J. (2010). As a Jew I was taught it was ethically imperative to speak up. *Haaretz*, February 24.
Dion, S. (2009). *Braiding histories, learning from Aboriginal peoples' experiences and perspectives*. Vancouver: University of British Columbia Press.
Dyson, M. E. (2003). Giving whiteness a black eye: Excavating white identities, ideologies and institutions. In *Open Mike: Reflections on race, sex, culture and religion* (pp. 99–126). New York: Basic Civitas Books.
Foley, G. (2000). *Assimilating the natives in the US and Australia*. http://www.kooriweb.org/foley/essays/essays_page.html%3E
Hart, V., & Whatman, S. (1998) Decolonising the concept of knowledge. In *Proceedings of HERSDA: Annual International Conference* (pp 1–11). Auckland, NZ, 7–10 July, http://eprints.qut.edu.au/27531/1/27531.pdf
Indigenous Higher Education Advisory Council (IHEAC). (2011). *National indigenous workforce strategy*. Available from ttp://www.deewr.gov.au/indigenous/HigherEducation/Programs/IHEAC/Pages/Home.aspx
Lipsitz, G. (1995). The possessive investment in Whiteness: Racialised social democracy and the "White" problem in American Studies. *American Quaterly 47*(3), 369–387.
Lipsitz, G. (2002). The possessive investment in Whiteness: Racialised social democracy and the "White" problem in American studies. *American Quarterly, 47*(3), September, 369–387.
Martin, K. L. (2008). *Please knock before you enter: Aboriginal regulation of outsiders and the implications for researchers*. Tenerife: Post Pressed.
Moreton-Robinson, A. (2009). Imagining the good indigenous citizen. *Cultural Studies Review, 15*(2), 61–79.
Nakata, M. (2007). *Disciplining the savages: Savaging the discipline*. Canberra: Aboriginal Studies Press.
Smith, L. (1998). *Decolonizing methodologies*. Otago: Zen Books.
Smith, L. T. (2012). *Decolonising methodologies: Research and Indigenous peoples* (2nd ed.). London & New York: Zed Books.
Spivak, G. C. (1988). Can the subaltern speak? In C. Nelson & L. Grossberg (Eds.), *Marxism and the Interpretation of Culture* (pp. 271–316). Champaign, IL: University of Illinois Press.

Stanton, S. (July 2013). *Talking both ways – Acting one way: looking to find the right balance.* Batchelor Institute, Northern Territory.

Steyn, M. (2012). The ignorance contract: recollections of apartheid chilhood and the construction of epistemologies of ignorance. *Identities: Global Studies in Culture and Power, 19*(1), 8–25.

WEBSITES

http://adb.anu.edu/biography/unaipon-david-8898 for details of David Unaipon's life.

https://theconversation.com/australias-history-wars-reignite-57065

http://www.haaretz.com/news/judith-butler-as-a-jew-i-was-taught-it-was-ethically-imperative-to-speak-up-1.266243

Kathryn Gilbey
College for Indigenous Studies, Education and Research
University of Southern Queensland, Australia

Tracey Bunda
College for Indigenous Studies, Education and Research
University of Southern Queensland, Australia

SUSANNE GANNON AND JO LAMPERT

15. ACADEMIC WRITING, CREATIVE PLEASURE AND THE SALVAGING OF JOY

INTRODUCTION

We met in a women's writing group in north Queensland[1] long before we became academics, but it seems the passions for writing otherwise that brought us together then have infused our writing ever since. Like many scholars, we began our academic careers not just *with* a love of but *because* of our love of writing. Indeed, writing helped defined us. It's how we knew we were smart, passionate, connected; yet writing is situated and having successfully navigated our way into the academy we find ourselves increasingly worried that the joy we had found as writers of fiction and poetry is being leached out of us. The desire to write still lives in our guts, but sometimes we wonder if academic work is endangering us. Way back then we spent our Saturday afternoons with other women laughing, weeping and writing together, now we are more likely to be alone at our desks rewriting academic journal articles, or disciplining other writers in our roles as peer reviewers and editors. In successfully becoming part of the "academicwritingmachine" (Honan, Henderson, & Loch, 2016), we ask ourselves what might we be losing and what strategies might help us to find pleasure in failing, feeling and having fun again in our writing. At this point in our chapter, on expert advice, we offer a warning to readers that you are likely to encounter sweeping statements, figurative and emotive language which will be used liberally and unapologetically throughout. We recognise that writing is an affect-laden process, e ngaging bodies, minds, desires through the artful deployment of the multiple capacities for making meaning that language offers. Through our writing we seek "affective attunements" or "resonances" (Gibbs, 2015) that differ from those of conventional academic prose.

In this chapter we consider the effects that "mastering" academic writing conventions has had on our writing trajectories and pleasures, and the extent to which our pleasures have been coopted not only by our institutions but by our own desires for success in academia. The two samples of writing that we include move in different directions and take different forms but are, at the same time, entirely contingent on our academic research. Each offers an alternative way of knowing, expressed not as scholarly, 'objective' writing but through fiction. One is a satiric, dystopic comment on the impact of neoliberalism on schooling; the other a poetic, sensual and affective response to Deleuzian theory. Before we turn to our separate sections – Jo and her short story, and Susanne and her poem – we interrogate some of the language we have used to frame our inquiry, and some of the scholars we have found helpful in thinking through what we want to say about writing. We conclude with a rough outline of the strategies we have found helpful in our own salvage operations.

We ask how have the desires to write that drove us to an old wooden hall through so many humid Saturday afternoons become infested by pressures that we sometimes think of as external to ourselves. As our collaboration developed we thought about the parasitical practices associated with academic writing. Our writing is shaped by algorithmic indices or software we do not understand (e.g. SCImago, Eigenfactor, SNIP, h-index) or institutional systems and processes (e.g. ERA) that favour certain outlets over others, or by the friendlier seeming alternatives that require our complicity as we voluntarily attach our publications outputs to our writing identities (e.g. Researchgate, academia.com, googlescholar etc.). These might be understood as practices of governmentality, in a Foucauldian sense, requiring "algorithmic self-regulation", in a diffuse and multidirectional "liquid and flowing sociomaterial assemblage" that reshapes both academic writing as product and reforms the subjectivities and desires of academic writers (Introna, 2015, p. 19).

AFFECT, JOY AND WRITING

For our consideration of "pleasures" in this chapter, we turn to feminist scholars who write about positive affects such as joy broadly, and about writing specifically. Claire Colebrook, for example, influenced by Bergson, Nietzsche and Deleuze, critiques happiness which she says is the "activity of the soul in accordance with virtue – so that we become what we ought to be" (2008, p. 95). Human happiness is driven by "meaningful" activity, and hooked to "narrative, to a sense of one's life as a whole, and to the subordination of pleasure" (p. 82). Happiness, even that which comes from work, or scholarly pursuits, is an intellectual activity, predicated on "utility and quantified pleasure" (p. 83). Considering ourselves as writers, we accept that through diligence and conformity to the generic and stylistic conventions of academic writing, we create coherent research profiles and publication track records. We constitute ourselves, and are constituted by our writing, as the sorts of recognisable and virtuous academics our institutions require us to be. We are likely to achieve satisfaction, perhaps even some happiness, in these achievements. However, Colebrook provokes us to think beyond mere happiness and invites us to reframe our writing through "joy" which for her is "the liberation of creation and potential from virtue" (2008, p. 95). She suggests that this will entail moving "beyond the human intellect of utility and quantified pleasure, to an intuition of movements and sympathies that are not our own" (p. 83). In particular, this requires a literary voice, an imaginative mode where point of view, image and narrative voice can move beyond *what is* towards what *might be*.

We turn to writing as a wild profusion of possibilities of forms and modes that move writers and readers affectively, corporeally and intellectually. This takes us outside the conventions of academic prose, which tend to flatten affect and disregard the body. In this reconceptualised approach, each instance of writing will find its own form, will find its way *through* writing as the writer draws on all the textual and stylistic affordances that arise in the moment of writing. Our guides here are feminist scholars who advocate courage and experimentation in writing. For qualitative researchers, the most well known of these is likely to be Laurel Richardson who has consistently argued from her influential book *Fields of Play* (Richardson, 1997) through to the compendium of her influences in *Permissions* (White, 2016), that writing is itself a method of inquiry through which we come to know, perhaps more, and certainly differently than in conventional academic prose. In St Pierre's contribution to this argument, "writing *is* thinking, writing *is* analysis, writing *is* indeed a seductive and tangled *method* of discovery" (Richardson & St Pierre, 2005, p. 967). Anna Gibbs considers "writing as method' in her work on affective modes of writing (2015). She argues that writing forms a "critical form of resistance" to current academic pressures, "including the injunction to write in ways codified by the academy" (2015, p. 222). This requires experiments that respond to singular problems and are always invented anew, where affect is engaged and writing is "driven by interest and desire, subject to frustration and misery as well as productive of joy and excitement" (2015, p. 223). Writing otherwise is a form of rapture, for bell hooks, for whom her childhood memories of overhearing "voices moved by spirits – voices caught in moments of divine rapture" (1999, p. 124) in Pentecostal tent-meetings in the rural south epitomise the sublime joys of succumbing to the demands of writing. Writing as submission, art, beauty, surprise. Like Nina Lykke and Mona Livholts, we aim for an other-than, even "post/academic" writing that might enable us to rediscover the "amazement … of letting the unexpected work on us" through writing (Lykke, in Livholts 2012, p. 138).

What were we discovering as we wrote the short fiction and poetry that we have included in this chapter? Perhaps that affects and bodies are never far away from our intellectual work, and that we need to give ourselves permission to let writing take us where it will. Moments of escape both in what might be considered our mainstream academic writing and in our writing of poetry and fiction, enable us to salvage joy from the wreckage of our successful academic lives. This post/academic writing is critical, reflective, creative, cross disciplinary, cross genre and affectively potent. Our use of the verb 'salvage' for these writing strategies draws attention to the tenuousness of such recovery operations. Like those cargoes, battered and dripping on a beach after a salvage operation, our strategies do not return us intact or pristine to the scene of academic writing. Nor do they return us to the pre-academic naïve and artful pleasures in writing, with and for each other and other women, on those humid Saturday afternoons in that community hall. Nothing is as it was, but we are committed to helping each other remember how to play.

CREATIVE/ACADEMIC WRITING

Jo on Writing Fiction

The academy is sometimes a serious and punitive place with little time for play. Each scholarly paper is written with the knowledge that each word will be scrutinised by a panel of 'peers'. If there is room for ambiguity, it must be spelled out (as in 'this point I now make is ambiguous – let me look at both sides of the story and provide evidence of my real point, lest you not understand my real point and reject my paper'). Unless, of course, you're happy for the paper to be accepted by a lesser journal – one with less rigorous peer review. But no self-respecting academic – at least none with any ambition to get ahead – feels happy to go down this road. It would be naïve at best not to care about impact factors: Scimago, academia.com; google scholar; eprint downloads; and whatever exists next year. The academic voice cannot help but exclaim, 'What if this is misunderstood? What if I say this (meaning that) and reviewers don't get my satire or irony? What if I go too far? What if I don't go far enough? What if there is an axe to grind? What if someone has said something like this before, but better? What if I am wrong?' The censoring voice has little sense of humour. Writing becomes careful and the critical voices in the head very loud. It's a wonder anything ever gets sent out for review. But as Laurel Richardson writes, those holding "dinosaurian beliefs that 'creative' and 'analytic' are contradictory and incompatible modes are standing in the path of a meteor; they are doomed for extinction" (Richardson & St Pierre, 2005, p. 962).

The truth is, in reclaiming pleasure, the works we present here are no less rigorous, and no less researched than anything else we write. This first unfinished short story[2] is the culmination of my knowledge of some of the issues imposing pressure on teachers in the current climate. These include pressures on teachers to test and produce endless data on student outcomes, to regulate their performance at every given moment of the working day; to perform themselves in ways that prove their 'quality'; to respond to never-ending new pedagogical frameworks (sometimes ludicrous); to go against their instincts and their training to comply with policy; and increasingly to teach to scripts. Writing about these pressures as fiction allows them to be newly framed. As bell hooks has written: 'The point is not to render ideas more complex – the point is to make the complex clear' (hooks, 1999, p. 5).

But in fiction, I do not have to be guarded. I can take things farther, push boundaries, transgress the conventions of academic objectivity (or the pretense of it). I can amuse myself, scare my readers and myself, go a little nuts. There is enormous pleasure to be had in "expressing and constructing textuality via writing that transcends academic belonging" (Livholtz 2012, p. 141). By fictionalising what I know about these pressures I also have the great pleasure of giving referencing the finger.[3] So here it is.

Robomentor

It was only after a week of more than the usual number of electric shocks that Darla decided to have the earpiece implanted after all. She was clearly getting it wrong since it wasn't only the amount of times she received the shocks but the increase in voltage too. This was putting her too on edge and it frightened the children to keep seeing her convulsing. She worried that they too thought they must be responsible. She had woken up on the floor last week to little Vagita fretting over her. "I'm sorry" the little girl had said, " I knew how to spell friend but I just forgot. I'm really really sorry". Darla felt terrible about this. It wasn't the children's fault at all. Maybe the earpiece would help her be a better teacher. Maybe the children's' literacy outcomes would improve and maybe there was less chance she would be decanted to another school. The Department of Education seemed to think an unmanned mentorbot would help. It was to be inserted today.

It was a relief when at 10:30am Darla had arrived at little break without incident. She had been very careful to follow the script to the letter. As always, she received the text at 6am, and managed to memorise it before her phone was taken from her at the front desk when she arrived at 7:45am. There was nothing unusual about the day, she was relieved to see. She was to begin by asking four children (two girls, two boys, at least one from a linguistically or culturally diverse background) to pass a 'clap' around the room. If the others didn't follow the clap in rhythm she was to intervene and clap it out. The clapping was only to occur for 30 minutes, transition to take place with the handing out of a healthy vegan snack (from the green/grey category). After clappies the serious literacy business was to begin, today Script Number Three from the Brilliance Publishing Inc! program Positive Readers (2). Today the class was learning the letter/sound connection 'G', with a brief discussion of the socio-political meaning of 'G'. The deconstruction of the alphabet always made Darla a bit nervous, since she wasn't really sure. But today she did well, and was careful to include God in her list of G words.

The word God might be on the Perception and Beliefs, Literacy and Maths (Pablum) Test, which all school children took once a month from birth to eighteen. Darla looked at her phone diary, suddenly worried she had missed the day, and breathed a sigh of relief to see that it wasn't until next week. She should have known that, since the darkened blinds had not yet been lowered and she had not yet dispensed the anti-anxiety pills to her young pupils. All was well then. She had reviewed God and, reviewing her script, still had time to prepare the children to draft a budget spreadsheet, something that had been on the grade two, April test for the last three years. In fact, the teachers had more or less been instructed to spend extra time this month on financial budgeting at their last TTT – Teach to the Test – staff meeting. And she certainly wasn't going to make the same mistake twice anyway. The zap she had received when she got mixed up and taught 'art' in February instead of waiting until after September when the real work was done taught Darla a strong lesson. She'd just gotten confused, that's all. She'd read that mandala colouring in books were good for relaxation, but somehow she hadn't quite understood that art was only for the good children, and only an add-on. No more art then, though secretly Darla had thought the colouring in very artistic indeed. But it was quite a lot of hard work to learn a new pedagogical framework by heart every year, but it was necessary, especially if Darla hoped not to be decanted to a new school. If she wasn't careful, it would not just be a new school in the same town, but they would put her on a Mystery Teacher Transfer list and she could end up anywhere. She had heard that sometimes teachers never saw their families again. So Darla had put her earphones on at night, and listened to the subliminal and dulcet tones of policy and pedagogy. This year, many schools in her region were using The Pay Pray and Play Pedagogical Framework. It was the best pedagogical framework she had ever learned, and was full of Innovative and Progressive strategies designed to support Behaviour, Bodies and Budgets. She felt sorry for every second school, who were instead using the Crap and Strap Framework. This was the worst pedagogical framework she had ever heard of. Unfortunately, that was the one they would adopt next year, while those other schools would swap to theirs.

At noon, Mary Myers arrived at Darla's classroom door with a briefcase, a tablet and her technician. "Are you ready, love?" she asked Darla. "Glad to see you've taken up this opportunity for lifelong learning and good to see you embracing the new technologies as an early adopter. Adoption means adaptation", she quipped. Darla was understandably a little nervous. While many of her colleagues had already taken the plunge, she hadn't had an implant before. She was reassured when Mary explained the procedure in some detail.

The first step involved a series of questions that would inform Mary as to which implants were required. Barry, the technician hooked her up to the lie detector to make sure her answers were correct and true. Mary then began with the Ten Priority Questions for Teachers[4]:

1. What are your failings and weaknesses?
2. Which of your practices most impact on the lifetime failure of your students?
3. What are your weakest attributes, skills and dispositions?
4. What do your students hate you for most?
5. Think of an example of your practice that has made your students cry or vomit
6. Think of an example of your practice that has made your students stupider than they already were
7. What do your colleagues mock you for?
8. When were you closest to being fired?
9. Tell about a time when you didn't know what you were doing
10. Which pedagogical and curriculum knowledge are you faking understanding?

Darla tried to answer all questions truthfully and was surprised when Edelweiss began playing through the lie detector after her answer to number 4. She had said her students hated her most for being strict, but it turned out they hated her most for being kind, which was her second answer. She was already growing from this intervention. She hadn't known this, and told herself to remember to be a little less kind in future. Nor had she realized her colleagues laughed at her for having *unusually small feet, but Mary wasn't sure this could be resolved in this first round of remedial pedagogy.*

"Excellent", Mary said. "We can help with many of these. Once we implant the effective teaching whisperchip you will be monitored 8 hours a day by one of our robomentors. Based on the answers you've just given, your robomentor can begin whispering improving practices in your ear as you go about your daily business. We'll start on this lite version, which may be enough to solve all your teaching failures. Think of your robomentor as your Sherpa. They'll carry your pack to lighten your load. If you say or do or teach the wrong thing, if your classroom activities don't match the curriculum or the plan, you'll simply get a whisper suggesting you do things otherwise. Its gentler than the shocks you've been receiving, and we think the positive reinforcement is much more helpful. Basically, it's just a way for you to receive feedback, and be able to respond to it immediately. If you don't 'correct' your ways in 30 seconds though of course you will receive that shock, as you always have. So now Darla how does this sound?"

"Great!" Darla said, with only slight trepidation. I'm actually excited. I've always wanted to be the best teacher I could be".

Darla had a great thought, which she shared with Mary. "Why don't they implant whispermentors for children too? Wouldn't that be great? Then if children misbehaved, or gave the wrong answer, or even if they bullied other children they could have a childmentor whisper corrections in their ears. That's probably the next phase, right?"

Mary's beaming smile shrank, and Darla, who experienced a sudden shooting pain behind her right eye, saw her write the word 'psychopath' on her tablet. She would have to think later about what had been wrong with her answer.

After a brief moment Mary struck a yoga pose, turned her palms upward, appeared to be listening for guidance and began speaking again. "Darla", she said, "We'll put in the implants now. First, can I get your banking password? "

"My banking password?" Darla looked momentarily worried. "Why do you need that?"

"You're such a dear", Mary smiled again. "Nothing to fear, you little worry wart. We won't use it for anything. It's just for security. In case the insert falls out and we need to get you a new one. It never happens, silly. It's just routine".

"Must I?" Darla asked. She had heard tales of teachers being sued by parents, their accounts debited.

"No, not at all", Mary said. "It's not required. Well at least not in Bogger Ponds where I believe you are down to be transferred".

"If I give you the details will I still be transferred?" Darla asked.

"Oh no, dear. We can make a note on your files that you would like to stay here".

Darla was very relieved. She felt she had dodged a bullet. She looked up her account number and password on her tablet, and passed them over to Mary, who entered them on her own phone.

SUSANNE ON WRITING POETRY

This section turns to a different mode of serious play with writing, to what Hélène Cixous (1986, 1993) calls *jouissance*, diffuse and abundant pleasures where the body is imbricated in writing and where writing runs like a river carrying writer, reader, sense, language forward in unexpected ways. But the poem in this section is as much about reading as writing.

Academic writing is always also a matter of academic reading. The texts that we produce take material form most often as lines dotted with quotation marks separating what we read from what we write, marking off what we make use of from elsewhere and what might be ours. This demarcation is maintained as clearly as possible, preserving originality whilst performing authoritative citationality, through a form of academic ventriloquism. The texts we cite are not usually the sort of pleasurable reading that sets pulses racing, changes our moods and feelings, opens us to new experiences. Academic reading is dry, neutral, disembodied. Formal, impersonal, objective. It requires a clear head and no body at all. These qualities also characterize academic writing. It is *formal* and *impersonal,* as this university website describes: "It is formal by avoiding casual or 'conversational' language, such as contractions or informal vocabulary. It is impersonal and objective by avoiding direct reference to people or feelings, and instead emphasising objects, facts and ideas" (University of Sydney, 2016). But what if what you read infuses more than what you write, what if it seeps into your senses, frames your world a little differently, if your body tries to comprehend what you are reading?

The poem in this section came when I was first struggling to read Deleuze and Guattari. I took a bag of them on holiday, back to my old home, that place of the humid afternoons and writing women. While their figurations intrigued me, and their prose intoxicated me, I could not find a route through my reading. The logic of academic discourse did not assist me, and the guides to their work that I had been dipping in and out of (e.g. Colebrook, 2002) tended to adopt an expository mode in order to define, summarize, explain, elaborate, clarify and pin down their slippery prose. But this did not work for me, not there and not then, rather the instability of affects and desires entangled with reading started to move me unexpectedly towards the poetic.

Here Cixous, writer, critic, dramatist, and inventor of a new language she calls *ecriture feminine* became my guide. For Cixous, writing is not about resolution, definition or explanation but about *not arriving*. Rather she says that, in writing, "[o] ne must go on foot with the body. One has to go away, leave the self. How far must one not arrive in order to write, how far must one wander and wear out and have pleasure? (Cixous, 1993, p. 65). Writjng, the body, dreams, desires, pleasures and subterranean movements of affect, emotion and imagery are inseparable. Writing, for her, is "the passageway, the entrance, the exit ... that tears me apart, disturbs me, changes me" (1986, pp. 85–86). The bag of books, the return to a home that was mine no more, to an almost-ended relationship, to intense presence and loss, and in not reading and reading Deleuze while I was on leave from work and work would not let me go, led me to this poem.

No one quite got it. The poets' group suggested a series (perhaps "Foucault in Forest Lake" could be next) but I can't write like that. The academics wanted footnotes and more accurate referencing, but that killed it for poetry. I couldn't show philosophers, and the lover never saw it. A version slipped (at the last minute, on the last page, in the Postscript section) into a book on writing playfully in academia (Lykke. 2014). Is it any good, on any of these counts? I doubt it, but nor does it matter to me. It feels somehow true, to me, to a moment, to that contingent and precise assemblage of reading/writing/living/place/time/bodies/affects.

On (not) reading Deleuze in Cairns
Lines of flight

From a jetty in Djibouti and the obscenity of leisure
in the west to a man, a gun, and a dog, in Ecuador.

A forest mandala and a parade of fog
and firewalking for the winter solstice

Coals are a poor conductor, you say
but your voice carries in the thick dark, your fingertips
touch the nape of my spine: burn

Haecceity

Time falls off
Just us now
tangled intaglio
etching bodylines
with our fine
chisels of flesh
and bone
our invisible ink
our breath

Univocity

Moon in your mouth
sound of the sea in me
coral driftwood weed
small creatures swim in us
crabs scutter at your wrists:
salt: we are almost all water
At the cellular level, our filaments drift apart
divide, multiply; our surfaces are
littoral zones, subject to moon
tide and the pulsing planet.

IN/CONCLUSION

If we were to conclude this chapter, though we have confessed already that we are committed to inconclusion, we might suggest that escape from institutional capture of writing is always possible. With varying success, we have found new writing groups in other places. Or we have written alone, when texts seek forms other than those that are conventionally endorsed by our institutions. We read and read and read, mixing it up so that most of all we can keep loving language and worrying at it, and taking pleasure in it, regardless of what we write or for whom. We collaborated on this chapter in ways we already knew would give us pleasure, having written together in the past. We hadn't entirely anticipated how much our "salvage strategies" would give us some direction to escape tedium but also provide us with a way to comply as well as subvert the expectations of "what counts" as scholarly writing. After all, here we are, getting an academic publication from our most pleasurable writing.

NOTES

[1] This women's writing group was initiated and facilitated by writer and teacher Inez Baranay (see inezbaranay.com) who remains a friend and mentor for both of the authors of this chapter.
[2] Pleasure! Imagine writing for the sheer joy of it, leaving it unfinished and not feeling guilty about it.
[3] Don't quote me. No, do quote me. Academics get great pleasure out of being cited, and we like to count our citations.
[4] Here we have a social survey.

REFERENCES

Cixous, H. (1986). Sorties: Out and out: Attacks/ways out/ forays (B. Wing, Trans.). In H. Cixous & C. Clement (Eds.), *The newly born woman* (pp. 63–134). Manchester, England: Manchester University Press.
Cixous, H. (1993). *Three steps on the ladder of writing*. New York, NY: Columbia University Press.
Colebrook, C. (2002). *Understanding Deleuze*. Crows Nest, Australia: Allen and Unwin.
Colebrook, C. (2008). Narrative happiness and the meaning of life. *New Formations, 63*, 85–102.
Gibbs, A. (2015). Writing as method: Attunement, resonance, and rhythm. In B. T. Knudsen & C. Stage (Eds.), *Affective methodologies: Developing cultural research strategies for the study of affect* (pp. 222–236). Basingstoke & New York: Palgrave Macmillan.
Honan, E., Henderson, L., & Loch, S. (2016). The production of the academicwritingmachine. *Reconceptualising Educational Research Methodology, 7*(2), 4–18.
hooks, b. (1999). *Remembered rapture: The writer at work*. London: The Women's Press.
Introna, L. (2016). Algorithms, governance, and governmentality. On governing academic writing. *Science, Technology, and Human Values, 41*(1) 17–49.
Livholtz, M. (2012). To fill academic work with political passion: Nina Lykke's cosmodolphins and contemporary post/academic writing strategies. (Interview with Nina Lykke). *Feminist Review, 102*, 135–142.
Lykke, N. (Ed.). (2014). *Writing academic texts differently. Intersectional feminist methodologies and the playful art of writing*. New York & London: Routledge.
Richardson, L. (1997) *Fields of play: Constructing an academic life*. Rutgers University Press.
Richardson, L. & St Pierre, E. (2005). Writing: A method of inquiry. In N. K. Denzin & Y. S. Lincoln (Eds.), *Handbook of qualitative research* (3rd ed., pp. 959–978). Thousand Oaks, CA: Sage.

University of Sydney. (2016). How is academic writing different to other kinds of writing? http://sydney.edu.au/stuserv/learning_centre/help/styleStructure/st_academicWriting.shtml

White, J. (Ed.). (2016) *Permission: The international interdisciplinary impact of Laurel Richardson's work*. Rotterdam: Sense Publishers.

Susanne Gannon
Western Sydney University, Australia

Jo Lampert
La Trobe University, Melbourne, Australia

JUDY GOUWENS AND KENNETH P. KING

16. FROM FRUSTRATION TO FLOW

Finding Joy through Co-teaching

INTRODUCTION

In June 2015, after our spring semester was finished, our grades were posted, and our offices organized for the summer (when neither of us was teaching), we were summoned to a meeting with our Dean. At the meeting, we were presented with predictions of low enrolment for the upcoming fall semester, which created the necessity for changing the courses we were scheduled to teach then. Although we were asked, it became clear in our discussion that the Dean's request for both of us to teach "Methods of Teaching Mathematics in the Elementary and Middle School" was not an option but an assignment. What follows is an account of how we moved from the frustration such "assignment" outside of our areas of academic preparation and expertise caused, to creating an effective learning experience for our students and enjoying working together, analyzed through the frameworks of Wenger's Communities of Practice (1998) and Csíkszentmihályi's Flow (1991).

For various reasons (Cochran-Smith, Piazza, & Power, 2013; Diverse Staff, 2011; Imig, Wiseman, & Imig, 2011; McKeown-Moak, 2013; Saunders, 2015), teacher preparation institutions throughout the US have experienced declining enrolment since 2010. Enrolment in teacher education programs in our state dropped by 57% from 2010 to 2015 (US Department of Education, 2016). At our institution, teacher education enrolment dropped from 808 to 411 students during the same time, a 49% drop.

The enrolment decline presented an immediate challenge addressed most visibly by not replacing faculty members who retired or left the institution. Long-time adjunct faculty members were no longer employed to teach in the program, with all courses in the program taught by full time faculty members, regardless of their areas of preparation. What we learned while negotiating the challenge of teaching outside our area of preparation – and what it taught us – is the story we explore here.

ANALYTICAL FRAMEWORK

Two constructs provide the analytical framework for our paper. Communities of practice, as defined by Wenger, serves as an analytical tool for exploring our working relationship while co-teaching the course, while Csíkszentmihályi's concept of flow provides us with a framework to describe the personal and professional growth we experienced from our collaboration.

Communities of Practice

Within Wenger's social learning system paradigm, he identifies three broad constructs – communities of practice, boundaries, and identities – that provide a framework for analysis and interpretation (2000). Communities of practice (COP) refers to groups of individuals who share a common purpose and learn how to pursue this purpose through interaction with one another. "The concept of COPs holds that knowledge is fundamentally relational, not individual, and that the primary way in which we learn is through interactions with others around shared experiences in the world" (Scanlan, Kim, Burns, & Vuilleumier, 2016, p. 9).

Communities of practice. We use COP as an analytical tool to examine the nature of the relationship between us as we negotiated and implemented teaching a new course.

Boundaries. LeCornu (2009) noted the importance of recognizing and crossing boundaries in the establishment of COPs. The factors of transparency, negotiation, and coordination of boundary interactions benefit from having a trusted colleague. This sort of support allows opportunities to discuss and reframe interactions to increase confidence and effectiveness in working together.

Identities. Within a teacher education milieu, teacher identity provides insight toward understanding why this construct might hold a central place in the professional practice of teachers (Harlow & Cobb, 2014). Teacher identity can be described as a self-attributed belief constructed through teaching experiences that affirm what it means to be a teacher, grounded in the opportunity to connect with other teachers, to gain a sense of professional effectiveness and expansiveness, defining the breadth and scope of one's identity (Wenger, 2000; Kwan & Lopez-Real, 2009).

Within each of these broad constructs (COP, Boundaries, and Identities) Wegner identified three dimensions, each with three modes of belonging, that describe forms of participation. Engagement describes interpersonal interactions; imagination describes expanding one's view of the world to conceive of new possibilities; and alignment describes coordination of activities so that actions have an impact beyond our ability to directly control them (Wenger, 2000)

Flow

The pathway we experienced as we negotiated designing and teaching the mathematics methods course led us from dealing with a professional challenge to an opportunity for professional growth – and personal satisfaction that we would comfortably characterize as joy, the notion of flow researched and described by Csíkszentmihályi.

Here we reflect on our experiences during this semester using Wenger's model to analyze the COP that emerged during our co-teaching and Csíkszentmihályi's concept of flow to analyze the personal growth that emerged. We present our experiences as a dialogue, framed by Wenger's and Csíkszentmihályi's frameworks, and reflect, in the end, on how the process ultimately helped us to achieve professional satisfaction and, in fact, a measure of joy.

REFLECTION ON PROCESS: ESTABLISHING A BASELINE – THE CHALLENGE

Ken: Looking back on the meeting in the dean's office, I left the room frustrated and angry. I appreciate that as an academic, I'm supposed to be good at learning – but the responsibility of teaching a course outside of my knowledge base left me stunned. It's bad for us as faculty – and it's bad for our students. They deserve experts. And professionally – I had just been required to vacate my office on the suburban campus and move my work to the Chicago campus. It was a combination of frustrations and, frankly, considerable anger. Adding to it was a deep sense of helplessness about what we were expected to accomplish.

Judy: My own feeling of helplessness was only somewhat assuaged by our being in this together. Looking back on that meeting makes me think of Wenger's notion of "perturbability" as a key factor in the initiation of a COP (1998). I was indeed perturbed!! Of course I had taught mathematics as a primary teacher, but that was nearly 30 years ago. So much has changed since then, both in what we know about children's learning and in the standards for mathematics learning.

Ken: In the beginning, I appreciate that neither of us would be alone during this experience. Having a sense of "shared misery" was appreciated, as at least we would have some empathy for one another and our shared plight.

Judy: We also possessed another factor Wenger identifies in the emergence of a COP – resilience. In our work together redesigning the elementary education program in our college, for example, our roles were often like the inflatable toys, weighted on the bottom, that when punched, right themselves, standing defiant and ready for the next punch. When faced with this enormous challenge, as frustrated as we were, we were ready to take it on.

REFLECTION ON PROCESS: A COMMUNITY OF PRACTICE

The framework below is based on the three dimensions of Wenger's construct of COP (2000).

Community Dimension: Enterprise, Mutuality, and Repertoire

We reflect here on how we became a COP, the result of respect and the vision we shared in this co-teaching experience. The dialogue explores the concepts of enterprise, mutuality, and repertoire.

Ken: I appreciate a point you made early in the process, that we both have backgrounds in curriculum and instruction, and that while there is quite a bit we don't know about math education as a discipline, we at least have a framework for understanding curriculum and instruction and can understand how math education fits into that larger framework.

Judy: We also both have had experience tackling projects that might, at the outset, seem daunting, but then completing them successfully. That base provided both the resilience that Wenger describes as necessary to a community of practice, and the skill that Csíkszentmihályi says is a key element of flow. We know how to plan for effective instruction and engage students.

Judy: In our process, we were fortunate to have a mentor who coordinates mathematics in a middle school. Our mentor scaffolded our learning in mathematics, suggested resources for us to use and share with our students, and, true to scaffolding, gradually released the planning process to us.

Ken: Speaking to my experience in the process, enterprise and imagination are pretty lofty constructs – I think that in the beginning, I was more focused on survival. While we were guided by the precepts of our conceptual framework, the realization that we could do this – and meet our students' needs – opened me up to possibilities in innovation that I could not perceive in the beginning.

Judy: We did have the conceptual framework of the program as a guide, as well as some textbooks, the Common Core State Standards for mathematics learning, and the Illinois Professional Teaching Standards for teaching mathematics: a defined agenda. Like you, I was also initially focused on survival, probably the most immediate personal goal, but we shared the overarching goal of facilitating students' learning to be competent and effective teachers of mathematics.

Judy: Something happened somewhere around the third or fourth week, for both of us. We began to develop the confidence to deviate from our plan and be innovative.

Judy: One concept that shaped our course was the idea of "worthwhile tasks", problems that were authentic, that could be solved in a variety of ways, and in some cases had a variety of possible answers. We also tried to incorporate children's literature about mathematics concepts whenever we could. One worthwhile task we shared began with Hutchins' book, The Doorbell Rang (1986). The story involves partitioning a set of cookies in a variety of ways based on the number of children sharing the cookies. To demonstrate how teachers might use manipulatives to help children develop understanding, we distributed paper "cookies" the students could use as we read the story aloud. The paper cookies then served as an optional tool for solving a subsequent worthwhile task that involved cookies.

Ken: I recall that class meeting well. Watching our students struggle with the problem – they approached it from the perspective of adults. Some students used algebra, for example, which demonstrated that there was a great opportunity to help them learn to think about teaching and learning and not just about finding answers to math problems. It was, for me, evidence that we could use what we know about teaching and learning, as well as our growing expertise in mathematics pedagogy, to help our teacher candidates grow.

Judy: We were both guided by the vision of changing our students' notion of mathematics as computation to the concept of mathematics as a problem-solving enterprise, with computation being a set of tools that might be used in problem-solving.

Judy: Since the class met Monday and Tuesday mornings, we typically planned to address specific concepts for the week, with activities that flowed from one day to the next. We asked students to reflect on their learning at the end of each class meeting, using a format for critical reflection (Henderson & Noble, 2015). We set aside time after each class meeting to reflect on what and how our students were learning, using our reflection and those of our students to guide our teaching in our next class meeting.

Ken: One of the things that I came to appreciate about our collaboration was, frankly, how collaborative it was. We came to quickly understand and appreciate the respective strengths we brought to the class and how we were able to use those skills to create a better experience for the students.

Judy: As we worked together, the leadership for the course seemed to be distributed fairly equally. We planned for our class meetings together, and we each prepared and selected materials to use. At every class meeting, we each took the lead in facilitating some of the activities. Interestingly, as the term proceeded, we began to facilitate activities together, not with a specific plan to do so, but because it seemed to evolve naturally.

Ken: I agree. This experience reflected a mutual vision for success. Looking back at the entire experience, one of the places I saw our mutual trust and sense of collegiality evident was when we had to contend with some students who were struggling beyond our ability to help them successfully pass the class. The students appealed their final grades in the course, and we met with them.

Judy: Early in the term, we had some students who had attended class irregularly or who were consistently arriving late. We decided to meet with those students individually to remind them of the on-time attendance policy we had set for the course and to determine what we could do to help them attend class or arrive on time. At our meeting with the first student, we learned that one of her parents was terminally ill and her absences were due to training for a job she had taken to assist with family finances. Talking with the student provided us the opportunity to experience directly our shared levels of empathy for students' life situations.

Ken: Reflecting on those discussions with students, I think it helped the class as a whole. Word does leak out that our focus is on their success as teacher candidates – and that we can be trusted to focus on their success and empathize with them. Of all classes I have taught, particularly at the undergraduate level, I sensed a real community developing during our class meetings. And that level of trust and community was present during our joint field experience observations as well.

Judy: I have an added personal and professional appreciation for our collaboration that extended to my recent promotion from associate professor to full professor. It's an expectation that faculty members demonstrate some degree of collaboration and that the candidate for promotion document an observation of teaching during the probationary phase. The letter you wrote, advocating for my promotion, was not one of the typical "one and done" observations, but was based on watching my classroom practice for an entire semester.

Judy: Collaborating as we did in teaching this mathematics methods course both deepened and strengthened my appreciation for you, Ken, personally and professionally. Before working so closely together, I would have described our relationship as professional colleagues, certainly based on trust that we shared a vision for our program and our college. Since co-teaching, I would add to my description that of friend.

Ken: And that process continued as we worked into the next semester. When, months later, we independently reviewed a student's work for feedback, the comments we made were identical to one another. That level of alignment and shared expectations is remarkable – and is ongoing.

Judy: One sign to me that we were aligned both philosophically and in practice was that in class we began to finish each other's sentences, add examples to each other's explanations, and respond to students' questions in the same way.

Ken: Reflecting on our co-teaching experience, I can see how it built upon our shared experience designing the new elementary education program, much in the same way that we worked so seamlessly with our students. I think that designing the program really opened up to each of us both what we had in common in our academic background, as well as differences, both of which contributed to the program design. We had the luxury of time designing the program; organizing the class put our shared experience a more rigorous test.

Ken: Looking ahead, this will serve us well in the next phase of program design as we begin to develop course content and experiences in detail. I think we achieved a high degree of trust through this process.

Judy: One component of the redesigned program that will require collaboration is a new set of field experiences for teacher candidates. As we plan for and facilitate those experiences, the reflection process that we shared during our co-teaching should serve us well. Our reflections were driven by a set of questions: What are our students learning? How are our students learning? What are we doing/did we do that facilitated that learning? What did we do that got in the way of our students' learning? The questions should help us to develop the worthwhile field experiences we envision.

Ken: I would add to that the language we developed to characterize the phases of the redesigned program of study – survival/orientation/innovation/inquiry – showed that we could develop a shared framework and language to describe our work to each other – and communicate it to a larger audience. Our deeper collaboration with this course will further develop our shared language.

Ken: One worry, resting uncomfortably in the back of my mind is to make sure that we do not become too insular. I think that our ability to communicate and operate with a shared point of view could run the risk of disenfranchizing other faculty members from the ongoing design process.

Judy: If we had the opportunity (is my sarcasm apparent here?) to co-teach this course again, I believe that we would begin with the shared expectations that we discovered and developed through our work together. If we co-teach again, I will enter that opportunity with great anticipation and optimism for working together and for the outcomes for our students that will be more than what either of us can bring about on our own.

Evident in the dialogue above are elements of enterprise, mutuality, and repertoire. The degree of interaction shared in the dialogue emphasises the concept of engagement. Working together, we carried out actions that guided the class's culture, as well as our own relationship. As Borgati (2004) noted, engagement requires more than simply assignment to a group; it requires a level of deep interaction. The shared work delivering the class was a culmination of experiences that began initially as colleagues but grew through additional shared responsibilities (program leadership, program design) that found its fullest expression by collaborating to deliver the class.

The concept of enterprise is evident as we focused on organizing and delivering the course to our students. As a common purpose, we had numerous levels of engagement ranging from (initially) week-to-week survival to a sense of professional accomplishment and growth as our shared proficiency grew. As Judy noted, "that personal connection cycled back into the teaching and planning experiences", providing a framework for both professional and personal growth.

Shared repertoire was evident as we built upon our professional skills in curriculum and instruction and grew in our knowledge of mathematics pedagogy. Borgati (2004) noted that shared repertoire represents an accomplished community of practice. The experience is built upon the experiences, shared history, and the sense of identity shared among the participants themselves. Judy's comments above noted an initial alignment in terms of philosophy and practice, and the overall narrative demonstrates how this shared point of view, when applied in collaboration to address a common challenge, contributed to the development of our community of practice.

BOUNDARY DIMENSION: COORDINATION, TRANSPARENCY, AND NEGOTIABILITY

Here we reflect on concepts related to boundaries in a COP: coordination, transparency, and negotiability.

Judy: I think that in co-teaching, we challenged the boundaries that were set up for us by the culture of our department and our college. In academia, opportunities to observe my colleagues' teaching have been rare; the opportunities I have had were one-time "official" observations for the purposes of supporting tenure and promotion decisions.

Ken: The concept of boundaries is evolving rapidly in teacher education. The impact of state and national initiatives and their impact on what we can do in the classroom is an ongoing challenge. Knowing what public school teachers have experienced over the last two decades, it was only a matter of time before the accountability movements set their sights on teacher education.

Judy: A positive outcome of co-teaching and of the community we developed is that we can think through the next steps together and ensure that our professional and personal identity is not lost as we move into the next accountability paradigm. Doing this alone would be incredibly difficult – it would lead rapidly to a place of frustration and even despair.

Judy: I know that Ken and I have spent more time in collaborative reflection on our teaching and on resolving student issues since co-teaching than ever before. For me, our semester of co-teaching set in place the habit of reflecting with a trusted colleague. In his book, *The Fifth Discipline*, Senge argued that a learning community sustains itself because of the commitment of its members. He said that a person who experiences the power of membership in a learning organization will seek out membership in such organizations for the rest of that person's life (1990). After experiencing the joy our community of practice produced for me, I intend to seek out ways to continue to produce that joy through collaboration.

Judy: Although our community of practice at this point includes only the two of us, I would hope that in the future we could grow the community to include others of our colleagues as we continue to work together.

Ken: I think that our ability to coordinate and align goals and methods into action was grounded in a common language of curriculum, instruction, and assessment. It is an interesting perspective that we used those same concepts to build a course that was focused on curriculum, instruction, and assessment in elementary math instruction. In many ways, we were using the skills that we were teaching.

Judy: Indeed, the curriculum, instruction, and assessment perspectives and understandings that we share, as well as our college conceptual framework, did help us align our goals and methods. When we began to design the course, and even when we began teaching it, I doubt that we realized just how much our common understandings would provide direction for the course. It is only in looking back now that I realize that we had much more to begin with than I considered initially.

Ken: Except for the early involvement of our math education mentor, we just had each other in this process. As a community of two, plus our students, we had to seek our own explanations and encourage each other. Every time we planned and taught class, it was always a joint operation with the entire process revealed to one another.

Judy: The time that we set aside to unpack, reflect, and plan was invaluable in developing explanations – we developed shared explanations, in coaching each other, and generally in making sense of what we were doing and where we were headed in the course. Having the opportunity to teach together provided windows into Ken's practice for me, and allowed us to traverse some boundaries.

Judy: As I think back on this experience, I am amazed at how we had almost no differences in perspectives and expectations. It is possible that expediency facilitated our agreement, but I think it is more likely that our common background in curriculum, instruction, and assessment provided the basis of our agreement. Perhaps there might have been more differences, had we been co-teaching a course that one of both of us had taught previously.

Ken: Absolutely. As I mentioned during our work together, I appreciate the very conceptual approach you take when you approach a problem. It complements my more methodical approach. You did so much to provide us with the vision and direction, which allowed me to organize aspects of the week-by-week content for the students in the course.

Ken: I think we often had the sense that the other was "doing more" with respect to the course – which is a different experience than, for example, dealing with resentment when someone is not contributing to a project.

Judy: I always felt that you were doing more, Ken. I so appreciated your detail-orientation and learned so much about the value of the detail you created. In many ways, it was the detailed planning you did that helped us move toward feeling competent. Those detailed plans even helped build our confidence to deviate from them, I think, because we always had a sense of where we were headed with them.

Coordination was evident in terms of the way we worked together to plan and organize the course experiences. The coordination across a single course was enhanced by curriculum design work that we had shared previously, but the mechanics of collaborating on the delivery of a single course offered the means to further develop an ethic and practice of collaboration and coordination of action.

Transparency was not only part of our working style, but the transparency led to a further seamless delivery of course work during the inaugural delivery of courses in a new program of study one year later.

The construct of negotiation presented itself, for example in Ken's comment that their approaches were complementary in nature: Judy approaches problems and program design from a very conceptual approach, whereas Ken sees his strengths and the development of incremental experiences that are more operational in nature.

IDENTITY DIMENSION: CONNECTEDNESS, EXPANSIVENESS, AND EFFECTIVENESS

The identify dimension in our community of practice provided the opportunity to reflect on our evolving sense of connectedness, expansiveness, and professional effectiveness.

Ken: We've been acquainted for the 10 years that I've been a faculty member in the college of education. It's only been the last few years that we've had a chance to work together more closely.

Ken: I know that when I assumed program chair responsibilities from you, you helped orient me quickly to the role, and two years ago, when we started the redesign process for the program, we spent much more time working together. I think that the redesign process really helped set a foundation for what we did during our co-teaching last fall.

Judy: I agree that our previous work provided a foundation for our co-teaching. But until then, we had had essentially two separate programs on different campuses. We worked together administratively, but not substantively. The redesign process, which ultimately fell to the two of us, demonstrated how similar our academic backgrounds and philosophies are.

Ken: Working with you was also helpful as I left our former suburban campus. While I am acquainted with all the members of the faculty, having a colleague on the Chicago campus was helpful as I settled in a new office and such. Having someone with whom I shared trust made a personally and professionally challenging experience much more humane.

Judy: For me, your moving to the Chicago campus has facilitated our work together and enhanced my own practice. We have had lots of "coworkers", but not many true colleagues. Being in residence at the same campus, with offices in close proximity, has strengthened our COP, for which I am grateful.

Ken: And it has opened up communication between us better than we might have imagined.

Judy: We do have great conversations. Often, when we are having one of them, I am left wondering why it took us nearly 10 years to develop our community and regretting not having had these conversations years ago.

Judy: We both believe strongly in our college's conceptual framework, based on enacting social justice through education, and that does inform our COP. While we haven't articulated a set of principles for our specific COP, I suspect that if we each set down some principles, they would be similar, if not identical.

Ken: I think what I would add is that I see our work as an extension of key ideas that are present in our college's conceptual framework. A quote from the conceptual framework – with the idea attributed to John Dewey – expresses well what we achieved during the class: "[a] meaningful education upholds the social standard of democracy and shared decision making, understood not merely as allegiance to representative government but as a method of social deliberation on problems of significance" (College of Education, 2006, p. 4).

Judy: Our program has always focused on making the conceptual framework a living document, not just on paper. Students learn from their first course in the program that we are about implementing the ideas presented in the conceptual framework. I suspect that if we did not follow the guidelines of the conceptual framework, our students would bring us back to them.

Ken: We are fortunately that we have students that would do this – to keep us grounded in the conceptual framework – as well as appreciating how it guides our practice and our relationships.

Judy: We negotiated this aspect of the experience – the personal and professional boundaries well – but I'm not sure that our program, more broadly, shares enough trust or vision to experience what we have. I hope I am wrong.

Judy: One aspect of boundaries Wenger identifies is the opportunity for professional recognition. Working together, I believe, provided us the opportunity to recognize each other's efforts and effectiveness. Co-teaching then provided a platform for recognition – and joy – that we typically do not have within our program or college.

Judy: As we implement the new program, into which we built many opportunities for faculty members to collaborate, we can also work to build the trust upon which the success of our collaboration depended so much.

Evidence of connectedness is documented as we discuss how out relationship evolved during the planning and delivery of the course, building on our prior collaboration as curriculum designers. The reference to the college's conceptual framework offered a common vision for preparing students to be effective teachers as well as a point of shared values and connection between us during our collaboration. Indeed, the level of collaboration and connection served to reinforce the values and dispositions present in the conceptual framework.

Expansiveness was enhanced during the formation of the community. Wenger's point that expansiveness serves to "enable action and participation" (2000, p. 240) is fully realized during the process of planning and collaboration. Collaboration on the shared math course further developed the shared experience established during the previous year's program design process – as barriers were eliminated and a new vision for teacher preparation was established – and continued a year after teaching the math methods course as we led the inauguration of the new education program with its first cohort of students.

Effectiveness was evident as the identity of the COP matured. One of the core aspects of effectiveness is based in the opportunity for action and participation. The development of an identity that is "socially empowering" (Wegner, 2000, p. 240) is evident through the entire dialogue. From frustration at the outset our arrival as highly coordinated collaborators demonstrates fully the construct of effectiveness in action.

REFLECTION ON PROCESS: EXPERIENCING FLOW

Engaging with the concept of flow serves as a personal and professional outcome for this experience. Anticipating only the need to complete the class and to prepare students to teach mathematics well, the community that we developed as we designed and implemented the course led to a degree of engagement in the course and its content that we rarely achieve. That degree of engagement led to unexpected happiness or what Csíkszentmihályi calls "flow" (1990). According to him, flow, or happiness "is not something that happens" to us, but rather "a condition that must be prepared for, cultivated, and defended privately by each person" (p. 2). He argues that flow "usually occur[s] when a person's body or mind is stretched to its limits in a voluntary effort to accomplish something difficult and worthwhile" (p. 3). Indeed, teaching the mathematics methods course stretched us to our limits, and, in reflection, we found that our experience met Csíkszentmihályi's conditions for flow. Csíkszentmihályi describes eight conditions that most people who experience flow describe:

1. A challenging activity that requires skills;
2. The merging of action and awareness;
3. Clear goals;
4. Feedback;
5. Concentration on the task at hand;
6. The paradox of control;
7. The loss of self-consciousness; and
8. The transformation of time. (pp. 49–67)

Teaching the course clearly met the first condition, "a challenging activity that requires skills" (p. 49). We both had the necessary skills to plan and teach a course; both of us had earned high ratings of our teaching, and students regularly describe our courses as challenging and engaging. Designing this particular course was challenging, as we have explained earlier.

Csikszentmihalyi's second condition, "the merging of action and awareness", is met when "people become so involved in what they are doing that the activity becomes spontaneous, almost automatic" (p. 53). When our practice evolved to the point that we deviated from the detailed plans for our class meetings, focusing instead on how our students were learning, our teaching became spontaneous, allowing the students' questions and our observations of their learning in the moment to drive our teaching. For example, during a break in one class meeting, students were guessing one another's Zodiac sign. In that class meeting, we were focusing on designing worthwhile tasks, and we used their interest in the Zodiac as content for worthwhile tasks.

The course was driven by the clear goal for the students to learn to teach mathematics effectively, we sought continuous feedback from the students, and we set aside time to reflect and give feedback to each other. That goal and the immediate feedback, the third and fourth conditions for flow, according to Csikszentmihalyi, made it possible for us to achieve the spontaneity and automaticity that evolved in our co-teaching.

In focusing on planning and facilitating the course, both of us quickly left behind the frustration and despair that we felt initially when assigned the course. Csikszentmihalyi describes this level of concentration as the fifth condition for flow. In our focus on teaching the course, we began early on to enjoy both the challenge of teaching the course and the COP that we were creating.

At the same time, as we saw ourselves succeeding in co-teaching the course, we stopped worrying about failure. This sixth condition of flow, having a sense of control, according to Csikszentmihalyi, is what motivates participants to continue on in the activity that ultimately produces happiness or joy.

Csikszentmihalyi's seventh condition of flow, "the loss of self-consciousness", for us became the loss of the sense of ego in our teaching. For both of us, the focus was not on our individual excellence in teaching, but on the students becoming successful teachers of mathematics. In other words, at a certain point, as we freely contributed our individual strengths to the joint effort, we gave up 'I' to 'we'.

Our work together also met the last condition of flow: "the transformation of time". At the beginning of the term, we both watched the clock during class meetings to make sure that we had enough activities to fill the allotted time, and we carefully scheduled time for us to reflect and plan together. But we soon found ourselves in a rhythm in class, concurring with the students when they were so engaged that they were surprised when it was time for the class meetings to end. Our reflection and planning, that we had so carefully scheduled at the beginning of the term, took on the same inattention to the clock, as we developed a rhythm for unpacking and reflecting on our teaching and the students' learning.

REFLECTION ON PROCESS: PERSONAL GROWTH-ACHIEVING JOY

Judy: When the semester was over and the course finished, to my surprise, I did not have the sense of relief that I had expected. Instead, I had almost a sense of loss at the experience being over, and at the same time an amazing sense of accomplishment and happiness. I realized that my experience in co-teaching the mathematics methods course had been one of most challenging in my tenure at the university, and at the same time, one of the most exciting and joyful. Certainly, we had succeeded in teaching the mathematics methods course and helping the students be prepared to teach mathematics. But we had accomplished something else in the process that was perhaps more important. We had become a real COP, with the potential for that community to extend both beyond the two of us and beyond the semester of the course.

Ken: I'll speak for myself, but too often, collaboration in work settings has been characterized by frustration and competing visions of what needs to be done – and the purpose for doing it. This experience was unlike any other I have experienced.

The collaboration and its outcome is not just something that took place in the past – it is something that will take us forward as colleagues, collaborators, and friends.

REFERENCES

Borgati, S. (2004). *Communities of practice*. Retrieved from http://www.analytictech.com/mb119/communities_of_practice.htm

Cochran-Smith, M., Piazza, P., & Power, C. (2013). The politics of accountability: Assessing teacher education in the United States. *The Educational Forum*. 77(1), 6–27. doi: 10.1080/00131725.2013.739015

College of Education. (2006). *Roosevelt University College of Education Conceptual Framework*. Retrieved from https://www.roosevelt.edu/~/media/Files/pdfs/COE/ConceptualFrameworkFull.ashx

Council for the Accreditation of Educator Preparation. (2013). The CAEP Standards. Retrieved from http://caepnet.org/standards/introduction

Csikszentmihalyi, M. (1990). *Flow: The psychology of optimal experience*. New York: Harper Collins.

Diverse Staff. (2011). Where do we go from here? *Diverse Issues in Higher Education, 28*(5), 13–16.

Harlow, A., & Cobb, D. J. (2014). Planting the seeds of teacher identity: Nurturing early growth through a collaborative learning community. *Australian Journal of Teacher Education, 39*(7), 70–88.

Henderson, R., & Noble, K. (2015). *Professional learning, induction and critical reflection: Building workforce capacity in education*. Basingstoke, UK: Palgrave Macmillan.

Imig, D., Wiseman, D., & Imig, S. (2011). Teacher education in the United States. *Journal of Education for Teaching, 37*(4), 399–408. doi: 10.1080/02607476.2011.611006

King, K. P., & Gouwens, J. (2016, April). *Program redesign through democratic participation: An iterative design process involving college faculty and public school partners.* Paper presented at the annual meeting of the Midwest Association for Teacher Education, Urbana, IL.

Kwan, T., & Lopez-Real, F. (2009). Identity formation of teacher–mentors: An analysis of contrasting experiences using a Wengerian matrix framework. *Teaching and Teacher Education, 26*(3), 722–731. doi: 10.1016/j.tate.2009.10.008

Lave, J., & Wenger, E. (1991). *Situated learning: Legitimate peripheral participation.* New York: Cambridge University Press.

Le Cornu, R. (2009). *Crossing boundaries: Challenges of academics working in professional experiences.* Paper presented at the annual conference of the Australian Teacher Education ATEA), Albury, New South Wales, Australia.

McKeown-Moak, M. P. (2013). The "new" performance funding in higher education. *Educational Considerations, 40*(2), 3–12.

Omidvar, O., & Kislov, R. (2014). The evolution of the communities of practice approach: Toward knowledgeability in a landscape of practice – An interview with Etienne Wenger-Trayner. *Journal of Management Inquiry, 23*(2), 266–275.

Saunders, D. B. (2015). Resisting excellence: Challenging neoliberal ideology in postsecondary education. *Journal for Critical Education Policy Studies, 13*(2), 391–413.

Scanlan, M., Kim, M., Burns, M. B., & Vuilleumier, C. (2016). Poco a Poco: Leadership practices supporting productive communities of practice in schools serving the new mainstream. *Educational Administration Quarterly, 52*(1) 3–44. doi: 10.1177/0013161X15615390

United States Department of Education. (2015). *Title II Reports.* Retrieved from https://title2.ed.gov/Public/Home.aspx

Wenger, E. (1998). *Communities of practice: Learning, meaning, and identity.* New York: Cambridge University Press.

Wenger, E. (2000). Communities of practice and social learning systems. *Organization, 7*(2), 225–246.

Judy Gouwens
Roosevelt University, Chicago, USA

Kenneth P. King
Roosevelt University, Chicago, USA

SAMUEL DAVIES AND PATRICK ALAN DANAHER

17. PLEASURE, PAIN AND THE POSSIBILITIES OF BEING AND BECOMING

Robustly Hopeful Reflections by an Australian Personal Fitness Trainer and His University Academic Client

For Milo
The cat who thought he was a dog and who kept Samuel company during a lonely year

For Rex Gato
Wise soldier, kindred spirit and fellow sojourner
"Courage, mon brave"

And for Felix and Pietmuis
"Los desaparecidos" (21 and 22 September 2016)
Patrick: "Mea culpa, mea culpa, mea máxima culpa"

INTRODUCTION

The personal and private dimensions of academics' lives have been a growing focus in the psychological and sociological literature pertaining to their work (Harreveld & Danaher, 2004). One manifestation of this scholarship is the deployment of ethnography to explore informal learning experiences by others that resonate with the researcher's newly developed interests, such as Delamont's (2005) analysis of classes for the Brazilian dance and martial art capoeira in the Welsh city Cardiff. By contrast, some of this literature has drawn on the research method of autoethnography to develop academics' and researchers' reflexive accounts of their contributions to a range of disciplines, including vocational psychology (McIlveen, 2007, 2008).

At one level, this attentiveness to the personal dimensions of academics' lives is directed at understanding more precisely the interplay between the public and private dimensions of their work. At another and more holistically encompassing level, this scholarship highlights the porous character of supposed binaries (please see also Midgley, Tyler, Danaher, & Mander, 2011) such as public/private and individual/collective and proposes instead a more complex, differentiated, fluid and situated understanding of academics' subjectivities and of the influences on and the effects of their aspirations and actions.

The book of which this chapter forms a part takes up this idea of academics' multiple and shifting subjectivities by tracing several manifestations of the experience of *pleasure* in academics' lives and work and by elaborating the significance of that pleasure in contemporary universities. The authors of this chapter contribute to that project in three distinctive ways. Firstly, the notion of pleasure is paired with that of *pain* – again not as a simplistic binary but rather as a mutually constitutive and interdependent analytical and experiential category that assists in understanding a specific manifestation of academic work and identity. Secondly, that same interdependence emerges as being crucial to the professional relationship between the authors and also to the second author's efforts at *being and becoming* a hopefully more effective academic as well as a healthier human being. Thirdly, these equally interdependent phenomena of being and becoming are demonstrated as exhibiting equivalent interdependence with the perspective of *robust hope* (Halpin, 2003; McInerney, 2007) in relation to future possibilities of more pleasurable and sustainable enactments of academics' work and of enhanced health and wellbeing in universities as contemporary sites of learning and development.

The chapter is structured around the following three sections:
– The study's combined literature review, conceptual framework and research design;
– Focussed reflections by the chapter author;
– Data analysis and implications of the study for understanding and maximizing the production of pleasure in the contemporary university.

LITERATURE REVIEW, CONCEPTUAL FRAMEWORK AND RESEARCH DESIGN

The book to which this chapter contributes is located in the broader and growing scholarly field pertaining to the identities and subjectivities of academics and researchers in contemporary universities (Ezer, 2016). This field exhibits a number of distinct strands. One such strand builds on the rich insights afforded by feminist and post-feminist theorizing that deconstructs such binaries as public/private and work/home (Acker, Webber, & Smyth, 2016). Another strand, which is sometimes intertwined with the feminist and post-feminist theorizing evident in the first stand (Acker & Webber, 2016), engages with the cluster of ideas associated with academic capitalism, corporate managerialism, globalization and neoliberalism (Clarke & Knights, 2015; Raaper, 2016).

Against the backdrop of this burgeoning scholarly field related to academics' and researchers' identities and subjectivities, and in many ways working against the grain of the assumptions and foci of that field, is a smaller but increasingly significant subfield concerned with the possibilities of contesting and resisting the dominant discourses framing contemporary universities, as well as with the diverse and multiple pleasures to be gleaned from academic work in such universities. For instance, a study of early career academics in Canadian universities (Jones, Weinrib, Scott Metcalfe, Fisher, Rubenson, & Snee, 2012) found that generally they "perceive[d[the academic workplace as reasonably positive and supportive" and that they reported "relatively high levels of satisfaction, institutional support and remuneration" (p. 189). Similarly, Meyer (2012) viewed increased requirements for academic accountability as constituting a valuable opportunity for professors to exercise leadership in assisting their less experienced colleagues to engage wholeheartedly with "supporting knowledge development and dissemination through research and teaching ... to ensure that universities contribute to the social good" (p. 207).

More specifically, the concept of pleasure has been taken up by several scholars exploring the identities and subjectivities of contemporary academics. For example, despite the acknowledged pressures of "hyperprofessionality" and working "in an 'always-on' environment" (Gornall & Salisbury, 2012, p. 135), academic staff members identified and celebrated a number of "unseen pleasures of academic work" (p. 135). Likewise, drawing on feminist theorising of universities as "greedy institutions" (p. 33), Hey (2004) distilled the ambivalent and "perverse pleasures" derived from "the complicities secured by the rewards and the displacements won by our repression" (p. 33).

As we noted above, the chapters in this book also take up this focus on pleasure in the context of academic work. As we also noted above, the distinctive theoretical contribution of this chapter to that broader intellectual project is three-fold, in keeping with the chapter's tripartite conceptual framework. Firstly, we pair pleasure with the notion of pain, not as a simplistic binary (Midgley, Tyler, Danaher, & Mander, 2011) but rather as an experiential category with a complex, interdependent and iterative relationship between the two phenomena. Secondly, we link this *pleasure–pain* paired category with that of *being–becoming*, understood as the ongoing and unceasing possibility and responsibility of sentient beings. Thirdly, we mobilize the concept of *robust hope* (Halpin, 2003; McInerney, 2007) both to assist in analysing our focussed reflections below and to elicit potentially more pleasurable enactments of academics' work and of enhanced health and wellbeing in universities as well as more broadly.

From that perspective, and against the backdrop of the uncertain and challenging contexts of contemporary universities and academic work, Halpin (2003) outlined a provocative call for a particular form of optimism with regard to the futures of education. While this call was directed specifically at schooling, in our view it applies equally urgently to higher education and to educational aspirations and activities more widely:

Basically, this attitude is one that entails the adoption of a militant optimism of the will in the course of which a form of *ultimate hope* is brought to bear on educational situations and problems through specific applications of the utopian imagination. (pp. 1–2; *emphasis in original*)

This notion of "*ultimate hope*" (Halpin, 2003, pp. 1–2; *emphasis in original*) has been elaborated as the idea of robust hope, which McInerney (2007) contrasted with "naïve optimism" (p. 257) and which he propounded as a theoretically rigorous means of "Sustaining a commitment to social justice in schools and teacher education in neoliberal times" (p. 257).

Understood in this way, robust hope has been deployed by a number of education scholars. For example, Halpin (2007) argued for the utility of robust hope in teacher education curricula and he explicated the values that he associated with such hope, including "human agency, collective action, sustainability, community and equity" (p. 243). Similarly, Sawyer, Singh, Woodrow, Downes, Johnston and Whitton (2007) explored the applicability of robust hope as a valuable analytical tool in interrogating teacher education policy, specifically in New South Wales, Australia. As we expound below, our interest in robust hope lies in its capacity to inform and extend our understandings of what might otherwise be seen as excessively individualized and solipsistic accounts of our separate and shared journeys of pleasure and pain and of being and becoming (please see also Danaher, 2014) with regard to health and wellbeing in our lives. From this perspective, robust hope affords particular insights into the constituents and effects of informal learning and the facilitation of that learning that we hope to explore at greater length in a future publication elsewhere.

Finally in this section of the chapter, the research design framing this study exhibited selected principles of autoethnographic, co-constructed, interpretivist, naturalistic, phenomenological and qualitative inquiry (Denzin, 2014; Ravitch & Mittenfelner Carl, 2016). This approach was predicated on the axiological, epistemological, methodological and ontological proposition that the two authors of the chapter shared certain perspectives and understandings of our joint personal fitness training sessions, developed through common experience and language, and also that equally some of one author's perspectives and understandings were likely to differ significantly from those of the other author, just as each author's perspectives and understandings changed over space and time. Moreover, we assumed that the process of co-authoring the chapter would be valuable to eliciting deeper insights that otherwise would remain unknown to both authors. We were aware also of the potential risks attendant on this research method, in the sense that we were careful to use language that was clearly intended to be constructive and positive, while still affording opportunities to develop more critical understandings of our separate and shared journeys of health and wellbeing.

More specifically, the process that we adopted was as follows. Firstly, we talked about the intended purpose of the chapter and its proposed contribution to the wider book project. Secondly, Patrick wrote his first focussed reflection (please see the next section of the chapter), seeking to place his personal fitness training sessions with Samuel in the broader context of selected aspects of his life, particularly since January 2011. Thirdly, Samuel used his reading of that reflection to write his own focussed reflection, again locating his personal fitness training of Patrick in relation to a reflexive account of his own life as well as of his training of other clients. Finally, the two authors wrote their second reflections in targeted response to what the other author had written and as part of the developing dialogue between their respective experiences and perceptions.

PLEASURE, PAIN AND THE POSSIBILITIES OF BEING AND BECOMING

FOCUSSED REFLECTIONS BY THE CHAPTER AUTHORS

Patrick

Monday, 10 January 2011 saw the development of flash flooding in the Australian inland regional city where I live and work that was called an "inland tsunami" and that sadly led to loss of life (http://www.abc.net.au/news/2011-01-11/toowoomba-swamped-by-deadly-inland-tsunami/1900720). At a personal level, on that same day I experienced medical symptoms (mostly a strong sense of nausea that prompted me to lie on my bed) that I had never felt previously, and that I considered to be concerning rather than alarming. These symptoms recurred the next day, prompting me to telephone local medical centres to seek an appointment to see a general practitioner. One receptionist informed me briskly that I should go to hospital rather than seeing a general practitioner, which prompted my best friend who was staying with me at the time and me to travel in a taxi to one of the local hospitals. The outcome was the diagnosis that I had experienced a heart attack, necessitating a stay in intensive care and undergoing a coronary angiogram, and subsequently a transfer to a hospital in the nearest metropolitan city and the insertion of a stent in my heart.

People were very kind and supportive, with greatly appreciated visits from friends and colleagues and telephone calls with family members. However, I felt to a considerable degree the sense of being a fraud (akin to what many academics say that they undergo in their work) because I did not *feel* that I had had the *experience* of a heart attack, which I associated (incorrectly) with significant chest pain. Indeed, I felt "disgustingly healthy", and I was able to take a lively interest in other patients and in the inevitable personality differences and clashes of viewpoints attending any human organisation, illustrated during the hand over at the end of each shift that I could not help overhearing.

More broadly, the events of January 2011 constituted a "wake up call" and a clarion call to action for me, if I were able to heed those calls. I was 51 years old at the time of my heart attack, and on the first day of that month I had been promoted to professor in my university. Sadly my father had died of a sudden heart attack at the age of 57, and his father had died at the same age (at the time of writing, I turned 57 just over one month ago). So I was conscious that I needed to learn from my heart attack if I were to avert a similar and more serious medical incident in a few years' time. At the same time, I experienced heightened doubts that I would be able to make the required changes to lifestyle and routine and, although the hospital provided other patients and me with comprehensive information about diet and exercise, I felt that I lacked the knowledge and skills necessary to mobilize this significant change to who I was and how I saw myself – a veritable transformation in my ongoing *being and becoming*.

During the next few years, I experimented with various attempts to change. I bought expensive sporting equipment (such as a treadmill, a weights machine, a rower and a stationary bicycle) that still reposes in my garage unused after the initial burst of enthusiasm had given way to a sense of boredom and futility. For most of 2012, I worked with a personal fitness trainer and I participated in a number of classes conducted by the gymnasium that he owned and managed. However, pressure of work in the second half of 2012 caused me to stay away from the gymnasium.

In 2013, I searched for another gymnasium and another personal fitness trainer. I met Samuel and we agreed that I would start working intensively with him in July 2013, after I had returned from two academic conferences in New Zealand. I recall feeling anxious about the delay; I wanted to start as quickly as possible to develop this new relationship that I saw as being crucial to my renewed efforts at *being and becoming* – not just as an academic, but also as a more fully developed and hopefully healthy human being.

More than three years later, I see Samuel as a good friend and as someone whom I admire enormously. I consider that he has a wise soul (and our shared fascination with cats is a useful indicator in that regard). I repose complete trust in Samuel's judgment about the organization and sequencing of our training sessions, and in his information about the appropriate weights of the various machines that I use in the gymnasium when I am not training with him, in ways that will challenge and extend my capacity without overtaxing my heart.Most recently, Samuel is advising me about food and nutrition. On the one hand, I feel embarrassed about having to ask for such advice from someone about 30 years younger than I am. On the other hand, it is for about 30 years that I have struggled with being overweight and obese, to little or no avail. I am grateful to Samuel for this additional element of our interactions, and I am determined to make a success of it. The character and settings of my interactions with Samuel have varied over the time that we have worked together. We spent over two years at the gymnasium where we started working together, then for about seven months we trained in a public park. For the past few months we have moved to a new gymnasium, with new routines to accommodate the different equipment. Recently I have become a member of this new gymnasium, and Samuel has devised a training program for me to complete when I am not training with him.

Samuel

My journey can be started at the age of 17, having completed high school as a morbidly obese teenager. I come from a family of sportspeople, with a dad who coaches athletics with multiple Australian representatives under his belt, and a sister who has been around the world representing Australia several times over for sprinting. Needless to say, as a rugby union lover I had an excellent source of expertise and support.

I always had a natural athletic ability, but I was always hindered by my overweight and unfit body. My childhood was full of all the usual that an overweight kid would expected, including bullying and depression. I aimed to change that and find a sense of identity. I began to focus on my big love in life, rugby union, and started playing for a local under 20s club. With the support of my dad, who never missed a game in my career, I started training hard. Again I always had a natural ability at sports, and I was exceptionally skilled at rugby. All I needed was my overweight body of 140 kilograms to stop holding me back. I found myself training six days a week, sometimes twice a day. I had a gym set up in my shed and went through a dozen training partners.

By the age of 19, I had been around Queensland representing the Darling Downs, and I was playing for the A grade at my local club. At 20, I suffered an ankle and back injury that ended my rugby aspirations and I had to leave the sport, but I left a different person from the person who went into it. I had lost 40 kilograms over the past few years, and more importantly I had become fit and healthy, which I noticed makes one feel good about oneself and more proactive, and in my case made me want to help others to feel this way, as I will always remember how it felt beforehand.

I got a Personal Trainer's qualification and began to help people at a local gymnasium. I was fairly successful at maintaining a personal training business and I had a large clientele, but I believe the key to my success was my drive to help my clients. Each of my clients had a unique story and background, with nevertheless at times similar but different goals.

My favourite sessions were with clients whom I would have to take special considerations with. For example, I had a female client who needed some very out of the box thinking to train, whether it was finding new uses for equipment that simply couldn't fit her or making mundane tasks interesting as she couldn't do the complex exercises. The biggest challenge was not getting her moving but to keep her moving once she had begun. She suffered from severe confidence issues, and I found myself digging deeply into my mind to say something motivational that could down out the voices in her head telling her how worthless she was. Many tissues were needed on a regular basis when we trained.

Or clients with knee problems or shoulder problems who needed rehabilitation, or in some cases the joint was completely shot and just had to be avoided; the list goes on. Although every once in a while I would encounter those perfectly healthy, fit clients who honestly didn't need a personal trainer or in fact were personal trainers themselves but wanted me to push them to a new level of pain and exhaustion, and I can tell you those clients are a heap of fun.

It was at the height of my success as a personal trainer that I met Patrick in July 2013. I can say from the start that he was like no other client I had had before. It was safe to say he was not an athletic man, nor did he fit the bill of an avid gym goer. He was a self-proclaimed "academic" who always wore a full tracksuit regardless of how hot it was; incredibly nice man. He struggled with even the most simple of exercises, especially ones that required coordination, and he couldn't do a single push up to save his life. But I thoroughly enjoyed training him as no matter how hard or difficult the task he would at least attempt it and always give it a go and never had a complaint or bad thing to say the whole time.

Training at times would have to be unorthodox, and unconventional goals had to be set up to ensure progress was made. The general client would set a goal as being to lose X kilograms, but in Patrick's case those goals were not getting met no matter how hard we tried, so we changed the figurative goalposts and began at the grassroots with the mastery of the most basic movements. First we learnt how to do one single, perfectly formed push up, how to do a bodyweight squat, how to do a wall sit. Then build on that with the next step being a set of push ups, barbell squats and wall sits for some time. We developed our ability to train, and we now use that ability to meet specific goals and can take some of the more complex workouts I throw at him.

In the process, Patrick has improved his health and wellbeing with a lifestyle that includes going to the gym by himself on non-PT days and healthy eating. He now has the results to show, with return trips from the doctor showing improved lung capacity, improved testosterone output and improved x-ray results. Patrick continued to train with me through several business changes, including the downsizing of my business, leaving the gymnasium to train at parks and the setup in a new gymnasium, which is where we still train three times a week.

Patrick

Several points occurred to me as I read Samuel's initial focussed reflection above. The first and most important was that I saluted his characteristic courage and generosity of spirit in sharing details of his life from high school through to the present day. Relatedly, I admired his commitment and determination as he encountered challenges and obstacles. For instance, he had developed a promising trajectory as an A grade rugby union player in a highly competitive field. When injury befell him, he transitioned into building up his personal fitness training business into a new and successful trajectory. Again when the business changed, Samuel devised new transitions, including university study. This complex interplay among trajectories, transitions and potential transformations (which we hope to elaborate in a future publication) is applicable to many if not most lifetime learners, but that fact does not lessen Samuel's commendable achievement in making these major adjustments to his life plans.

Samuel's courteous comments about his initial and subsequent impressions of my efforts to derive pleasure from what I saw as the pain of my training sessions (understood as an agglutination of physical discomfort, embarrassment and a sense of futility) also generated a number of responses in me. Firstly, they represent an apt remembrance that our reminiscences are always and necessarily limited and partial, and also that another's good-hearted insights into one's experiences immeasurably enrich one's analysis of those experiences. Secondly, they remind me that – possibly in common with many others – I tend to suppress memories of events that I find painful to recall. Yet Samuel's memory of how I looked and of my inability to perform basic exercises is important, both because it provides another and an invaluable perspective and because it helps to establish a baseline for the success of our subsequent training together.

Occasionally I ask Samuel when and how he devises his training programs and sessions for his other clients and for me. This is not merely idle curiosity; I see Samuel as an instinctive and intuitive educator with the power to construct enabling and transformative learning experiences for others. Therefore I was fascinated to read more fully about his highly considered and individualized strategies for working with each of his clients. In my case, I appreciated and benefited from his knowledgeable scaffolding of breaking seemingly simple physical movements into smaller skills that took account of my lack of physical coordination. I also enjoyed the pleasure attending the mastery of progressively more complex exercises and movements resulting from this successful scaffolding.

Finally in my response to Samuel's reflection, his reference to our goals not being met evokes what I see as a tendency towards self-sabotage in my character, as well as an enduring sense of futility about losing weight. I did achieve some weight loss thanks to Samuel's training. However, that limited progress was undermined by my poor diet. It is only since Samuel has generously provided me with a program of health eating (again skilfully scaffolded, starting with breakfast and moving through the other meals of the day and night) that I have started to lose weight in a healthy and sustainable way.

Samuel

Patrick's journey is definitely a "then and now" story, where you can compare the "then", with Patrick's bad eating habits, self-consciousness and self-proclaimed sabotaging of himself, with the "now", where he is active in his own health, making those tough, healthy choices on his own. Reflecting on Patrick's input into this chapter, it is evident that he has come a long way; most notable is the hard work he does when not with his personal trainer. This includes his willingness to train a number of times a week on his own between personal training sessions, overcoming his self-consciousness and being able to push himself when there is no-one around to push him.

I believe Patrick has reached the point where he understands that the avoidance of the discomfort and pain that a session brings, which I consider a "good pain" as it is necessary for the body to adapt and improve, heavily outweighs the initial pleasure of avoiding exercise that is followed by a deep feeling of regret at missing an opportunity to improve oneself by not turning up to the gym at all. Now he knows that, although exercises are tough, the pain and discomfort are only for moments and will go away almost immediately, whereas the knowledge that you deliberately avoided the healthy option of going to the gym can eat away at your mind till the next time you go to the gym.

A similar mindset is brought to the adherence of a healthy diet. In Patrick's case, this is not a diet in the sense of those health fads that are on the TV with strict rules of being able to eat only at a specific time and based on calorie counts, but merely a template that has ideally spaced times to eat, with a long list of healthy options of foods that one can pick and choose at will as blanks that can be filled in by the person eating. This is generally a lot tougher than adhering to an exercise regime, as exercise is but an hour a day, whereas one must think about every meal of the day from breakfast to dessert.

Patrick is currently following a full regime of exercise and healthy eating and is seeing results in all aspects of his health. He is at a transitional point, where the goals have been met and are being changed from mobility and fat loss to gaining of muscle, which includes a complete restructure of his training program. Patrick has come a long way and has broken down his self-imposed barriers and now has the ability to make healthy decisions on his own, including differentiating between pleasure and good pain.

DATA ANALYSIS AND IMPLICATIONS

The book of which this chapter forms a part is focused on the production of pleasure in the contemporary university. This chapter contributes to that focus by exploring the indispensable role in the pleasures of academic work played by influences that lie outside the formal domain of universities but that nevertheless are vital for the success and sustainability of that academic work. More specifically, this exploration has highlighted Patrick's parallel journeys towards pleasure and wellbeing: one directed at his responsibilities at the university where he works; and the other concentrated on his efforts to attain health and wellbeing in his non-working life. This exploration has also demonstrated Samuel's crucial role in facilitating the effectiveness of both those journeys. In turn, Samuel's reflections have revealed his own strategies for enhanced pleasure (understood as success, health and wellbeing), including in his current university studies.

With regard to *pleasure–pain*, the paired analytical category that constitutes the first element of the tripartite conceptual framework informing this study, the focussed reflections in the previous section of the chapter afforded evidence of this category's applicability to the experiences of both authors of the chapter. Samuel has experienced a number of career changes owing to sporting injury and alterations to his personal fitness training business; he has had to transition from previously identified and no doubt pleasurable trajectories to new challenges and opportunities that again no doubt have generated some pain and uncertainty but that have also no doubt brought about the excitement of previously unconsidered directions and prospects for his life journey. Similarly, Patrick's heart attack in January 2011 necessitated a hoped-for life-sustaining shift from the undoubted pleasures but ultimately unhealthy prognosis of his sedentary lifestyle that enabled pleasurable absorption in his academic work at the cost of his health and wellbeing. Patrick's struggles to develop a more balanced and healthy lifestyle has certainly involved pain, both the physical pain of new exercise regimes and more recently the unaccustomed self-discipline of nutritious eating, and the psychological sense of futility and the absence of self-efficacy about being able to make this fundamental transition in his life (which Samuel is helping Patrick to overcome).

In relation to *being–becoming* (see also Danaher, 2014), the second element of the study's conceptual framework, the focussed reflections of both Samuel and Patrick highlight the unceasing and unfinished character of this paired phenomena. Rather than constituting a predictable, progressive and regular unfolding of a teleological process of self-actualization, these reflections demonstrate that seemingly certain trajectories sometimes necessitate transitions into new directions, often as a result of events beyond the individual's control. Likewise, the attendant learning is often not the expected assimilation of new knowledge into existing knowledge frameworks, but instead can entail the unlearning (Clem & Schiller, 2016) of previously developed habits and routines that turn out to be unproductive or unsustainable (as in the case of Patrick's sedentary lifestyle and unhealthy eating habits). Being and becoming emerge from this analysis as limited, partial, tentative and uncertain – but also as potentially agential, powerful and productive.

Finally, in terms of *robust hope* (Halpin, 2003; McInerney, 2007), the third element of the study's conceptual framework, we acknowledge that this notion is more commonly associated with broader policy and social issues such as schooling and teacher education. Nevertheless, we contend that robust hope – conceptualized as affording "resources of hope" rather than as being derived from "naïve optimism" (McInerney, 2007, p. 257) – can assist in generating relevant insights at personal and psychological levels into how individuals can and do make significant shifts in their lives in ways that embrace wholeheartedly the interdependent and co-constructed phenomena of pleasure–pain and being–becoming.

CONCLUSION

The German poet Heinrich Heine (1982) distinguished between what he called "Hellenism" and "Nazarenism", respectively physical enjoyment and spiritual elevation. One interpretation of this distinction is to contrast the pleasure and enjoyment of hedonism with the pain and self-denial of asceticism. Yet our focussed reflections in this chapter highlight a different interpretation of pleasure, one that sees it as a complex and situated phenomenon, capable of generating extremely productive outcomes but also liable to draw one into experiences of flow (Csíkszentmihályi, 2014) that, while they can be enjoyable and generative, can also restrict the breadth and depth of one's experiences of the other domains of life.

Our analysis in this chapter has placed the production of pleasure in contemporary universities in a broader perspective, encapsulated by Patrick's struggles to achieve something of a work–life balance in his academic role, and enlivened by Samuel's efforts as a personal fitness trainer to facilitate those struggles as well as by Samuel's own changing career trajectories and transitions. In the process, *pleasure–pain*, *being–becoming* and *robust hope* (Halpin, 2003; McInerney, 2007) have emerged as three among several conceptual resources that can provide new insights into the aspirations and outcomes of individuals and communities, whether in higher education or more generally.

ACKNOWLEDGMENTS

The authors are grateful to Associate Professor Peter McIlveen, whose work in integrating the personal and scholarly dimensions of pleasure and pain is exemplary. Professor Michael Singh and Professor Bobby Harreveld introduced the authors to the productive concept of robust hope. The chapter's clarity and coherence have been enhanced by the editorial commentary of Dr Marcus Harmes. More broadly, the second author acknowledges with gratitude the efforts of a number of people who have previously worked with him over many years to improve his health and wellbeing.

REFERENCES

Acker, S., & Webber, M. (2016). Uneasy academic subjectivities in the contemporary Ontario university. In J. Smith, J. Rattray, T. Peseta, & D. Loads (Eds.), *Identity work in the contemporary university: Exploring an uneasy profession* (Educational Futures: Rethinking Theory and Practice, Vol. 1) (pp. 61–75). Rotterdam, The Netherlands: Sense Publishers.

Acker, S., Webber, M., & Smyth, E. (2016). Continuity or change? Gender, family, and academic work for junior faculty in Ontario universities. *NASPA Journal about Women in Higher Education, 9*(1), 1–20. doi: 10.1080/19407882.2015.1114954

Clarke, C. A., & Knights, D. (2015, December). Careering through academia: Securing identities or engaging ethical subjectivities? *Human Relations, 68*(12), 1865–1888. doi: 10.1177/0018726715570978

Clem, R. L., & Schiller, D. (2016, May). New learning and unlearning: Strangers or accomplices in threat memory attenuation? *Trends in Neurosciences, 39*(5), 340–351. doi: 10.1016/j.tins.2016.03.003

Csíkszentmihályi, M. (2014). *Applications of flow in human development and education: The collected works of Mihály Csíkszentmihályi*. Dordrecht, The Netherlands: Springer.

Danaher, P. A. (2014). Seeming, being and becoming: Lifelong learning and teacher transformation. In J. K. Jones (Ed.), *Weaving words: Personal and professional transformation through writing as research* (pp. 220–235). Newcastle upon Tyne, UK: Cambridge Scholars Publishing.

Delamont, S. (2005). Four great gates: Dilemmas, directions and distractions in educational research. *Research Papers in Education, 20*(1), 85–100. doi: 10.1080/0267152052000341345

Denzin, N. K. (2014). *Interpretive autoethnography* (2nd ed.). Los Angeles, CA: Sage Publications.

Ezer, H. (2016). *Sense and sensitivity: The identity of the scholar-writer in academia* (Imagination and Praxis: Criticality and Creativity in Education and Educational Research, Vol. 6). Rotterdam, The Netherlands: Sense Publishers.

Gornall, L., & Salisbury, J. (2012, April). Compulsive working, "hyperprofessionality" and the unseen pleasures of academic work. *Higher Education Quarterly, 66*(2), 135–154. doi: 10.1111/j.1468-2273.2012.00512.x

Halpin, D. (2003). *Hope and education: The role of the utopian imagination*. London, UK: Routledge/Falmer.

Halpin, D. (2007). Utopian spaces of "robust hope": The architecture and nature of progressive learning environments. *Asia-Pacific Journal of Teacher Education, 35*(3), 243–255. doi: 10.1080/13598660701447205

Harreveld, R. E., & Danaher, P. A. (2004, June). Private and professional lives, pedagogical work and situated learning: The multiliteracies of distance education. *Malaysian Journal of Distance Education, 6*(1), 129–142.

Heine, H. (1982). *History of religion and philosophy in Germany* (P. L. Rose, Ed.). Townsville, Qld, Australia: Department of History, James Cook University of North Queensland.

Hey, V. (2004). Perverse pleasures: identity work and the paradoxes of greedy institutions. *Journal of International Women's Studies, 5*(3), 33–43. Retrieved from http://vc.bridgew.edu/jiws/ vol5/iss3/4/

Jones, G., Weinrib, J., Scott Metcalfe, A., Fisher, D., Rubenson, K., & Snee, I. (2012, April). Academic work in Canada: The perceptions of early-career academics. *Higher Education Quarterly, 66*(2), 189–206. doi: 10.1111/j.1468-2273.2012.00515.x

McIlveen, P. (2007). The genuine scientist-practitioner in vocational psychology: An autoethnography. *Qualitative Research in Psychology, 4*(4), 295–311.

McIlveen, P. (2008, Winter). Autoethnography as a method for reflexive research and practice in vocational psychology. *Australian Journal of Career Development, 17*(2), 13–20.

McInerney, P. (2007, August). From naïve optimism to robust hope: Sustaining a commitment to social justice in schools and teacher education in neoliberal times. *Asia-Pacific Journal of Teacher Education, 35*(3), 257–272. doi: 10.1080/14780880701522403

Meyer, L. H. (2012, April). Negotiating academic values, professorial responsibilities and expectations for accountability in today's university. *Higher Education Quarterly, 66*(2), 207–217. doi: 10.1111/j.1468-2273.2012.00516.x

Midgley, W., Tyler, M. A., Danaher, P. A., & Mander, A. (Eds.). (2011). *Beyond binaries in education research* (Routledge Research in Education, Vol. 59). New York, NY: Routledge.

Raaper, R. (2016). Academic perceptions of higher education assessment processes in neoliberal academia. *Critical Studies in Education, 57*(2), 175–190. doi: 10.1080/ 17508487.2015.1019901

Ravitch, S. M., & Mittenfelner Carl, N. (2016). *Qualitative research: Bridging the conceptual, theoretical, and methodological*. Los Angeles, CA: Sage Publications.

Sawyer, W., Singh, M., Woodrow, C., Downes, T., Johnston, C., & Whitton, D. (2007). Robust hope and teacher education policy. *Asia-Pacific Journal of Teacher Education, 35*(3), 227–242. doi: 10.1080/13598660701447197

Samuel Davies
University of Southern Queensland, Australia

Patrick Alan Danaher
University of Southern Queensland
and
Central Queensland University, Australia

FRED DERVIN

18. "DON'T CRY – DO RESEARCH!"

The Promise of Happiness for an Academic Killjoy

Don't impose on us the dirty word of happiness.
(Buddhist monk M. Ricard, 2012, heard from his critics)

Happiness is overrated. Life is miserable. (comment online)

A: Where did you find that? I've been searching for it everywhere.
B: (Holding a pot of happiness) I created it myself. (cartoon online)

INTRODUCTION

This volume has set the ambitious and noble goal of reflecting on producing pleasure within the contemporary university. As the negativity pusher or the academic killjoy that I feel I have become, it took me longer than expected to start writing this chapter, fending off a writer's block for weeks. Several times during the writing process did I feel *frustrated, furious* and *frantic* about research worlds. There are several reasons for this. Let me mention two related to my context, Finnish academia.

First, 2016 marked the termination of employment contracts of 371 employees at my university, a trend that will continue until the end of 2017, with the number of fixed-term staff gradually decreasing. Then there was a letter sent by the Minister of Education and Culture Grahn-Laasonen to Finnish universities, reprimanding us for "using resources inefficiently", which angered the academic community. The corporate and techno-scientific discourses and phenomena of new funding structures, rankings, metrics-based appraisals of performance and quality, etc. that accompany these unfortunate events, make things even worse. In his great piece on research training and the production of ideas, Jan Blommaert (2016) argues that "Einstein would, in the present competitive academic environment, have a really hard time getting recognized as a scientist of some stature" (n.p.): his field of research was marginal; his work was not empirical; he wrote in German and he published in not so prestigious journals …

How can one find and produce pleasure in such circumstances of 'survival' that millions of scholars have experienced, are experiencing or will experience globally?

My second source of disappointment and frustration relates to my own field of research: intercultural communication and education. Since the end of summer

2015, like other countries around the world, Finland has been welcoming asylum seekers from the Middle East. The arrival of refugees has coincided with a very weak Finnish economy, and since 2015 there have been differing reactions from academics, decision makers and the general public. While some people welcomed refugees (for example the campaign *Welcome Refugees*) and volunteered to help them; others responded by demonstrations, sometimes with overtly racist overtones. The 2015 September event in Lahti, which was reported widely around the world, saw around 30 demonstrators throwing stones and fireworks at a bus of refugees, with one demonstrator wearing a Ku Klux Klan robe. The Finnish government has firmly condemned such racist acts. In 2016 there were also reports of refugee centres being burnt down. Suddenly it also seemed that intercultural/multicultural education became popular: many scholars wanted to 'help' refugees and to start doing research on them in the context of education. Some wanted to teach them about 'Finnish culture' from a very ethnocentric and xenophobic perspective, others wished to teach them Finnish with methods that would give many applied linguists and sociolinguists around the world headaches. Many were awarded funds to help teachers deal with the influx of refugees but what I saw was a wheel reinvention, urgency pushing people to act without thinking.

This all drained my energy and made me even more of a killjoy ... My multiple trips to Asia saved me from losing my intellectual and emotional sanity at the time.

But I would like to apologize to the reader and to the editors for these first paragraphs, which deviate from the noble objective of discussing pleasure in academia. When I told my Swedish colleague Andreas Jacobson about this chapter, and the incapability I felt to write it, he mentioned that his wife had just retrieved a book about Women's studies from 1979, published in Sweden, entitled "Don't cry – Research!" (*Gråt inte – forska!*, Westman Berg, 1979). Inspired by this I decided to 'stop crying' and to get on with this piece. I also remembered these words from Edward Said (1993, p. 82), which are encouraging, "To my mind the Western university (...) still can offer the intellectual a quasi-utopian space in which reflection and research can go on, albeit under new constraints and pressures". Of course, in 2016, we should drop the word *Western* and substitute it with *global*.

As I am using discussions on happiness in this chapter to engage with the topic of producing pleasure within the university, I would like to say a few things about happiness in general. Since the study of human happiness was put at the centre of psychology research and theory in the 1990s, thousands of studies and books have been published on the subject matter. Not a week passes without the media reminding us of its importance, based on 'scientific research' and mere happiness-speak: Happier people help others to become happier; they are also less likely to engage in risky behavior; happiness could the key to success (The Guardian, November 2014). Since 2012 the World Happiness Report published by the United Nations Sustainable Development Solutions Network presents a measurement of happiness in different countries and suggests ways to help guide public policies. The criteria are: *GDP per capita, social support, healthy life expectancy, freedom to make life choices, generosity and trust* (http://worldhappiness.report). In her book *The Happiness Myth*, the philosopher Hecht (2008) explains that these often misrepresent people's (sense of) happiness.

In what follows I reflect on my own work as an interculturalist and the happiness that goes with it. The philosopher Henri Bergson (1932/2001, p. 449) writes that the word happiness "is commonly used to designate something intricate and ambiguous, one of those ideas which humanity has intentionally left vague, so that each individual might interpret it in his own way". The first path that I will take is a definitional one: What are the meanings of happiness in academia, beyond the negative issues described at the beginning of this introduction? Then, based on my recent experiences in the field of intercultural communication and education, I reflect on the happiness that I have felt in researching and teaching about the topic. The article is autobiographical in nature and contains auto-ethnographic observations.

THE CONUNDRUM OF HAPPINESS IN ACADEMIA

Just as happiness is a difficult intuition to categorize in general (Hecht, 2008), happiness in academia is one of the most difficult conundra as it can cover many aspects of being a scholar. It is easy to imagine that scholars experience different types of happiness. Following Hecht (2008), we might also argue that some types of happiness experienced in academia may even conflict with one another, and with those outside academia. But how to obtain information about *this* happiness? If we simply ask scholars about their 'well-being', as Borowiecki (2013, p. 6) argues: "The respondent's answer might not be accurate due to her wishful thinking and various mechanisms of defense".

In order to get very concrete definitions, I started by searching Google for "the pleasure of doing research" and "the joy of doing research". The somewhat random results included portraits of researchers from different fields and "paratexts" (acknowledgment sections of books and dissertations). Although this is not a systematic analysis of the results, I think it is a good way to start reflecting on happiness.

Two comments that I collected were very straightforward, but also interesting, and did not really give any indication as to what it is about: "the pleasure of doing research can't be defined in words" and "just do research for the pleasure of doing research".

Many items refer to working with others and sharing academic activities: "The pleasure of learning new things and working with bright minds is usually immediate"; "Part of the pleasure of doing research is having co-authors whom one can enjoy as friends"; "Always feeling welcome greatly enhanced the pleasure of doing research". They are also utterances hinting at the joy, happiness and/or pleasure of working in a given location (e.g. at a library at Oxford). Some netizens also mention that the joy of doing research "lies on that you have the freedom to decide what research to do and what problems to solve". It is important to note here that in 1999 the United Nations stipulated that academic freedom is part of a human right to education. For Rajagopal (2015, p. 5) academic freedom has both individual and collective dimensions.

References to the intellectual features of doing research are also very much represented:

> "The joy of doing research comes in discovery, of asking questions and using one's ingenuity and technical ability to answer those questions".

> "But I guess that's the joy of doing research: you develop a theory, you test it, you see what you learn. And slowly, slowly, you maybe begin to understand".

> "Still, the joy of doing research and yes, there is joy in doing research, is being able to crack some of these issues, despite the fact that they drive you nuts".

These features include specific skills, discovery, and being led to understand. In these quotes one can also sense a feeling of uncertainty related to the pleasure of doing research. This is very well exemplified in the following excerpt:

> So you float a question and then wait to see where it leads someone, which may be somewhere you would have never imagined. For me, that's the joy of doing research. But you have to be willing to have your framework shifted. You have to tolerate the uncertainty of not knowing.

Discovery is thus related to what this same individual refers to as "moving through darkness". The hypothesis of serendipity (i.e. accidental discoveries in research) represented archetypically by e.g. the discovery of x-rays or Newton's theory of gravity, often goes hand in hand with the pleasure of curiosity and perseverance in academia (Roberts, 1989, p. 288).

So defining happiness in academia seems to lead to describing common and somewhat loose features. I believe that happiness in this context also relies on the way(s) we understand what research is about, how and why it should be done. There are, of course, several answers to these questions, depending on one's own ideologies, training, fields, paradigms, gurus ...

In his 2006 article, in which he explains how to resist the 'academic enemies' of scientism, technicism and economism in today's university (values I do not associate with but of which I am a victim like many others, J. J. Venter provides us with important arguments about what happiness could entail. First he begs for us to rehumanize the university, in order to promote critical reflection and creative alternatives (2006, p. 217). Venter also suggests moving away from the "rationalistic" reduction of human life and "naturalistic" reduction (through which nature is only associated with brutality and danger) in research work – approaches that are being privileged worldwide regardless of post-modern, queer, post-colonial thought (ibid.). This means that the researcher needs to be flexible and nuanced enough to both enjoy his work and trigger more happiness in those who benefit from it. Furthermore, Venter argues that the push for 'rationality' "institutionalises a (manipulated) survival struggle that replaces collegiality with strongly egocentric behavior" (2006, p. 283; about the importance of collegiality for happiness, see the comments found on Google above). The centering on the self does not "encourage meditative, reflexive maturation" but goes hand in hand with competitiveness in academia (2006, p. 207). It also, implicitly, pushes for generating research in the shortest possible time, which can be a killjoy.

Complementary to Venter is Edward Said's work on the Representations of the Intellectual (1993). This book is very inspiring to ponder happiness within the university. Said confronts different figures of the intellectual, of whom the scholar is a representative. He argues that certain 'habits of mind' run counter to 'a passionate intellectual life' (1993, p. 101). Using the metaphor of the *amateur* to describe the ideal enthusiastic and joyful intellectual, Said (1993) can allow us to determine further aspects of happiness within the university. The first important aspect concerns the necessary avoidance of 'passive attitudes', taking on political stances instead. Said explains (1993, p. 66):

> Nothing in my view is more reprehensible than those habits of mind in the intellectual that induce avoidance, that characteristic turning away from a difficult and principled position which you know to be the right one, but which you decide not to take. You do not want to appear too political; you are afraid of seeming controversial; you need the approval of a boss or an authority figure; you want to keep a reputation for being balanced, objective, moderate; your hope is to be asked back, to consult, to be on a board or prestigious committee, and so to remain within the responsible mainstream; someday you hope to get an honorary degree, a big prize, perhaps even an ambassadorship.

This leads Said to argue that the intellectual/scholar should be a concerned and committed member of a society who raises, exposes and engages with ideas, values and moral issues (1993, p. 76). In order to problematize further those 'habits of mind', Bernstein's pragmatic fallibilism, an important epistemological doctrine that rejects the grand Either/Or between relativism and foundationalism (2005, p. 43), is inspiring. Bernstein defines fallibilism as "the belief that any knowledge claim or, more generally, any validity claim – including moral and political claims – is open to ongoing examination, modification, and critique" (ibid.). In other words, "inquiry (sh/c/ould be) a *self-corrective enterprise*" (ibid.). I claim that it is through this 'enterprise' that academic work brings a lot of satisfaction and happiness to scholars.

Based on my own beliefs concerning the work of a scholar, what Venter, Said and Bernstein describe corresponds to my perception of the kind of happiness I would wish to experience within the university. The figure below summarizes the components described in this section.

Figure 1. Some components of Academic Happiness

HAPPINESS DOUBLED WITH PAIN AND DISCOMFORT

Phone conversation with a 'confirmed' researcher in Finland who just started researching multicultural education – a field she was unfamiliar with)

(her) I want to change the situation in Finland … I want to borrow multicultural practices from other countries where they have a longer and more successful tradition …
(me) Many researchers have tried to do that before without much success. I am not sure that there is a single country in the world where they are doing this … Have you reviewed the literature?
(her) I want to help teachers to integrate newcomers.
(me) What do you mean by *integrate*?
(her) The kids feel comfortable in Finland.
(me) And from whose perspective?
(her) Well you see in Sweden they are very successful at integrating migrants…
…
(I hang up)

Second apology of this chapter: I need to delve back into negative matters. I remember very few lines from the poems that we were made to learn when I was a child. This line from Apollinaire's Mirabeau Bridge (1912) has always stayed in my mind: "After each sorrow joy came back again". A promise.

All the elements listed in Figure 1 do not happen overnight and can be very unstable, some being more relevant than others at times. For the feminist scholar and social activist bell hooks (1994), who has worked extensively on systems of oppression and class domination, emotions and passions (including confrontation and conflict) are central to academia. She explains (1994, p. 39):

> I have not forgotten the day a student came to class and told me: "we take your class. We learn to look at the world from a critical standpoint, one that considers race, sex, and class. And we can't enjoy life anymore": Looking out over the class, across race, sexual preferences, and ethnicity, I saw students nodding their heads. And I saw for the first time that there can be, and usually is, some degree of pain involved in giving up old ways of thinking and knowing and leaning new approaches. I respect that pain. And I include recognition of it now when I teach, that is to say, I teach about shifting paradigms and talk about the discomfort it can cause.

Academic work includes creativity as one of its important tenants (Figure 1), the "Big-C" (Kaufman & Beghetto, 2009). For Kaufmann (2015, p. 141) "creativity essentially involves the development of a novel idea or solution to a problem that has value for the individual and/or a larger social group". Creativity has many 'dark sides' that cannot be ignored, even if they are deemed to be controversial, especially in academia (Borowiecki, 2013).

Although we need to bear in mind that happiness does affect creative performance (see for example Barsade & Gibson, 2007), drawing on a large Swedish sample, Kyaga et al. (2013) show that people in creative professions are linked to an increased risk of manic depression. In an article from 2008 Akinola and Berry Mendes explain that vulnerability to experiencing negative affect and intense negative emotions can influence (artistic) creativity. Referring to clinical, empirical and biographical studies they show how individuals involved in the creative arts suffer from higher rates of mood disorders (ibid.). The authors are specifically interested in previous studies on mood, affect and creativity such as Kaufmann and Vosburg (1997), which demonstrate that negativity can enhance creativity with tasks that require concentration, divergent thinking and problem solving – which we scholars experience most of the time. Ideally, as argued by Kaufmann (2015) a state of mixed 'mood' might influence creativity more than negative/positive emotions. It is also important to note that situational variables, in combination with moods, can also affect creativity (ibid.).

In a very interesting study, the economist Karol Jan Borowiecki (2013) analysed letters written to their friends, colleagues and family by three composers (Amadeus Mozart, Ludwig van Beethoven and Franz Liszt). Comparing the emotions emerging from these documents and their compositions, he shows that there is a clear link between periods of negative emotions (sadness, anger) and artistic brilliance. Borowiecki thus demonstrates that an increase in negative emotions represents an increase in (quality) works created the following year. To my knowledge there is no such study about contemporary intellectuals and scholars.

Going back to the discussion with the researcher who called me, reproduced earlier, this kind of unpleasant moment, when one feels one is not being listened to, see patronized, because of a lack of interest or pure ignorance about a field (multicultural education) where everyone is entitled to have a say, is a painful and uncomfortable episode. Although I am a strong believer in Bernstein's pragmatic fallibilism, that is to say "ongoing examination, modification, and critique" (2005, p. 43), my interlocutor and I failed to negotiate meaning and understanding. Yet, this is the kind of episode that can trigger reflexive maturation (*how come we can't really speak to each other? Are we speaking the same language? Was hanging up the only option?*), criticality and engagement (*my refusal to accept that one uses the word 'integration' in academic fields without problematizing it for the sake of those whom it is supposed to cover*). This unfortunate event also contributed to my motivation to continue writing this chapter.

HAPPINESS IN DOING RESEARCH ON THE INTERCULTURAL

The fields of intercultural (multicultural) communication and education have a short history, going back respectively to the 1950s and 1970s. Over this short period, they have experienced tremendous epistemological and methodological changes. However, be it in research, political parlance or daily discourses there are still problematic 'outdated' ideas that colonize our imagination about it: solid identity, (hidden) forms of ethnocentrism coupled with other -isms (nationalism, racism, sexism, ageism, etc.), "pornographies of difference" such as exoticism, etc. (Dervin, 2016). As such this warning from Said (1993, p. 33) is still not a 'norm' in these fields:

> With regard to the consensus on group or national identity it is the intellectual's task to show how the group is not a natural or a God-given entity but is a constructed, manufactured, even in some cases invented object, with a history of struggle and conquest behind it, that it is sometimes important to represent.

Although I could spend the rest of this chapter writing about pleasure of cooperating with wonderful colleagues from around the world or the joy of being able to use creativity in both research and teaching I concentrate on correcting enterprises here. Over my short career, I have experienced many instances of "self-correcting enterprise" that have guided my engagement with the intercultural in both my public and private lives. Reading through my work I become aware of the processes of shifting from essentialism-culturalism (where culture explains all) to a form of janusianism (in reference to the double-faced God) through which I contradicted myself by being both essentialistic and (co-)constructivist (*e.g. we need to bear in mind that people have multiple identities that they negotiate but Finnish people tend to be this or that*). My work also witnessed a movement from what I now call idealistic interculturality, which resembles universalism and a loose form of constructivism, to a more realistic form of intercultural understanding, symbolized by the notion of simplexity, a portmanteau word that combines simplicity and complexity and that reminds us that neither are accessible – only a process in between (Dervin, 2016). This approach also takes into account *the Real*, that is to say economic and material reality enriched with dreams and imaginaries (Maffesoli, 2016). The ensuing conviction that there is no real panacea for intercultural encounters – or worse: quick fixes – but just never-ending reflexive and critical engagement with self-others and a commitment to change, may sound like cowardice to some. Yet I believe that a lot of research on interculturality (mine included) has contributed to more damage to intercultural relations than good and that modesty and reflexive maturation are needed more than ever. Being increasingly aware of this and trying to lessen our negative influence would surely trigger more happiness.

There is some kind of satisfaction and contentment in being able to engage in this lifelong process of redefining, and re-appropriating the intercultural. Like Foucault (2000, p. 131) put it during an interview:

> When people say, "Well, you thought this a few years ago and now you say something else", my answer is, [Laughter] "Well, do you think I have worked like that all those years to say the same thing and not to be changed?

Finding like-minded scholars and students but also collegially disagreeing with those who don't share my 'ideologies' has also been a source of joyful inspiration. Recent encounters with students from around the world, who have questioned my ideas or with whom I have discussed my views and research on interculturality, have brought much happiness to me. In the USA, a few months ago, as I was about to deliver a keynote on study abroad and interculturality, I started talking to a minority student who was representing her 'ethnic group' in the exhibition hall. When I asked about her experiences on an American campus and how she felt about what I considered to be an 'ethnic performance', she was overly positive. I was very eager to try to find the 'hidden' in what she was saying. Her position was somewhat ambiguous: She had been posted there to represent a 'club' that promoted 'her' culture on the campus. After several exchanges, the student changed her discourse and started revealing that she had faced discrimination and racism on the campus, also admitting that what she was performing on that day (a specific 'race' or 'ethnic identity') did not correspond to her beliefs about who she was, but more to the imaginaries of those she was expecting to meet on that day. This was an exhilarating encounter that tested both my skills in entering into dialogue while respecting the other and my commitment to reflexive engagement. This was also an example of 'self-correcting enterprise' both for the student and myself. My intention was not to patronize the student but to help her to understand that it is fine to be political about one's (imposed) positions. This encounter also helped me to do further interpretative work on the strategies used by the other to 'keep up appearances'.

When one works within the fields of intercultural communication and education, any encounter outside academia is potentially part of one's ongoing learning process. Over the past few months, I have experienced such random encounters, which have led to fascinating discussions and that have helped me to reflect further on my attempt to be more realistic and modest about the intercultural. One such encounter took place in Beijing, in an antique centre. I noticed beautifully decorated tea cups in one of the shops. As I entered a shop, I asked the old man who was sitting inside if he spoke English. He replied negatively, saying *"Vous parlez français?"* (Do you speak French?). Never before had I used French in China, especially in a shop. We then started interacting. I spent many hours in the shop, drinking pu-erh tea with the man and listening to his fascinating stories of his time spent in France in the 1980s. On several occasions, maybe to bring up 'easy' topics and to cover the intermittent silence, I could hear myself uttering silly stereotypes about the French and the Chinese. To my joy, the old man would systematically question my assumptions, claiming that "Chinese people are not all the same", "there is no typical French person", and so on. What a great lesson of modesty and interculturality! I had maybe wrongly and patronizingly assumed that, as an old Chinese man, he would easily fall into the trap of what I have denounced in my work, failing to apply the principles mentioned in figure 1… I can still see myself smiling from inside… realizing how biased I had been. To me this is a pure moment of happiness: The realization that I can be challenged (and need to be challenged), that I don't have 'the truth' and that, regardless of my knowledge, I am not better than others.

CONCLUSION: DO RESEARCH, 'AUCTOR' YOUR HAPPINESS AND … REMEMBER TO CRY!

In this chapter, I have discussed various aspects of happiness within the university. It has become clear throughout the different sections that happiness is not a state but a process, and that different scholars might experience it with different people, in different ways and through different times and contexts. It is thus important to bear in mind that there is not one way of feeling happy in this context. I have also explained that 'negative' moods and emotions complement happiness to stimulate potential academic creativity and that it is important to recognize the power of 'constructive negativity'. In that sense I disagree with the French writer André Gide (1949, p. 172) who reminds us that happiness is "rare, more difficult, and more beautiful than sadness". He adds: "Once you make this all-important discovery, you must embrace joy as a moral obligation" (ibid.). Happiness and negative emotions are both valuable in the work of scholars and should thus *both* be cherished. *However…*

The current invasion and dictatorship of the 'happiness' business in Finnish universities (and elsewhere), with positive psychologists being given too much influence to my taste, can be counterproductive and infantilizing. Can an institution decide what happiness is/should be? Should it intervene? Who should/can benefit from their definition? Who decides? For a critical interculturalist like me, who is a migrant himself, the reactions of universities to our troubled times, are fascinating as they reflect ideologies but also politico-economic pressure in relation to internationalization.

After the repeated bomb attacks in France in 2015–2016, the Occupational Safety Officer (!) of my university sent me the following automatic message for every bomb attack. It was entitled *"We want to offer the option of debriefing to our French staff"*:

While the XXX terrorist attack have (sic) shocked our whole community, we especially want to offer the option of debriefing to our French staff. The University's occupational health care provider XXXX's professionals are on stand-by to give you support now and also later. To make an appointment please contact XXXX or call +358 XXXX

My first reaction was that of non-understanding. *What does 'debriefing' mean? Why would a university get involved in an individual's life? Is there the fear that, by being potentially 'traumatized' by such events, s/he will not be able to work properly, be productive and/or happy enough?*

Then I became angry: *why contact people based on one of their nationalities? Is terrorism a national thing? Do we still live in times when a mere passport means that people are still 'attached' to a place, a country? Were all the people who died in these tragic events French?*

The message also trigged an avalanche of questions: *Does the university contact (and care about?) those from e.g. Syria on a daily basis to 'offer debriefing'? What is the hidden agenda of offering this service (ticking a box for an international strategy)? Why believe that 'health care providers' only can offer 'support'?*

What this kind of approach suggests is a rationalist approach to happiness, well-being (and production!) coupled with unproblematized methodological nationalism. This proves to lack imagination, which, as Gaston Bachelard (1884-1962) a professor of epistemology and the history and philosophy of science argued, needs to be "reestablished in its living role as the guide of human life" (1943/2011, p. 209). I believe that scholars should thus be empowered to become the 'auctors' (a portmanteau word composed of *authors/actors*, Bauman, 2007, p. 53) of their happy and not so happy academic lives ... and to cry if they want to!

REFERENCES

Akinola, M., & Berry Mendes, W. (2008). The dark side of creativity: Biological vulnerability and negative emotions lead to greater artistic creativity. *Personality and Social Psychology Bulletin, 34*(12), 1677–1686.

Bachelard, G. (1943/2011). *Air and dreams: An essay on the imagination of movement.* Dallas TX: Dallas Institute Publications.

Barsade, S., & Gibson, D. E. (2007). Why does affect matter in organisations? *Academy of Management Perspectives, 21*, 36–59.

Bergson, H. (1932/2001). *The two sources of morality and religion.* University of Notre Dame, IN: University of Notre Dame Press.

Bernstein, R. J. (2005). *The abuse of evil: The corruption of politics and religion since 9/11.* Cambridge: Polity.

Blommaert, J. (2016). Research training and the production of ideas. *Ctrl+Alt+Dem. Research on alternative democratic life in Europe.* https://alternative-democracy-research.org

Borowiecki, K. J. (2013). How are you, my dearest Mozart? Well-being and creativity of three famous composers based on their letters (December 19, 2013). *Discussion Papers on Business and Economics, University of Southern Denmark, 20*/2013. Available from http://ssrn.com/abstract=2368863 or http://dx.doi.org/10.2139/ssrn.2368863

Dervin, F. (2016). *Interculturality in education.* Basingstoke: Palgrave MacMillan.

Foucault, M. (2000). *Essential works of Michel Foucault.* Vol. 3. New York: The New Press.
Gide, A. (1949/1967). *Journals 1889–1949.* London: Penguin Books.
The Guardian. (2014). *Why does happiness matter?* 3 November.
Hecht, J. (2008). *The happiness myth: The historical antidote to what isn't working today.* San Francisco: HarperOne.
hooks, bell. (1994). *Teaching to transgress.* New York: Routledge.
Kaufmann, G. (2015). The mood and creativity puzzle. In Jing Zhou (Ed.), *The Oxford handbook of creativity, innovation, and entrepreneurship* (pp. 141–158). Oxford: Oxford University Press.
Kaufmann, G., & Vosburg, S. K. (1997). "Paradoxical" mood effects on creative problem-solving. *Cognition and Emotion, 11*(2), 151–170.
Kaufman, J. C., & Beghetto, R. A. (2009). Beyond big and little: The four C model of creativity. *Review of General Psychology, 13*(1), 1–12.
Kyaga, S., Landén, M., Boman, M., Hultman, C. M., Långström, N., & Lichtenstein, P. (2013). Mental illness, suicide and creativity: 40-year prospective total population study. *Journal of Psychiatric Research, 47*(1), 83–90.
Maffesoli, M. (2016). *La parole du silence.* Paris: Editions du CERF.
Rajagopal, B. (2015). Defending academic freedom as a human right. *International Higher Education, 33,* 3–5.
Roberts, R. M. (1989). *Serendipity: Accidental discoveries in science.* New York: Wiley.
Said, E. (1993). *Representations of the intellectual.* New York: Vintage.
Venter, J. J. (2006). A human(e) 'uni-versity': Resisting scientism, technicism, and economism. *Koers, 71*(1), 275–316.
Westman Berg, K. (Ed.). (1979). *Gråt inte – Forska!* Stockholm: Prisma.

Fred Dervin
University of Helsinki, Finland

ABOUT THE AUTHORS

Thomas Banhazi is an Associate Professor at the University of Southern Queensland and his expertise is related to various aspects of animal production. He participated in excess of 40 research projects throughout the years both in Australia and Europe, and published in excess of 200 book chapters, journal and international conference papers.

Ali Black is an arts-based and narrative researcher in the School of Education, University of the Sunshine Coast. Her research and scholarly work seeks to foster connectedness, community, wellbeing and meaning-making through the building of reflective and creative lives and identities. Ali is interested in storied and visual approaches for knowledge construction, representation and meaning-making and the power and impact of auto-ethnographic, collaborative and relational knowledge construction.

David Bright is a lecturer in the Faculty of Education at Monash University, Australia. His research, teaching, and engagement are focused on questions of difference and identity, exploring how teachers and students encounter each other in diverse contexts. David's current research interests include post qualitative research methods and writing as a method of inquiry.

Tracey Bunda is a Ngugi/Wakka Wakka woman and current Head of the College for Indigenous Studies Education and Research. Her research interests extend to Indigenous Knowledges as a critical theoretical foundation for centering Indigenous voices and interrogation of white ideologies and institutional and individual practice.

Jennifer Charteris is Senior Lecturer of Pedagogy and has been working in the University of New England School of Education since 2013. She conducts research in the area of the politics of teacher and student learning, identity and subject formation. Critical, poststructural and posthuman theories influence much of her work and she is interested in how theories of affect and materiality can be used to inform education research.

Pauline Collins, Associate Professor, teaches dispute resolution in the Bachelor of Laws and Juris Doctor at the University of Southern Queensland. Pauline has a number of teaching awards. Pauline's PhD was in the area of civil-military relations and the role of the courts (University of Queensland). She has research interest in and has been published in academic journals on matters such as legal education, IR laws, alternative dispute resolution, international law and private military companies. Prior to joining USQ Pauline was a legal practitioner in South Australia working in general practice, Parliamentary Counsel, the Crown Solicitors Office, and the office of the Director of Public Prosecution. In addition to her legal

ABOUT THE AUTHORS

qualifications Pauline has degrees in visual arts, public relations and is a Nationally Qualified mediator.

Gail Crimmins is an Early Career Researcher at the University of the Sunshine Coast, Australia. Prior to moving to Australia Gail was a UK-based actor, director and casting director and taught Drama at universities and conservatoires. Gail's research combines the arts with narrative inquiry in arts-informed research projects which explore the lived experiences of various marginalised women, such as women casual academics, mothers with rheumatoid arthritis, and women survivors of domestic and family violence.

Patrick Alan Danaher is Professor in Educational Research in the School of Linguistics, Adult and Specialist Education at the Toowoomba campus of the University of Southern Queensland, Australia, where he is currently Associate Dean (Research and Research Training) in the Faculty of Business, Education, Law and Arts. He is also currently Adjunct Professor in the School of Education and the Arts in the Higher Education Division at CQUniversity, Australia. Email: patrick.danaher@usq.edu.au

Samuel Davies is a personal fitness trainer who has been running his own business for the past five years. He worked successfully out of a large commercial gymnasium with an extensive clientele before choosing to downgrade to work on a more personal level with only a handful of chosen clients. Samuel is currently studying a Bachelor of Civil Engineering (Honours) degree at the Toowoomba campus of the University of Southern Queensland, Australia. Email: samuel_davies_01@hotmail.com

Fred Dervin is Professor of Multicultural Education at the University of Helsinki (Finland). Professor Dervin specializes in intercultural education, the sociology of multiculturalism and student and academic mobility. Dervin has widely published in international journals on identity, the 'intercultural' and mobility/migration. He has published over 40 books.

Erich C. Fein is a Senior Lecturer of Psychology at the University of Southern Queensland. He completed his PhD in psychology at the Ohio State University with a focus on quantitative methods, organisational psychology, and individual differences. His research programs focus on motivation and performance, training and development, work life balance, and occupational health, and include the coordinated supervision of numerous PhD students.

Rahul Ganguly has two decades of experience in disability rehabilitation, with specific expertise in supporting individuals with emotional and behavioural disabilities. Currently, he is a Senior Lecturer at USQ, where he teaches post-graduate courses in special education and conducts Australian Government funded research on resilience among University students with disabilities.

ABOUT THE AUTHORS

Susanne Gannon, Associate Professor, is Deputy Director and Equity strand leader in the Centre for Educational Research at Western Sydney University. She is a prolific publisher with interests in diverse fields of educational research including gender equity and diversity; creative writing pedagogies; media and cultural studies in educational research and educational policy. She uses a range of qualitative methodologies including autoethnography and narrative methodologies, collective biography, discourse analysis and she is particularly interested in how theories of affect and materiality are reshaping feminist theories and research methodologies in education.

Kathryn Gilbey is an Alyawarrye woman and a passionate educator who believes in the transformative effect of education designed by and for Aboriginal peoples. She is an academic at the College for Indigenous Studies Education and Research co-ordinating the Preparatory Pathways program for Aboriginal and Torres Strait Islander students seeking entry into the university.

Judith A. Gouwens earned the EdD degree from the University of Kansas and is professor of education at Roosevelt University, Chicago, Illinois. Her research interests are qualitative research methods, education of underserved children, and education of migrant farmworkers' children. She has published books about migrant education and education reform.

Marcus K. Harmes is a senior lecturer at the University of Southern Queensland's Open Access College with particular interests in the history of education and popular culture studies. In the latter field has he has published on a range of topics including science fiction and horror cinema as well as the use of television as an educational medium.

Linda Henderson is a Senior Lecturer in the Faculty of Education at Monash University. Her research draws on post-structural and post-humanist ideas, methodologies and practices. Through her work she aims to foster connectedness with all living matter in an effort to create a world that values connectedness, heterogeneity and multiplicity. Her work includes poetry, narrative and creativity with the aim of generating new and just imaginaries for education and society.

Robyn Henderson, Associate Professor, teaches and researches in the field of literacy education at the University of Southern Queensland, Australia. She is particularly interested in the impact of student mobility on literacy learning. In working in initial teacher education, she is also curious about the university context and how it works.

Andrew Hickey, Ph.D., is Associate Professor in Communications in the School of Arts and Communications at the University of Southern Queensland. Andrew is a critical ethnographer and has undertaken large-scale research projects exploring community, and the role of place and social harmony with various government

ABOUT THE AUTHORS

partners and community organisations. His most recent books, The Pedagogies of Cultural Studies (Routledge) and Cities of Signs: Learning the logic of urban spaces (Peter Lang) chart the public pedagogical formations that organise contemporary life. Andrew can be contacted at: andrew.hickey@usq.edu.au

Eileen Honan is a senior lecturer at The University of Queensland in the School of Education. Her particular research interests include: the connections between teachers' practices and curriculum guidelines; the interactions between home and school literacy practices particularly in relation to digital literacies; and the development of new rhizomatic methodologies in educational research.

Cecily Jensen-Clayton is a director of Lifelong Conscious Living, is an academic, theologian, philosopher, educator, linguist, and psychoanalyst. Cecily's work, scholarship, and publishing are underpinned by a feminist consciousness that includes mentoring and offering spiritual guidance to research students and women for effective leadership in our complex age.

Janice Jones is a Senior Lecturer (Expressive Arts) in the School of Linguistics, Adult and Specialist Education at the University of Southern Queensland. Janice's research interests include narrative, creative and arts-informed research including auto-ethnography. Janice values and facilitates creative and reflective practice for personal and professional growth.

Marguerite Jones is a lecturer and researcher in the School of Education, University of New England School of Education since 2013. Her research areas include innovations to pre-service teacher professional experience, teacher mentoring, and the politics of casual teaching, gifted education, and higher education. She liaises with professionals in schools across New South Wales and Australia to enhance leader and teacher practice.

Kenneth P. King earned his EdD in curriculum and instruction from Northern Illinois University. Dr. King is a professor of education at Roosevelt University in Chicago, Illinois. His research interests are in the areas of history of science education and in developing inquiry-rich science teaching materials. He is the author of two books on science teaching.

Jo Lampert is a Professor of Education at LaTrobe University in Melbourne. She has a national and international reputation in the fields of social justice, Aboriginal and Torres Strait Islander Education, and teacher education for high poverty schools. She also has a background in cultural studies.

Sarah Loch is an Honorary Associate with the Faculty of Arts and Social Sciences at the University of Technology, Sydney. She has worked in education for over twenty years, in both schools and academia. Her scholarly work draws on poststructuralist writing and a commitment to listening to others. Sarah's research is in the area of girls' education, middle schooling and poststructural research.

Rena MacLeod's PhD research focuses on gendered violence. In response to this issue Rena has developed a unique liberatory and interpretive model that engages biblical narratives as both formative and transformative texts. Her liberatory and interpretive model facilitates interrogation of women's and men's experience of gendered violence today in order to make transformation possible.

Adele Nye is a Senior Lecturer at the School of Education, University of New England. She researches and publishes in the areas of reflective practice, higher education and historical thinking. In her work with Teacher Education students, Adele focuses on research methods and reflective practice in schools.

Stewart Riddle is a Senior Lecturer in the School of Teacher Education and Early Childhood at the University of Southern Queensland. His research interests include social justice and equity in education, music-based research practices and research methodologies. He also plays bass in a band called Drawn from Bees.

Carol A. Taylor is Professor of Gender and Higher Education in the Sheffield Institute of Education, Sheffield Hallam University, and co-editor of the journal *Gender and Education*. Her research utilizes feminist, neo-materialist, and posthumanist theories and frameworks to explore gendered inequalities, spatial practices, and participation in a range of higher education sites. She shares her home with Patrick, Hermann and Frankie, without whom ...